Palgrave Studies in Victims and Victimology

In recent decades, a growing emphasis on meeting the needs and rights of victims of crime in criminal justice policy and practice has fuelled the development of research, theory, policy and practice outcomes stretching across the globe. This growth of interest in the victim of crime has seen victimology move from being a distinct subset of criminology in academia to a specialist area of study and research in its own right.

Palgrave Studies in Victims and Victimology showcases the work of contemporary scholars of victimological research and publishes some of the highest-quality research in the field. The series reflects the range and depth of research and scholarship in this burgeoning area, combining contributions from both established scholars who have helped to shape the field and more recent entrants. It also reflects both the global nature of many of the issues surrounding justice for victims of crime and social harm and the international span of scholarship researching and writing about them.

More information about this series at
http://www.palgrave.com/gp/series/14571

Kerstin Braun

Victim Participation Rights

Variation Across Criminal Justice Systems

palgrave
macmillan

Kerstin Braun
University of Southern Queensland
Toowoomba, QLD, Australia

Palgrave Studies in Victims and Victimology
ISBN 978-3-030-04545-6 ISBN 978-3-030-04546-3 (eBook)
https://doi.org/10.1007/978-3-030-04546-3

Library of Congress Control Number: 2018962760

This Palgrave Macmillan imprint is published by the registered company Springer Nature Switzerland AG
The registered company address is: Gewerbestrasse 11, 6330 Cham, Switzerland

Dedicated to my father Karl-Heinz Braun

Preface

The so-called rediscovery of the crime victim in many Western jurisdictions in the 1970s and 1980s has resulted in the subsequent emergence of numerous laws and policies focusing on victims and their treatment in the criminal justice system. On the national and international level, multiple strategies have been proposed on how to best enhance the role of victims in criminal procedure. The introduction of information, protection and other service rights for victims has largely been well perceived in many states. However, the idea of affording victims active participation rights during various stages of proceedings in order to improve their experiences has frequently been met with considerable criticism. Concerns raised not only relate to the impact of victim participation rights on defendants' rights but also revolve around the consistency of victim participation with the underlying aims of traditional criminal justice. Nevertheless, many Western governments reiterate that victims need to be reintegrated into the criminal justice system.

Victim-related law reforms occur at ever-increasing intervals in many jurisdictions, resulting in the fast-paced amendment and transformation of existing national laws concerning victims of crime.

Furthermore, as it is up to each individual state to decide what the role of victims should be in its national criminal justice system, approaches to victim participation vary between jurisdictions with different legal traditions and backgrounds. The result is a largely opaque framework on the national level. Only a small number of scholars have examined the particulars of victim participation rights during different trial stages from a comparative perspective. Yet, questions concerning the integration of victims in criminal procedure are of considerable interest both from a theoretical but also practical perspective. This book aims to contribute to filling this research gap and to initiate further academic debate on this topic.

One major goal of the volume is to provide detailed analysis of the scope of victim participation at the pre-trial, trial and post-trial phase in different adversarial and non-adversarial criminal justice systems. These systems include: England and Wales, the US and Australia with a mostly adversarial background; Germany and France, mainly influenced by the inquisitorial tradition; and Sweden and Denmark, which are frequently referred to as mixed adversarial and inquisitorial systems. The point of this exercise is to provide a more holistic understanding of existing victim participation rights in different legal systems during the main procedural stages and thus the role victims have been afforded in criminal justice. This is done in the hope of informing the development of future strategies aimed at enhancing the experience of crime victims. An additional goal of the book is to highlight the way victims' participatory rights are perceived in adversarial and non-adversarial systems. Therefore, a detailed case study is undertaken on the understanding of criminal justice and the victims' role in Germany, a largely inquisitorial system, and Australia, a mostly adversarial system. The findings for the two systems may be indicative of other jurisdictions belonging to either legal tradition. Building upon the analysis, a third goal of the book is to provide insight into what consequences the prevailing understanding of the victims' role in criminal procedure could have for future law and policy reforms in this area. The book ponders whether, at this stage in time, a greater focus on victim protection rather than on active procedural rights could be more beneficial to enhancing the overall experience of victims in the criminal justice system. In this context, the volume takes a close look at the merits of introducing or expanding legal representation schemes for victims.

While the book is theory based, it is also practical in its application. By providing a detailed comparative analysis of victim participation possibilities at different trial stages in different systems and how such participation is perceived in the national context, the book aims to contribute to a better understanding of the ever evolving and transforming landscape of victims' rights. Furthermore, it provides research on the treatment of victims in different legal systems which may be relevant to those contemplating law and policy reform in this area through a comparative lens. The volume is targeted to the academic audience, as well as practitioners, professionals and law and policy makers interested in the role of victims and victims' rights.

This work has benefitted greatly from my research stay at the Max-Planck Institute for Foreign and International Criminal Law in Freiburg im Breisgau, Germany, and its extensive library collection. I would like to thank Dr. Michael Kilchling, Dr. Johanna Rinceanu and Dr. Gunda Wößner for their hospitality, support, guidance and inspiration. Furthermore, I am grateful to Prof. Paul Cassell for his valuable insights and his patience with my many questions and Associate Prof. Tyrone Kirchengast for his encouragement along the way.

I wish to express my gratitude to my husband Seamus Tovey and our growing family for their patience and support during the time of writing.

Brisbane, Australia Kerstin Braun

Praise for *Victim Participation Rights*

"Victim participation in criminal justice has a long history in different of the world's legal systems but has been comprehensively displaced by state authorities. Kerstin Braun provides detailed analysis of the participatory traces that remain. Her book will be essential reading for those seeking to re-engage with these old ways of doing justice and to re-engineer participatory opportunities for victims into the future."

—Dr. Robyn Holder, *Griffith University, Australia*

"This volume provides a comprehensive insight into the different concepts of victim representation in criminal proceedings. The comparison of model justice systems demonstrates that it is primarily victims who face unequal procedural treatment. For defendants, it makes very little difference whether they are tried in Brisbane or Paris, London or Frankfurt, Chicago or Stockholm: in principle, their procedural standing remains the same. For victims, however, the location of a trial can have a significant effect on their representation. Kerstin Braun's book is a valuable resource that offers condensed and well-selected information about why this is the case and illustrates ways forward."

—Dr. Michael Kilchling, *Senior Researcher, Max-Planck-Institute For Foreign And International Criminal Law, Germany*

"Kerstin Braun's new book, Victim Participation Rights: Variation Across Criminal Justice Systems, thoughtfully explicates a revolutionary (but often overlooked) recent development in criminal justice systems around the globe: Participation by crime victims in criminal justice processes. As Braun explains, crime victims' voices are increasingly being heard in criminal cases, in systems as divergent as America's, England's, and Australia's. Anyone interested in understanding contemporary criminal justice will find much to learn from Braun."

—Paul G. Cassell, *S.J. Quinney College of Law at the University of Utah, USA*

Contents

Abbreviations

AJA	Administration of Justice Act, Retsplejeloven (Denmark)
Bundesregierung	Bundesregierung der Bundesrepublik Deutschland
CCP	*Code de Procédure Pénale*, Code of Criminal Procedure (France)
Code for Victims	Code of Practice for Victims of Crime (UK) 2013
CVRA	Crime Victims' Rights Act (US)
Declaration	UN Declaration of Basic Principles of Justice for Victims of Crime and Abuse of Power in Resolution 40/34
DPP	Director of Public Prosecutions
EU	European Union
EU Directive 2012	EU Directive on Minimum Standards on the Rights, Support and Protection of Victims of Crime
EU Directive on Victims	European Union Directive of the European Parliament and of the Council (2012). 2012/29/EU, 25 October 2012. Establishing Minimum Standards on the Rights, Support and Protection of Victims of Crime, and Replacing Council Framework Decision 2001/220/JHA

GVG	Gerichtsverfassungsgesetz, Court Organisation Act (Germany)
MPC	Model Criminal Code
NSW	New South Wales
NT	Northern Territory
PAP	Private Accessory Prosecutor
Qld	Queensland
RB	Rättegångsbalken Code of Judicial Procedure (Sweden)
Recommendation 85/11	Council of Europe Recommendation R 85/11 on the Position of the Victim in the Framework of Criminal Law and Procedure
SA	South Australia
SPPS	Swedish Prison and Probation Service
StPO	Strafprozessordnung, Code of Criminal Procedure (Germany)
Tas	Tasmania
UK	United Kingdom
UN	United Nations
US	United States
USA	United States of America
USC	US Code
Vic	Victoria
VIS	Victim Impact Statement
VPS	Victim Personal Statement
WA	Western Australia

1
Victim Participation in Criminal Procedure: An Introduction

1 Introduction

During most of the twentieth century, victims of crime played a limited role in criminal proceedings in many jurisdictions.[1] It was not until the 1970s and 1980s that scholars and policy makers started to challenge the diminished role victims held in the justice process (see in general Ash 1972; McDonald 1976; Shapland et al. 1985). Historically, victims had not always had such minimal impact. During the Early Middle Ages, victims of crime played a significant role in the administration of criminal justice by actively participating as private prosecutors (see in general Grakawe 1994, 2003; Kirchengast 2006; Sankoff and Wansbrough 2006). Over the centuries, however, the victim was marginalised from criminal trials in both common law and civil law jurisdictions and the victim's role became mainly that of a witness (Garkawe 2003; Henkel 1937; Hubig 2008; Kilchling 2002; McDonald 1975; Rosenfeld 1900; Wemmers 2009). In this role, victims had little opportunity to present their views and concerns during proceedings and to participate actively at trial unless when testifying. One of the first

K. Braun, *Victim Participation Rights*, Palgrave Studies in Victims and Victimology, https://doi.org/10.1007/978-3-030-04546-3_1

scholars to acknowledge the situation was McDonald (1975, 650) who described the victim as 'the forgotten man' in criminal procedure.[2]

Sometime between the late 1960s and early 1980s, the perception of victims and their needs underwent significant change in many Western states. During this time, scholars first started to notice and address the absence of victims from the criminal justice system and to highlight problems associated with their treatment (Ash 1972; Christie 1977; McDonald 1976; Schneider 1975).[3] Enhanced academic debate on, and increased public awareness of, victims and their role in the criminal justice system contributed to the adoption of an international instrument. In 1985, the United Nations (UN) General Assembly unanimously adopted the *UN Declaration of Basic Principles of Justice for Victims of Crime and Abuse of Power* (*Declaration*) in Resolution 40/34,[4] emphasising that 'millions of people throughout the world suffer[ed] harm as a result of crime and the abuse of power and that the rights of these victims ha[d] not been adequately recognized' (General Assembly Resolution 40/34 1985, [2]).

The General Assembly nominated a number of basic principles of justice for victims ('basic principles') that Member States should adopt in order to reduce secondary victimisation,[5] and secure justice and assistance for victims. The Declaration outlines four avenues of redress for victims of crime: access to justice and fair treatment (Declaration ss 4–7), restitution (Declaration ss 8–11), compensation (Declaration ss 12–13) and assistance (Declaration ss 14–17). Many basic principles enshrined in the Declaration are concerned with the provision of 'services' for victims. Such 'service-rights' include treating victims with respect, providing them with information about proceedings as well as the progress of their individual case and offering opportunities to receive reparation from the offender or compensation from the state for losses suffered from a criminal act (Ashworth 2000, 18; Sanders et al. 2001; Groenhuijsen 2004, 63). These 'service-related' basic principles are largely undisputed in Member States. One basic principle contained in Section 6(b) concerning giving victims a voice in the criminal justice system, however, was strongly debated during the drafting of the Declaration. Section 6(b) of the Declaration explicitly sets out that:

> The responsiveness of judicial and administrative processes to the needs of victims should be facilitated by: (b) Allowing the views and concerns of victims to be presented and considered at appropriate stages of the proceedings where their personal interests are affected, without prejudice to the accused and consistent with the relevant national criminal justice system.

During the drafting process of the Declaration, Member States reacted differently to the proposal of introducing victims' participatory rights in the respective national criminal justice systems. Some Member States were concerned about potential risks for the procedural guarantees of defendants if victims were allowed to present views and concerns.[6] Others argued that victims had not been given the right to present views and concerns in their system in order to protect victims from proceedings which could otherwise be traumatic (Seventh United Nations Congress on the Prevention of Crime and the Treatment of Offenders 1985, 157). Despite these concerns, the Declaration was unanimously adopted by the General Assembly in 1985 without a vote and without any reservations by Member States.[7]

2 The Focus on Victim Participation

The question arises why victim participation, as enshrined in Section 6(b) of the Declaration, emerged as an important concept in improving the situation for victims in the criminal justice system. According to the Seventh Congress when drafting the Declaration, one major aim of providing victims with adequate justice mechanisms, including being able to present views and concerns, was to avoid further trauma for victims. The drafters of the Declaration explicitly pointed out that, particularly with regard to criminal proceedings, the lack of suitable arrangements for victims during the trial process could not only lead to the disassociation of victims from the outcome of the trial but could also cause secondary victimisation. It was feared that if victims' views remained irrelevant to the process vigilantism and other undesirable responses could occur (Seventh United Nations Congress 1985, 142).

In light of these considerations, the introduction of Section 6(b) could be seen as an attempt to avoid any further victimisation during criminal proceedings. Additional victimisation could potentially be reduced if victims perceived proceedings and outcomes as fairer due to the possibility of partaking in decision-making processes (Orth 2002, 314). The possibility for victims to present views and concerns could strengthen the victims' perception that they have an important role to play in proceedings (Orth 2002, 321–324).

A second reason for the introduction of Section 6(b) could be assisting victims in obtaining therapeutic benefits, such as closure, through the criminal trial itself. As a consequence of the criminal act, victims can be left feeling unsafe and insecure (Richter 1994, 58).[8] The feeling of insecurity may be reduced through the victims' perception that they play an important part in criminal procedure by being able to make their views and concerns known and by knowing that their views are deemed important (Richter 1994, 62). It has been found that consideration and acknowledgement are factors that can contribute to the healing process of victims and allow them to reach a form of closure (see Burkhardt 2010, 65 for explanations on victims' needs in international criminal court proceedings). During discussions of the Seventh Congress, Member States' representatives pointed out that having confidence in the criminal justice processes was essential for the individual victim but also for the general community to avoid any negative social impact. Furthermore, it was proposed that the lack of suitable participation arrangements for victims during the trial could lead to their 'disassociation' with the outcome of the trial (Seventh United Nations Congress 1985, 143). The above suggests that victim involvement in the process was considered an important concept to reduce victim alienation from the criminal justice system and to ultimately contribute to providing victims with therapeutic benefits.

While the Declaration seems to propose that being heard and being able to express an opinion to a decision maker during proceedings can have a positive effect on victims, very little empirical work is available internationally on whether and to what extent participation can impact a victim's experience in the criminal justice system, and whether it is likely to do so in a positive or negative way (Volbert 2012, 198–199).

Some scholars have turned to procedural justice theory to explain why victims may perceive proceedings as more fair when they are afforded an opportunity to participate (see in general Van Camp and De Mesmaecker 2014). This explanation is based on the understanding that victims may perceive outcomes of particular decisions taken in the criminal justice system as unfair where their expectations are not met (on procedural justice theory, see Thibaut and Walker 1975).[9] This could then lead to secondary victimisation, meaning additional harm sustained through the victims' experiences in the criminal justice system (Orth 2002, 315). As per the theory, however, a person's perception of fairness does not solely depend on an outcome itself but also on other elements in the decision-making process (see discussion in Laxminarayan et al. 2012, 261; O'Hear 2007).[10] One important element for the perception of fairness is whether the people involved in the process are given the opportunity to be heard on the issue in question (Leventhal 1980, 27; O'Hear 2007). It has been proposed that the perception of voice and the possibility to present an issue to authorities can promote the acceptance of decisions as fair, even where these decisions are not favourable to the individual person involved. In regard to victims of crime, this may be the case, for instance, where sentence lengths are shorter than desired by the victim (Erez et al. 1997, 41). The possibility to present views to a decision maker could allow victims to perceive proceedings as fairer and potentially assist in avoiding secondary victimisation even where the outcome is not as they envision (Tyler and Lind 2001, 65). Furthermore, the possibility to be heard could positively impact on the victim's self-esteem and self-reliance and strengthen the perception that they do play an important role in criminal proceedings (Wemmers 1998, 65). It may be reassuring and a positive experience for some victims to know that decision makers value their input in the decision. The possibility to participate, so it is argued, could therefore provide victims with a sense of importance which might have been damaged by the initial experience of the criminal act (Erez et al. 2011, 20). Other scholars rely more on the potentially therapeutic effects trials could have on participating victims and the notion of 'therapeutic jurisprudence' in explaining why victims should have a role in procedure (see in general Wexler 2000; Casey and Rottman 2000). Regardless of the underlying justifications for victim involvement in proceedings, what exact role victims can play in practice in the national context is up to each criminal justice system to decide.

3 Participatory Rights in National Criminal Justice

Even though the Declaration calls upon Member States to allow victims to present views and concerns, the basic principle is qualified in that such opportunities should only be provided where this form of participation is consistent with the national criminal justice system. It follows that the extent to which victims can participate during domestic criminal trials is up to national law and policy makers to decide and is likely to differ between jurisdictions with different legal systems and traditions.

While in the past calls have been made that victims' participatory rights need to be enhanced in national criminal justice systems, especially those of adversarial nature (see Pizzi and Perron 1996), some scholars suggest that criminal justice processes today may be paying more attention to the needs of victims and are being progressively modified to allow victim involvement at different stages to a greater extent (Kirchengast 2016b, 1). As a result, it may be that criminal justice is currently in the process of transforming by affording victims greater avenues for participation during proceedings (see discussion in Kirchengast 2016b, 3).

To what degree victims can participate in national criminal justice systems is difficult to gauge. Law reform in this area has occurred rapidly in many jurisdictions resulting in the hasty introduction, change and amendment of potential rights. In Europe, such reforms may have been initially driven by the Council of Europe, which has issued numerous victim-related standards since the 1970s including, in the mid-1980s, the non-binding Council of Europe Recommendation R 85/11 on the Position of the Victim in the Framework of Criminal Law and Procedure (*Recommendation 85/11*). This included recommendations for the treatment of victims in national criminal justice systems. With the turn of the millennium, the pace of supra-national victim standards was accelerated by the European Union firstly with the adoption of the legally binding Framework Decision on the Standing of Victims in Criminal Proceedings in 2001 which, in 2012, was replaced by its successor legislation the EU Directive on Minimum Standards on the Rights, Support and Protection of Victims of Crime (*EU Directive*). As a consequence, especially in Europe, a myriad of national statutes and provisions containing victims' rights has rapidly emerged in an attempt to bring national laws in line with relevant supra-national obligations. Kirchengast (2016a, 79) notes the following in the context of victims' participatory rights at different stages of proceedings in national criminal justice systems:

> There is increased international concern over the role of the victim throughout the phases of the criminal justice process. This includes a concern over the role and participation of the victim in the investigation, the trial, from pretrial through to sentencing and appeal procedures, and the post-conviction phase, including punishment of the offender and parole. While victims have always been concerned with the entire process as relevant to their particular matter, much of the criminal trial has remained hidden from the public gaze of what constitutes the trial process, which has tended to focus on the hearing or jury trial phase alone. Thus, greater concern for the rights and powers of victims across the whole of the criminal trial, writ large, is bringing attention to those parts of the trial that were once identified as of little relevance to the victim.

Given all the political, scholarly and legislative attention victims have received on the national and supra-national level, the situation for victims seems to have changed significantly since the first half of the twentieth century. Being tough on criminals and fair to victims is a political slogan which has been popular with many political parties and Western governments for the past 20 years. These political catchphrases frequently go hand in hand with the enthusiastic promise to reintegrate victims into criminal procedure, perhaps through participation or service rights, although the exact strategy for said reintegration often remains unclear and unaddressed.

This book provides a detailed analysis of possibilities for victim participation in criminal proceedings by considering what rights victims have been afforded in different criminal justice systems during three distinct phases of the criminal trial: the investigation and pre-trial phase, the trial and sentencing phase, and the post-trial phase in light of appeals and early-release decision making. It assesses the availability of selected participatory rights for victims in different jurisdictions with diverging legal traditions and backgrounds. In so doing, it considers the situation in the United States on the federal level, England and Wales, and Australia. These judicial systems are mainly adversarial in nature and their laws originate from common law. Furthermore, it contemplates the participation possibilities in the continental European and largely inquisitorial systems of Germany and France.[11] Lastly, analysis is provided for the Scandinavian countries Denmark and Sweden with their mixed inquisitorial-adversarial systems, whereby the investigation and pre-trial phase is characterised by inquisitorial elements and the trial phase is more of an adversarial nature.

The analysis in this volume seeks to clarify to what extent victims have been integrated as participants into criminal trials at different stages by focusing on available statutory rights.[12] The chapters identify relevant norms and procedures in respective jurisdictions and build on existing (comparative) literature and empirical studies on victims' rights, where available. The assessment of victims' rights is informed by a comparative legal research method focusing on the similarities and differences between the selected criminal justice systems. The purpose of this exercise is to identify whether a holistic strategy for victim participation is traceable in the analysed criminal jurisdictions and to find out what the current status quo of victims' participatory rights is. In this context, the volume also contains a detailed case study on the position of victims, especially in light of national criminal policy, in two countries on either end of the criminal legal-tradition spectrum: Germany, a largely inquisitorial system, and Australia, a mainly adversarial system. The aim is to expose whether criminal trials, in inquisitorial, adversarial and mixed systems, are accommodating victims to a greater extent when it comes to participation and what potential underlying barriers can be identified in this regard in the national context. The argument is subsequently advanced that at this point in time there may be greater benefit in focusing on less contested and less controversial victims' rights than those associated with active procedural participation, including the better protection of victim witnesses. This is the case, as the possibilities for a successful expansion of victims' participation rights appear currently limited in national criminal justice systems due to various reasons identified in this volume.

What is to follow in this chapter is the introduction of the jurisdictions selected for examination in this volume, including a brief introduction to their criminal justice systems.

4 Introduction to Selected Jurisdictions

4.1 Inquisitorial Systems: Germany and France

Germany and France are both civil law systems originating from Roman law in which the main criminal procedure rules and principles are codified. While few systems appear to remain exclusively inquisitorial or adversarial, criminal procedure in Germany and France remains heavily governed by inquisitorial elements (Hermann 1987, 123; Weigend 2011, 257).[13] Briefly that means that criminal proceedings are not party—but judge dominated. For example, in both Germany and France much of the work in preparation of a trial is carried out by the judge and not the individual parties (in the French context see Steiner 2018, 195). Also, the trial proper and the examination of evidence are heavily judge-led. As a consequence, for example, cross-examinations of witnesses by the parties, which are standard practice in the adversarial context, are the exception in inquisitorial systems (Steiner 2018, 195). Goldstein and Marcus (1977, 247) explain the reasons for the significant involvement of judges in inquisitorial proceedings at the pre-trial stage as follows:

> Inquisitorial theory recognizes that the key to overall judicial supervision is control of the investigation of crime. Unless the judge plays a role in determining how investigations should be conducted, or what charges should be filed, his supervision will be limited to the cases that survive for trial as a result of decisions by others.

A brief general overview of the key aspects of the two criminal justice systems is provided below.

4.1.1 Germany

The Federal Republic of Germany, a federal parliamentary democracy, is located in north-central Europe and, with a population of around 82.3 million, is the most populated EU country (European Union 2018). The German President (*Bundespräsident*) holds the highest office and acts in a representative manner with limited reserve power. The executive power is vested in the cabinet formed by the German Chancellor (*Bundeskanzler*) and other ministers. The German Chancellor acts as head of government thus determining government politics. Parliament, a two-chamber legislature, consists of the elected *Bundestag*, mainly responsible for voting and passing bills, and the appointed *Bundesrat* (comparable to an upper house or second chamber), representing the interests of the federal states. It becomes mostly involved in legislative processes which affect the interests of the states. The state power is divided between the federal level (*Bund*) and the 16 federal states (*Bundesländer*) as per the principles set out in the Basic Law (*Grundgesetz*), the German Constitution. Each federal state has its own state parliament called *Landtag*.

In Germany, the core legislation governing criminal trials is the German Code of Criminal Procedure (*Strafprozessordnung, StPO*).[14] Criminal law and procedure fall under federal jurisdiction in Germany and therefore apply equally to all federal states.[15] In addition to the StPO, general guidelines have been issued in order to unify court and prosecution practices in German criminal trials. The StPO is divided into six books, each relating to particular aspects and stages of proceedings. The public prosecution (*Staatsanwaltschaft*) is independent of the judiciary (Court Organisation Act, *Gerichtsverfassungsgestz, GVG*, s 150) and organised in accordance with the court system into federal and state prosecution services. The investigative work is generally carried out by the police who answer to the prosecution in the context of investigations. Due to its dominant role, the prosecution is often called the master of pre-trial proceedings (*Herrin des Vorverfahrens*). Criminal matters in Germany can be dealt with by the lower courts (*Amtsgericht*), the regional courts (*Landgericht*) or the higher regional courts (*Oberlandesgericht*). Which court has jurisdiction is set out in the GVG. The lower courts usually have jurisdiction if a sentence of less than four years is expected as this is the maximum sentence they can impose. Where the sentence is expected to be less than two years, the matter will be dealt with by a single judge in the lower court. In all other cases, the lower court judge will sit with two lay persons (*Schöffen*) to decide over the case at hand (GVG ss 24–25, 29). The regional court generally has jurisdiction over criminal matters in which the expected sentence is greater than four years and which do not fall under the original jurisdiction of the higher regional court (GVG ss 73–74). A specific chamber of the regional courts, the *Schwurgericht*, comprised of three professional judges and two lay judges, has specifically been vested with the power to decide on serious offences including homicide offences. The chamber and its name, which roughly translates to 'sworn-in court', is a reference to the time during which jurors still took part in German criminal procedure—up until 1924 (Bohlander 2012, 37). The higher regional court in its original jurisdiction is tasked with deciding matters of state security (GVG ss 120–121) including homicide offences if committed in this context.

4.1.2 France

Located in northwestern Europe, the French Republic is the largest country in the EU in terms of area (Pfuetzner et al. 2013, 79). Its population is estimated to be around 67.2 million (The National Institute of Statistics and Economic Studies 2018),[16] making it the second most populated EU Member State (2018). The French system has been described as a democracy with a semi-presidential system of government. In this system, the President's function is to act as a guardian and to watch over the Constitution and different institutions while having far-reaching powers. The government consists of the prime minister as well as the cabinet ministers. The parliament, which is vested with legislative powers, consists of two chambers, the National Assembly (*Assemblée Nationale*) as well as the Senate (*Senat*).

The Criminal Code (*Code Pénal*) is one of the main sources governing criminal law in France, while the Code of Criminal Procedure (*Code de Procédure Pénale, CCP*) applies to criminal procedure aspects.[17] Chapter 4 outlines the distinction between police investigations and judicial investigation in France in detail. Suffice to say at this stage that investigations in France can be carried out by the police (*enquete policiere*) or there can be, and in certain cases must be, a judicial investigation (*instruction/information judiciaire*). Prosecutions in criminal cases (*poursuite*) are usually initiated by the public prosecutor (*l'action publique*) (Pfuetzner et al. 2013, 87–91). The French court system is divided between ordinary and administrative courts. Criminal courts form part of the ordinary courts. Kirchengast (2016a, 142) describes the structure of the French court system in the following way:

> The criminal courts include the police tribunal, or tribunal de police, which disposes of minor contraventions; the criminal court or correctional court, or tribunal correctionnel, for more serious offences, such as délits, the less serious felonies, and misdemeanours; the assize court, or *cour d'assises*, for the more serious felonies; the appeal court, or *cours d'appel*, which hears appeals; and the supreme appeals court, the court of cassation or *cour de cassation*, for final appeals on questions of law.

4.2 Mixed Criminal Justice Systems—Sweden and Denmark

Together with Norway, which is not analysed in this book, Sweden and Denmark form part of the Scandinavian countries. Scandinavian legal systems have great similarities due to their joint history and culture (Husabo 2010, 20). While France and Germany are classified as mainly inquisitorial systems, Denmark and Sweden are generally considered mixed criminal justice systems as the investigation phase is distinctly inquisitorial while the trial phase is now defined as adversarial (Cornils 2013, 167; Wergens 2002, 428; Ortwein II 2003, 428). The adversarial aspects of the criminal justice system and the participation of juries were introduced in Denmark in 1916 with the Danish Procedures Act, which came into force in 1919 (Husabo 2010, 21; Anderson 1992, 183). Similarly, in Sweden accusatorial elements were introduced in criminal procedure through the adoption of the Swedish Procedures Act in 1942. In contrast to Denmark, however, lay participation was already possible in Sweden prior to that time (Husabo 2010, 21). Therefore, the main trial features are adversarial, and the trial is seen as a dispute between the state and the defendant (Husabo 2010, 26). Thus, while judges continue to be actively involved in the main trial in Sweden and Denmark (Husabo 2010, 26), the parties play a much greater role especially in relation to introducing and examining evidence than their counterparts in Germany and France (Ortwein II 2003, 429). In addition, similar to Germany and France, Sweden and Denmark are generally associated with the civil law tradition meaning that their legal system is mainly based on written laws enacted by parliament (Ortwein II 2003, 411). The below provides a brief introduction to key aspects of the criminal justice systems in Sweden and Denmark.

4.2.1 Sweden

Located in northern Europe, the Kingdom of Sweden is the EU's third largest country in terms of area (Cornils 2013, 133–134). Yet, its population is estimated at only 10.4 million (Statistics Sweden 2018), making it one of the EU's least densely populated members (European Union 2018). Sweden is a constitutional monarchy with a parliamentary form of government in which the King has an exclusively representative function (Ortwein II 2003, 410). It is divided into 21 counties (*Laen*) with each one having a governor and a county council (Cornils 2013, 137).

In Sweden, criminal law and procedure are governed by a number of laws including the Code of Judicial Procedure (*Rättegångsbalken, RB*)[18] and the Swedish Penal Code (*Brottsbalken*).[19] The RB contains procedural provisions for civil as well as criminal proceedings and is supplemented by other laws, including, for example, the law on the treatment of young offenders. The main investigative authorities are the public prosecutor (*Aklagarmyndigheten*) and the police (*Polisen*). While more simple matters are usually investigated by the police, such as traffic offences, public prosecutors can take over investigations where required (Cornils 2013, 138). The actual investigative work, however, remains with the police even where the prosecution takes over. The Swedish court system is made up of three tiers: the district courts (*Tingsrätt*), which are comprised of one legally trained judge in addition to between three to five lay judges; the courts of appeal (*Hovrätt*), comprised of three professional and two lay judges; and the Supreme Court (*Högsta Domstolen*), which consists of five professional judges (Cornils 2013, 140). Most criminal matters are initially heard by the district courts, and appeals against their decisions are dealt with in the courts of appeals.

4.2.2 Denmark

The Kingdom of Denmark is located in northern Europe, bordering Sweden, and has a population of approximately 5.8 million (Statistics Denmark 2018). Consequently, it is one of the least densely populated countries in the EU (European Union 2018). Denmark is a constitutional monarchy with a parliament consisting of one chamber. While the Sovereign reigns, the executive power is vested in ministers. Denmark consists of five regions which each have their own locally elected council (Langsted et al. 2014, 17).

Substantive criminal law is regulated in Denmark by the Danish Criminal Code (*Straffeloven*). In comparison with many other jurisdictions, Danish law does not differentiate between felonies, misdemeanours and contraventions but treats all offences in the same way (Langsted et al. 2014, 18). Rules relating to civil and criminal procedure are set out in the Administration of Justice Act (*Retsplejeloven*,

AJA). The Danish judicial system comprises 24 districts in the first instance (*Byret*) excluding the Faroe Islands and Greenland (Langsted et al. 2014, 17). In addition, two High Courts exist, the Eastern and the Western High Court, which mainly have appellate jurisdiction. The highest Danish court is the Supreme Court. Each judge has the power to deal with civil and criminal matters and no specific criminal courts exist (Langsted et al. 2014, 20). In contrast to many other jurisdictions, the Danish system integrates police and prosecution services. This means that the Police Chief Constable at the police district level is the head of the prosecution. This differs at the regional level, where the regional prosecutor (*Statsadvokaten*) is responsible for jury trials and appeals to the High Court.

4.3 Adversarial Systems

England and Wales, the US and Australia are all considered largely adversarial criminal justice systems. Kirchengast (2016a, 158) comments on the nature of adversarial systems as follows:

> Adversarial systems of justice are characterised by an accusatorial, common law process dependent on the testing of the state or Crown case. This tends to occur through an independent prosecutor, who is briefed by the police, who brings charges against an accused. The accused may remain silent until proven guilty. The accused has the right to counsel in pursuit of the right to test the prosecution case. The defence is not compelled to offer any evidence at trial, although most do so in order to enhance their changes of acquittal.

The below provides a brief outline of the key aspects of the criminal justice systems in Australia, England and Wales and the US.

4.3.1 Australia

Australia, an island continent located in the Southern hemisphere, has a population of approximately 24.7 million (Australian Bureau of

Statistics 2018). Australia is a constitutional democracy, the head of state being the Sovereign, with a federal division of powers between the federal Commonwealth government and state, territory and local governments. While federal law is applicable in the whole of Australia, state and territory laws generally only operate within state and territory boundaries (Cumes 2013, 9). Federal parliament is made up of two chambers, the House of Representatives (lower house) and the Senate (upper house). Most States also follow a bicameral system.

In Australia, jurisdiction over criminal matters is mainly vested in the eight states and territories—New South Wales, Queensland, South Australia, Tasmania, Victoria, Western Australia, the Australian Capital Territory and the Northern Territory—and, to a limited degree, in the Commonwealth. The Australian states and territories are divided between those which have adopted a criminal code enshrining the principles of criminal law in statute—Queensland, Western Australia, Tasmania, the Northern Territory and the Australian Capital Territory—and those which continue to rely on common law with only some codifications—New South Wales, Victoria and South Australia. Even in code-states, however, common law is relevant for the interpretation of the law. Each Australian jurisdiction has established its own police and prosecution authority as well as court and corrections system. Criminal investigations are mostly carried out by the police in accordance with the rules of the individual jurisdiction. While police can carry out prosecutions mostly for summary matters, the main prosecution agency is the Office of the Director of Public Prosecutions (ODPP) controlled by the Director of Public Prosecutions (DPP). The lowest level courts in Australia are called 'local' or 'magistrates' courts or courts of summary jurisdiction. It is in these courts that most criminal matters commence. In addition, each jurisdiction has superior courts which deal with more serious offences. Juries in criminal trials operate in all Australian jurisdictions although laws in some jurisdictions now allow for judge-only trials under certain circumstances. The highest court in each jurisdiction is the Supreme Court. The High Court of Australia is the highest court in the Australian court hierarchy.

4.3.2 England and Wales

England and Wales are two of four countries which make up the United Kingdom of Great Britain (UK), with Northern Ireland and Scotland being the remaining two. They are located off the northwestern coast of the European mainland (Forster 2013, 3). Overall, the UK has a population of approximately 65.6 million (Office of National Statistics 2017a),[20] with England and Wales having a combined population of 58.4 million (Office of National Statistics 2017b). The UK is a constitutional monarchy with the authority of the state falling to the monarch. Yet, the authority is exercised by ministers who are accountable to parliament. The central parliament is located in London, referred to as the *Westminster Parliament*, with regional parliaments and authorities in place in Wales, Scotland and Northern Ireland. Central parliament is divided into the House of Commons (lower house) which is elected by the people and the House of Lords (upper house) which is not subject to democratic elections.

Criminal law in England and Wales is common law-based but a range of offences have since been enshrined in statute. While some jurisdictions have one criminal code containing most offences this is not the case in England and Wales. Rather offences have been codified across a range of acts including, for example, the *Sexual Offences Act 2003* (UK) and the *Theft Act 1968* (UK). The codification of criminal procedure, however, has never been attempted in England and Wales (Forster 2013, 48). Criminal proceedings are governed by some acts including the *Police and Criminal Evidence Act 1984* (UK) and by practice directions as well as rules issued by the courts, the so-called *Criminal Procedure Rules* (see Kirchengast 2016a, 159). In England and Wales, the police are the general investigation authority, and the Crown Prosecution Service (CPS) the main prosecution authority. While in some of the analysed jurisdictions, for example, Germany, Sweden and Denmark, the police are subject to directions of and supervision by the public prosecution during the investigation stage, in theory, the two authorities are entirely independent from each other in England and Wales. Only after the police investigation has been conducted will the CPS take over. In practice, however, the authorities work closely together and the CPS may take up an advisory role during investigations (Forster 2013, 8). The court system in the first instance consists of magistrates' courts and Crown Courts. Magistrates' courts will generally hear less serious matters while more serious offences go to the Crown Court, which usually sits with a single judge and a 12-person jury. Appeals can be heard by the High Courts (Queen's Bench Division) and the Court of Appeal (Criminal Division). Lastly, the Supreme Court acts as the highest and final appeal court.

4.3.3 USA

The United States of America (USA or US) is a federal republic located in North America. The country consists of 50 federal states as well as the District of Columbia, a separate federal district. Area-wise the US is the world's third largest country with a population of 327.72 million (US Census Bureau 2018). Governmental powers are divided between the federal and state governments. A bicameral system is vested with the legislative power exercised by the Senate and the House of Representatives. The President, head of government and head of state, has the executive power.

British common law forms the basis of the US legal system. While common law principles remain important in the US, much of the law has now been codified in statutes. Criminal jurisdiction is divided in the US between the individual states and the federal level. On the federal level, the Constitution sets out that the federal judiciary has the power to adjudicate 'all cases, in law and equity, arising under this Constitution, the laws of the United States, and treaties made, or which shall be made under their authority' (US Constitution, Article 3(2)). Furthermore, federal courts deal with conflicts arising between a state and a citizen of another, as well as with conflicts between citizens of different states. In the context of criminal law, that means that federal courts are concerned with crimes which go beyond state borders and, therefore, have a wider impact (Broyles 2015, 27). The main statute for substantive criminal law on the federal level is the US Code (*USC*), while each state can enact their own criminal provisions. In an effort to streamline criminal norms, the American Law Institute drafted the Model Penal Code, which has so far been adopted by around 34 states (Broyles 2015, 40). No comparable model code for criminal procedure exists.

Federal courts include the US district courts, the US circuit courts of appeal and the US Supreme Court.[21] The federal district courts are the trial courts on the federal level with each US state having at least one court hearing civil as well as criminal matters of national concern. In these courts, matters are generally heard by judge and jury. An exception are pre-trial matters including warrants, preliminary hearings, bail and other pre-trial motions which are generally presided over by a federal magistrate (Kirchengast 2016b, 170). State courts, on the other hand, will hear matters involving their own citizens which are limited to the interests of the respective state. Similar to the federal level, a court hierarchy also exists on the state level. The number of tiers, however, depends on the size of the state.

The prosecution on the federal level is controlled by the Office of the Attorney General and the Department of Justice. One US Attorney is appointed by the President for each of the federal judicial districts and carries out the duties under the directions of the Attorney General.

While the above provided a brief introduction to the selected jurisdictions and their criminal justice systems the below traces and clarifies the scope of this volume.

4.4 Scope of This Book: Victim Participation Rights Variations Across Criminal Justice Systems

It is undisputed that victims have received and continue to receive much attention on the national and international level including the promise by many Western governments to reintegrate them and to strengthen their role in criminal procedure. Despite these promises, this book argues that no holistic and systematic strategy to allow for victim participation during the different trial stages can generally be detected in the analysed adversarial, inquisitorial and mixed systems. This finding may be indicative of the situation in other European and non-European jurisdictions. The volume suggests that the traditional understanding of criminal justice, in which crime is seen as an offence against the state and criminal procedure as a de-privatised conflict, may pose a significant hurdle to the systematic expansion of victims' rights in criminal proceedings. For this reason, at the moment, greater benefits may lie in focusing on other, perhaps less contested, victims' rights rather than pursuing participation rights which arguably do not fit well with the current understanding of national criminal justice.

This chapter provided a brief introduction to the changed role of victims in criminal procedure and set out the legal background of the jurisdictions selected for analysis in this volume. The remainder of this book critically assesses what participatory role victims have been afforded in the different legal systems, what underlying problems are associated with introducing or strengthening participation rights and what implications this may have for future law and policy reform. As such, the next two chapters, Chapters 2 and 3, provide context for the subsequent analysis by tracing the historical developments regarding the victims' role in national criminal justice systems and in traditional criminal theories. Chapters 4–6 thereupon examine what participatory rights are available to victims at the pre-trial stage, the trial stage and the post-trial stage in each of the selected jurisdictions. In the pre-trial context, Chapter 4 focuses on four distinct decision-making processes whose results could severely affect victims. These are: the non-investigation and the non-prosecution decision, the decision to grant pre-trial release (bail) as well as the decision to enter into a plea agreement. It examines whether and to what extent victims can participate in these decision-making processes and what limitations remain. Chapter 5 assesses opportunities for victims to participate during the trial proper and sentencing phase while taking into account the particulars and structural limitations of the different legal systems. Participation possibilities identified in the analysed jurisdictions include the adhesion procedure, private accessory prosecution, Victim Impact Statements, as well as participation as a victim witness via a legal representative. Finally, Chapter 6 considers possibilities to partake in proceedings after verdict and sentence have been handed down. The analysis focuses on victims' rights to complain against pre-trial and trial decisions directly affecting them, to appeal the verdict or sentence issued against the defendant in the particular case at hand, as well as the possibility for victims to take part in early-release decision making. The findings of the three chapters offer a broad picture of available victim participation rights at the pre-trial, trial and post-trial stage in adversarial, inquisitorial and mixed criminal justice systems and make existing limitations transparent.

Chapter 7 then draws on these findings and contemplates whether the introduction of victims' participatory rights in Germany, a mainly inquisitorial system, and Australia, a largely adversarial system, may signify a changed understanding of criminal justice and a reconceptualisation of the existing criminal justice system. In doing so, it considers possible underlying reasons for the introduction of victim participation rights in the two countries and examines whether a societal consensus towards reintegrating victims in criminal trials can be detected in either system. The discussion includes analysis of explanatory memoranda to victims' rights bills, statements made by members of parliament as well as opinions uttered by legal and political bodies and in academic scholarship.

Drawing on themes arising from the previous analysis, Chapter 8 contemplates whether, at present, it may be more beneficial to focus on better protecting victim witnesses rather than continuing to pursue participation rights which may be ill-fitting with the current understanding of criminal justice. For this purpose, it considers the possibility of introducing or enhancing legal representation schemes for victim witnesses in the respective jurisdictions in order to improve the experience of victim witnesses during proceedings. The chapter examines the status quo of legal representation schemes in order to identify which countries are currently lacking this type of support. It subsequently assesses the merits of these schemes by contemplating risks and benefits, and analyses concerns associated with legal representation for victims in countries in which this form of representation is already available.

The last chapter, Chapter 9, brings together all previous discussion and findings in order to provide a holistic examination of victim participation in the selected jurisdictions, its limitations and possible implications for future law and policy reforms. This includes further contemplation of whether continuous advocacy for the expansion of victim participation rights in national criminal justice systems is likely to yield the envisioned results. Ultimately, the book concludes that the methodical advancement of victim participation rights cannot occur in a legal vacuum but requires a changed understanding of crime and criminal justice and a related attitude change of actors in the criminal justice system. Where such an understanding cannot be reached (yet), focusing on other, perhaps less contested, victims' rights, including legal representation for victim witnesses, may have a greater practical impact on crime victims' experiences in the criminal justice system.

Notes

1. Aspects of the research in this volume are an extension of the author's prior doctoral research at the University of Queensland, Australia, on the role of victims in criminal proceedings in Germany and Australia finalised in 2014. The original thesis can be accessed via the UQ e-space library.
2. The phrase 'forgotten man' or 'forgotten person' was repeated frequently in subsequent literature. See, for example, Shapland et al. (1985, 1).
3. For a short overview of the historical development of the victims' role, see Wemmers (2009), Hubig (2008), and Garkawe (2003).
4. The numbered sections of the Declaration containing the Basic Principles of Justice are referred to as sections in this volume.
5. Secondary victimisation has been defined as the 'negative social or societal reaction in consequence of the primary victimization', see Orth (2002, 314).
6. For example, the Netherlands expressed concerns regarding violations of defendants' rights in case victim participation was introduced in the criminal justice system. The opposition of the Netherlands contributed to the inclusion of the phrase 'Without Prejudice to the Accused' in Section 6(b). This is further discussed in Aldana-Pinell (2004, 657).
7. A reservation concerning Section 6(b) by the UK which can be found in the Report of the Seventh Congress was not upheld when the General Assembly adopted the Declaration.

8. For criticism on therapeutic terms such as 'closure' and their use in therapeutic jurisprudence, see Pemberton and Reynaers (2011, 235).
9. For the psychological effects of criminal proceedings and procedural justice theory, see also: Laxminarayan (2012).
10. Research on procedural justice does not only focus on victims but also on other actors in the criminal justice system. See, for example, Tyler (2003, 30) and Tyler and Huo (2002, 326).
11. It is acknowledged that few jurisdictions remain strictly adversarial or inquisitorial. However, Germany and France continue to be heavily influenced by the inquisitorial tradition. See Weigend (2011, 257).
12. When analysing victims' participatory rights in Chapters 4–6, this volume does not focus on victim-related law reform introduced to improve the situation for vulnerable witnesses when testifying at trial such as the possibility to testify outside the trial and to prerecord the evidence. This is not considered an active participation right in the sense of this book. These rights have been considered in detail by others elsewhere, see Kirchengast (2016a). These rights, however, are addressed in the context of legal representation schemes for victim witnesses in Chapter 8.
13. Explaining that no criminal justice system today is just inquisitorial or just adversarial is Freiberg (2011).
14. An English translation of the German StPO is available on the German Ministry of Justice website: https://www.gesetze-im-internet.de/englisch_stpo/.
15. Germany consists of 16 states (*Bundeslaender*) with 16 state and 1 federal jurisdictions. In Germany, criminal law and criminal procedure are federal matters, regulated by a (federal) criminal code and criminal procedure code, which apply equally to all states. The states generally do not have the constitutionally granted legislative power to enact their own legislation regarding criminal law and procedure.
16. The figures relate to the year 2017.
17. An unofficial 2006 English translation of the French Code of Criminal Procedure is available online: http://www.legislationline.org/documents/section/criminal-codes/country/30.
18. No complete official or unofficial English translation of the AJA is available online.
19. The following English translations of the acts available on the Swedish government website were used for this book: Code of Judicial Procedure:

http://www.government.se/49e41c/contentassets/a1be9e99a5c64d1bb93a96ce5d517e9c/the-swedish-code-of-judicial-procedure-ds-1998_65.pdf and Swedish Penal Code: http://www.government.se/49cd60/contentassets/5315d27076c942019828d6c36521696e/swedish-penal-code.pdf.
20. The figures relate to the year 2016.
21. Also referred to as Article III courts in light of Article III of the US Constitution.

Legislation and Related Sources

Administration of Justice Act (Denmark), Retsplejeloven
Brottsbalken (Sweden), Penal Code
Code de Procédure Pénale (France), Code of Criminal Procedure
Council of Europe, Recommendation R 85(11) on the Position of the Victim in the Framework of Criminal Law and Procedure (28 June 1985)
European Union, European Council Framework Decision. (2001). 2001/220/JHA, 15 March 2001, Standing of Victims in Criminal Proceeding
European Union, Directive of the European Parliament and of the Council (2012). 2012/29/EU, 25 October 2012. Establishing Minimum Standards on the Rights, Support and Protection of Victims of Crime, and Replacing Council Framework Decision 2001/220/JHA
Gerichtsverfassungsgesetz (Germany), Court Organisation Act
Offences Against the Person Act 1861 (UK)
Police and Criminal Evidence Act 1984 (UK)
Rättegångsbalken (Sweden), Code of Judicial Procedure
Sexual Offences Act 2003 (UK)
Strafprozessordnung (Germany), Code of Criminal Procedure
Theft Act 1968 (UK)
United Nations Declaration of Basic Principles of Justice for Victims of Crime and Abuse of Power, General Assembly Resolution 40/34 of the General Assembly, 29 November 1985
United Nations General Assembly Resolution 40/34, UN GAOR 40th sess, 96th plen mtg, supp no 53, UN Doc A/RES/40/34 (29 November 1985).

References

Aldana-Pinell, R. (2004). An Emerging Universality of Justiciable Victims' Rights in the Criminal Process to Curtail Impunity for State-Sponsored Crimes. *Human Rights Quarterly, 26,* 605–686.

Anderson, S. (1992). The Transition from Inquisitorial to Adversarial Criminal Procedure in Denmark. *Scandinavian Studies, 64*(2), 181–198.

Ash, M. (1972). On Witnesses: A Radical Critique of Criminal Court Procedures. *Notre Dame Lawyer, 48,* 386–425.

Ashworth, A. (2000). Victims' Rights, Defendants' Rights and Criminal Procedure. In A. Crawford & J. Goodey (Eds.), *Integrating a Victim Perspective Within Criminal Justice: International Debates* (pp. 185–204). Aldershot: Ashgate.

Australian Bureau of Statistics. (2018). 3101.0—Australian Demographic Statistics, December 2017, Figures for 2017. Retrieved from http://www.abs.gov.au/AUSSTATS/abs@.nsf/mf/3101.0.

Bohlander, M. (2012). *Principles of German Criminal Procedure.* Oxford: Hart Publishing.

Broyles, S. (2015). *Criminal Law in the USA.* Alphen aan den Rijn, The Netherlands: Kluwer Law International.

Burkhardt, M. (2010). *Victim Participation Before the International Criminal Court* (Doctor Iuris thesis). Humboldt University, Berlin, Germany. Retrieved from https://edoc.hu-berlin.de/bitstream/handle/18452/16887/burkhardt.pdf?sequence=1&isAllowed=y.

Casey, P., & Rottman, D. (2000). Therapeutic Jurisprudence in the Courts. *Behavioural Sciences and the Law, 18,* 445–457.

Christie, N. (1977). Conflicts as Property. *British Journal of Criminology, Delinquency and Deviant Social Behaviour, 17*(1), 1–15.

Cornils, K. (2013). Sweden. In U. Sieber, K. Jarvers, & E. Silvermann (Eds.), *National Criminal Law in a Comparative Legal Context, 1.1: Introduction to National Systems, Schriftenreihe des Max-Planck Instituts fuer Auslaendisches und Internationals Strafrecht* (pp. 133–204). Berlin: Duncker & Humbolt.

Cumes, G. (2013). Australia. In U. Sieber, K. Jarvers, & E. Silvermann (Eds.), *National Criminal Law in a Comparative Legal Context, 1.2: Introduction to National Systems, Schriftenreihe des Max-Planck Instituts fuer Auslaendisches und Internationals Strafrecht* (pp. 1–84). Berlin: Duncker & Humbolt.

Erez, E., Ibarra, P. & Downs, D. (2011). Victim Welfare and Participation Reforms in the United States: A Therapeutic Jurisprudence Perspective. In E. Erez, M. Kilchling, & J-A. Wemmers (Eds.), *Therapeutic Jurisprudence and Victim Participation in Justice* (pp. 15–40). Durham: Carolina Academic Press.

Erez, E., Roeger, L., & Morgan, F. (1997). Victim Harm, Impact Statements and Victim Satisfaction with Justice: An Australian Experience. *International Review of Victimology, 5*, 37–60.

European Union. (2018). *Living in the EU*. Retrieved from https://europa.eu/european-union/about-eu/figures/living_en#tab-1-3.

Forster, S. (2013). England and Wales. In U. Sieber, K. Jarvers, & E. Silvermann (Eds.), *National Criminal Law in a Comparative Legal Context, 1.1: Introduction to National Systems, Schriftenreihe des Max-Planck Instituts fuer Auslaendisches und Internationals Strafrecht* (pp 3–72). Berlin: Duncker & Humboldt.

Freiberg, A. (2011). Post-adversarial and Post-inquisitorial Justice: Transcending Traditional Penological Paradigms. *European Journal of Criminology, 8*(1), 82–101.

Garkawe, S. (1994). The Role of the Victim During Criminal Court Proceedings. *The University of New South Wales Law Journal, 17*(2), 595–616.

Garkawe, S. (2003). The History of the Legal Rights of Victims of Crime in the Australian Criminal Justice System. In Victims of Crime Bureau, NSW Attorney-General's Department (Ed.), *Raising the Standards: Charting Government Agencies' Responsibilities to Implement Victims' Rights* (pp. 35–42). Sydney: Victims of Crime Bureau.

Goldstein, A., & Marcus, M. (1977). The Myth of Judicial Supervision in Three Inquisitorial Systems: France, Italy, and Germany. *Yale Law Journal, 87*, 240–283.

Groenhuijsen, M. S. (2004). Victims' Rights and Restorative Justice: Piecemeal Reform of the Criminal Justice System or a Change of Paradigm? In H. Kaptein & M. Malsch (Eds.), *Crime, Victims and Justice: Essays on Principles and Practice* (pp. 63–79). Aldershot, Hampshire: Ashgate.

Henkel, H. (1937). Die Beteiligung des Verletzten am kuenftigen Strafverfahren. *Zeitschrift fuer die Gesamte Strafrechtswissenschaft, 56*, 227–254.

Hermann, J. (1987). The Federal Republic of Germany. In G. F. Cole, S. Frankowski, & M. G. Gertz (Eds.), *Major Criminal Justice Systems: A Comparative Survey* (2nd ed., pp. 106–138). Beverly Hills: Sage.

Hubig, S. (2008). Die historische Entwicklung des Opferschutzes im Strafverfahren. In F. Fastie (Ed.), *Opferschutz im Strafverfahren- Psychosoziale Prozessbegleitung bei Gewalt- und Sexualstraftaten* (2nd ed., pp. 285–302). Leverkusen Opladen: Verlag Barbara Budrich.

Husabo, E. J. (2010). History and Tendencies in the Development of Criminal Procedure Law in the Scandinavian Countries, and in Norway in Particular. *Law & Justice Review, 1*(1), 19–34.

Kilchling, M. (2002). Opferschutz und der Strafanspruch des Staates-ein Wiederspruch. *Neue Zeitschrift fuer Strafrecht, 22,* 57–63.

Kirchengast, T. (2006). *The Victim in Criminal Law and Justice*. New York: Palgrave Macmillan.

Kirchengast, T. (2016a). *Victimology and Victim Rights: International Comparative Perspectives*. Oxon, UK: Routledge.

Kirchengast, T. (2016b). *Victims and the Criminal Trial*. London, UK: Palgrave Macmillan.

Langsted, L. B., Garde, P., & Greve, V. (2014). *Criminal Law in Denmark* (4th ed.). Alphen aan den Rijn, The Netherlands: Kluwer Law International.

Laxminarayan, M. (2012). Procedural Justice and Psychological Effects of Criminal Proceedings: The Moderating Effect of Offense Type. *Social Justice Research, 25*(4), 390–405.

Laxminarayan, M., Henrichs, J., & Pemberton, A. (2012). Procedural and Interactional Justice: A Comparative Study of Victims in the Netherlands and New South Wales. *European Journal of Criminology, 9*(3), 260–275.

Leventhal, G. (1980). What Should Be Done with Equity Theory? In K. J. Gergen, M. S. Greenberg, & R. H. Willis (Eds.), *Social Exchange: Advances in Theory and Research* (pp. 27–55). New York: Plenum Press.

McDonald, W. F. (1975). Towards a Bicentennial Revolution in Criminal Justice: The Return of the Victim. *American Criminal Law Review, 13,* 649–673.

McDonald, W. F. (1976). *Criminal Justice and the Victim*. Beverly Hills: Sage.

O'Hear, M. (2007). Plea Bargaining and Victims: From Consultation to Guidelines. *Marquette Law Review, 91,* 323–347.

Office of National Statistics. (2017a). *Overview of the UK Population: July 2017*. Retrieved from https://www.ons.gov.uk/peoplepopulationand-community/populationandmigration/populationestimates/articles/overviewoftheukpopulation/july2017.

Office of National Statistics. (2017b). *Freedom of Information (FOI): UK Population 2017*. Retrieved from https://www.ons.gov.uk/aboutus/transparencyandgovernance/freedomofinformationfoi/ukpopulation2017.

Orth, U. (2002). Secondary Victimization of Crime Victims by Criminal Proceedings. *Social Justice Research, 15*(4), 313–325.
Ortwein, B. M., II. (2003). The Swedish Legal System: An Introduction. *Indiana International and Comparative Law Review, 13*(2), 405–445.
Pemberton, A., & Reynaers, S. (2011). The Controversial Nature of Victim Participation: Therapeutic Benefits in Victim Impact Statements. In E. Erez, M. Kilchling, & J.-A. Wemmers (Eds.), *Therapeutic Jurisprudence and Victim Participation in Justice* (pp. 229–248). Durham: Carolina Academic Press.
Pfuetzner, P., Adams, S., Neumann, L., & Walther, J. (2013). France. In U. Sieber, K. Jarvers, & E. Silvermann (Eds.), *National Criminal Law in a Comparative Legal Context, 1.4: Introduction to National Systems, Schriftenreihe des Max-Planck Instituts fuer Auslaendisches und Internationals Strafrecht* (pp. 79–174). Berlin: Duncker & Humbolt.
Pizzi, W., & Perron, W. (1996). Crime Victims in German Courtrooms: A Comparative Perspective on American Problems. *Stanford Journal of International Law, 32*, 37–64.
Richter, H. (1994). Wie erleben und verarbeiten Opfer den Strafprozeß?-Erste Befunde aus einer Untersuchung des Max-Planck-Institutes für ausländisches und internationales Strafrecht Freiburg in Zusammenarbeit mit dem Weissen Ring. In D. Eppenstein (Ed.), *Taeterrechte-Opferrechte: Neue Gewichtung im Strafprozess* (pp. 57–64). Mainz: Weisser Ring Gemeinnützige Verlags-GmbH.
Rosenfeld, E. H. (1900). *Die Nebenklage des Reichsstrafprozesses: Ein Beitrag zur Lehre von den Rechten des Verletzten im Strafverfahren*. Berlin: Guttentag.
Sanders, A., Hoyle, C., Morgan, R., & Cape, E. (2001). Victim Impact Statements: Don't Work, Can't Work. *Criminal Law Review, 6*, 447–458.
Sankoff, P., & Wansbrough, L. (2006). *Is Three Really a Crowd? Thoughts About Victim Impact Statements and New Zealand's Revamped Sentencing Regime*. Paper Presented at the 20th International Conference of the International Society for the Reform of Criminal Law Brisbane, 2–6 July.
Schneider, H. J. (1975). *Viktimologie: Wissenschaft vom Verbrechensopfer*. Tuebingen: Mohr.
Seventh United Nations Congress on the Prevention of Crime and the Treatment of Offenders. (1985). Milan 26 August–5 September 1985. Report Prepared by the Secretariat. UN Doc A/Conf.121/22/Rev.1.
Shapland, J., Willmore, J., & Duff, P. (1985). *Victims in the Criminal Justice System*. London: Gower Publishing.

Statistics Denmark. (2018). *Population in Denmark*. Retrieved from https://www.dst.dk/en/Statistik/emner/befolkning-og-valg/befolkning-og-befolknings fremskrivning/folketal.

Statistics Sweden. (2018). *Population Statistics—Figures as of March 2018*. Retrieved from http://www.scb.se/en/finding-statistics/statistics-by-subject-area/population/population-composition/population-statistics/.

Steiner, E. (2018). *French Law: A Comparative Approach* (2nd ed.). Oxford: Oxford University Press.

The National Institute of Statistics and Economic Studies. (2017). *Population by Sex and Age on 1st January 2018, France Demographic Balance Sheet 2017*. Retrieved from https://www.insee.fr/en/statistiques/2382597?sommaire=2382613.

Thibaut, J., & Walker, L. (1975). *Procedural Justice: A Psychological Analysis*. Hillsdale, NJ: Erlbaum.

Tyler, T. (2003). Procedural Justice, Legitimacy, and the Effective Rule of Law. In M. Tonry (Ed.), *Crime and Justice: A Review of Research* (pp. 283–357). Chicago: University of Chicago Press.

Tyler, T., & Huo, Y. (2002). *Trust in the Law: Encouraging Public Cooperation with the Police and Courts*. New York: Russell Sage Foundation.

Tyler, T., & Lind, A. (2001). Procedural Justice. In J. Sanders & L. Hamilton (Eds.), *Handbook of Justice Research in Law* (pp. 65–92). New York: Plenum.

United States Census Bureau. (2018). *U.S. and World Population Clock*. Retrieved from https://www.census.gov/popclock/.

Van Camp, T., & De Mesmaecker, V. (2014). Procedural Justice for Victims of Crime—Are Victim Impact Statements and Victim-Offender Mediation Rising to the Challenge? In I. Vanfraechem, A. Pemberton, & F. M. Ndahinda (Eds.), *Justice for Victims, Perspectives on Rights, Transition and Reconciliation* (pp. 277–299). London: Routledge.

Volbert, R. (2012). Geschaedigte im Strafverfahren: Positive Effekte oder Sekundaere Viktimisierung. In S. Barton & R. Koebel (Eds.), *Ambivalenzen der Opferzuwendung des Strafrechts: Zwischenbilanz nach einem Vierteljahrhundert opferorientierter Strafrechtspolitik in Deutschland* (pp. 197–212). Baden-Baden: Nomos.

Weigend, T. (2011). Germany. In K. Heller & M. Dubber (Eds.), *The Handbook of Comparative Criminal Law* (pp. 252–287). Stanford, CA: Stanford University Press.

Wemmers, J.-A. (1998). Procedural Justice and Dutch Victim Policy. *Law & Policy, 20*(1), 57–76.

Wemmers, J.-A. (2009). Where Do They Belong? Giving Victims a Place in the Criminal Justice Process. *Criminal Law Forum, 20*(4), 395–416.
Wergens, A. (2002). The Role and Standing of the Victim in the Face of Criminal Procedure Sweden. *Revue internationale de droit pénal/International Review of Penal Law, 73*(1), 259–300.
Wexler, D. B. (2000). Therapeutic Jurisprudence: An Overview. *Thomas Cooley Law Review, 17,* 125–134.

2
Victim Participation: A Historic Overview

1 Introduction

Famous nineteenth-century German historian, Johann Gustav Bernhard Droysen (1868), remarked in the context of fully understanding the present that '[i]t is undoubted, that we will fully understand what is, as soon we realise how it came into being' (quoted in Luederssen 2002).[1] Therefore, prior to considering the current role of victims in criminal procedure in Chapters 4–6, this chapter explores the historic evolution of the role of victims from the Middle Ages until the twenty-first century. It groups together inquisitorial and mixed criminal justice systems on the one hand and adversarial jurisdictions on the other hand to provide a brief historical overview. In so doing, the chapter highlights the once strong role victims held in adversarial and non-adversarial justice systems alike. The main aim of the chapter is to trace and compare the evolution of the victims' role in the legal systems selected for analysis in this volume. Due to its specific focus and for the sake of brevity, the chapter makes no claim to be an exhaustive historic account but rather seeks to emphasise key developments. It subsequently shows how the victims' role deteriorated over the centuries to mainly that of a witness

K. Braun, *Victim Participation Rights*, Palgrave Studies in Victims and Victimology, https://doi.org/10.1007/978-3-030-04546-3_2

in both systems—a development leading to the victim being called the 'forgotten man' in criminal procedure in 1970s scholarship. The chapter then investigates the influence of different victims' rights movements on the role of victims between the 1960s and 1980s, ultimately leading to the rediscovery of victims; their rights and needs. It stops short of tracing the current status quo of victims' participatory rights in the selected jurisdictions as this is undertaken in detail in subsequent chapters.

2 The Role of the Victim in Common Law Systems Until the Twentieth Century

2.1 England

In the Early Middle Ages (circa 600 until 900), state-based criminal justice systems did not exist in most communities in England. An offence was considered a wrong against the individual or their kinship group and not against the state. The victim or their kin sought revenge directly against an offender through warfare (Sidman 1976; Strang 2002, 3). Prosecutions by the victim were at least partially motivated by the prospect of receiving monetary compensation from the offender.[2] The overall belief was that justice could best be achieved if it was left to the victim and their families (see Cardenas 1986, 359). The prosecution procedure changed during the High Middle Ages (circa 900–1300) with the introduction of 'trial by battle'. Although a victim was still solely responsible for prosecuting felons on their own motion, now a judge would decide over facts presented to them. The victim (or any individual citizen who wanted to prosecute the crime) was responsible for stating facts relating to a wrongdoing which had occurred to them and for offering proof thereupon 'by his own body', while the accused would deny the accusation and try to establish their innocence by the same means (Laughlin 2009, 360). If the dispute was declared proper by a judge, the parties would carry out a duel until death or concession of one person (Rubin 2003, 263; see also Parkinson 2010, 71).

From the tenth century onward, the establishment of the authority of the monarch introduced the concept of crime against the king in comparison with the earlier concept of crime against the individual (Sidman 1976, 757; Cardenas 1986, 359). Private prosecutions were seen not only as a citizen's privilege but also as their communal duty to accomplish justice and preserve the 'King's Peace' (Burns 1975, 271). The idea behind this can be described as a communal approach to crime control, where the individual is responsible for policing, instead of a state-oriented approach, where this falls into the responsibility of state authorities. Due to the lack of a public prosecution and police service comparable to today's, private prosecution was necessary to control crime in those times (see Kirchengast 2006, 23).

During the reign of Henry the Second from 1154 to 1189, the trial process changed from 'trial by battle' to a more procedural-based trial with a jury (Laughlin 2009, 361–362). In these trials, the judge exercised more power over the conflict in comparison with the 'trial by battle'. A shift away from private and towards public prosecution during the time is first noticeable in the Assize of Clarendon (see reprint in Stubbs 1870, 134–140), introduced by Henry the Second in 1166. The Act sets out that 'twelve men from each hundred or four from each township' should be assembled by royal order to declare under oath if anyone in their hundred or township was suspected of a crime. This declaration served as the indictment and the men had a role similar to today's jurors during the trial. Since the accuser in these cases was the Crown, indicted persons could no longer choose to defend themselves via battle but had to defend themselves in court. Yet, the nature of the trial remained adversarial between victim and offender and not between Crown and offender (Rubin 2003, 272). The introduction of the Assize of Clarendon, however, demonstrates the beginning of a shift in the understanding of crime as an offence against the king rather than against the individual. An increase in courts and cases during the thirteenth century led to the establishment of the King's Attorneys (*Attornatus Regis*), called Attorney Generals from the fifteenth century onwards, who were responsible for conducting particular litigations in royal courts to uphold the interests of the king (Cooley 1958, 304–305).

The steady growth of Crown (state) involvement in criminal trials led to an increase of state-ordered punishments (payment of compensation in the form of a fine to church, king or community) (Klerman 2001, 6), and a decrease of state-ordered restitution to the victim (Joutsen 1987, 42). Lawyers and judges in English royal courts between 1200 and 1500, therefore, started to distinguish between the civil law of torts, created to resolve disputes between individuals with the aim of awarding restitution to the complainant, and criminal law, designed to protect the public interest by punishing unacceptable behaviour against the state (Seipp 1996).[3] By the eighteenth century, the division between criminal law and civil tort law had become an established principle under common law. In that regard, William Blackstone (1768, 2) remarked in his commentary on the laws of England that

> wrongs are divisible into two sorts or species; private wrongs and public wrongs. The former are an infringement or privation of the private or civil rights belonging to individuals … the latter are a breach and violation of public rights and duties, which affect the whole community ….

The transformed view on crime as an act against the state and not the individual caused another slight shift from private to public prosecution in 1555 with the introduction of the Marian Committal Statute (1555) during the reign of Queen Mary. This statute gave the justice of the peace, a local magistrate, a role that would be equivalent to today's public prosecutor. Despite this development, historians describe criminal proceedings in England from the sixteenth to the early eighteenth centuries as lacking public prosecution counsel and thus as still being greatly, although not exclusively, reliant on private prosecutions (King 1984, 27–34; Langbein 1973, 316–317; 2003, 11–13; Sidman 1976, 758). Only when there were no private prosecutors or it appeared that there was not going to be sufficient evidence, would the justices of the peace investigate, bind witnesses and conduct prosecutions (Langbein 1973, 323). The academic literature of the time offers no positive explanation as to why it was preferable to have private instead of public prosecution. Legal historians believe that private prosecution was merely accepted in order to avoid establishing and financing a public prosecution service (Langbein 2003, 12) or that it was simply a result of unplanned historical circumstances (Stephen 1883, 496–497). Prosecution by public prosecutors such as the Attorney

General or the police force (Kurland and Waters 1959, 494) instead of victims themselves became more and more common during the last part of the eighteenth century[4] and the early nineteenth century with the introduction of modern police services and prosecution authorities (Burns 1975, 272; see also Corns 2000, 284; Douglas and Snyder 1989, 46).[5] Yet, some describe the right to initiate and carry out private prosecutions as the 'paradigm of prosecution in England all the way up to the middle of the Nineteenth Century' (Cardenas 1986, 360).

The below first traces similar victim-related developments in Australia, a former British colony, whose laws originate in English common law, before considering the situation in colonial America.

2.2 Australia

In the eighteenth century, Britain occupied Australia under the principles of international law used by Britain for acquiring uninhabited territories or those that were treated as uninhabited (Castles 1982, 20). With the arrival of the 'first fleet' in Sydney on 26 January 1788 and the following establishment of the convict colony of New South Wales and later on the other five colonies,[6] fundamentals of English common law and the principles of eighteenth-century policing were taken over from England and implemented into the colonies' criminal justice systems (Chestermnan 1999, 70; Parkinson 2010, 63). It is, therefore, unsurprising that first Australian legislation allowed private prosecutions in criminal proceedings, a practice which had been the standard in England for centuries.[7] Role and responsibilities of the Attorney General as a prosecutor for more severe crimes were also introduced into the colonies' and later on into the Australian states' criminal justice systems.[8] Although there is limited historical evidence, legal historians believe a shift in the colonies away from private and towards public prosecution occurred with the introduction of a modern police force in the mid-nineteenth century and the increased prosecution of offences by the Attorney General in the higher courts (see Corns 2000, 288).[9] Even though the police force had mostly taken over prosecutions from private persons by the late nineteenth century, legal scholars at the time did not consider this as sidelining private prosecutors. For example, Sir James Fitzjames Stephen (1883, 494) in his 1883 book on the history of criminal law in England stated that:

> In England, and so far as I know, in England and in some English colonies alone, the prosecution of offenses is left entirely to private persons or to public officers who act in their capacity of private persons and who have hardly any legal powers beyond those which belong to private persons.

In 1901, the existing six Australian colonies[10] transferred into states in the Commonwealth of Australia under the Commonwealth Constitution, entering into force on 1 January 1901. The legislative power in regard to criminal law and procedure, however, remained vested within the states for most cases.[11] Therefore, prosecutions initiated by the police force continued as they had during colonial times. Although private prosecutions under common law remain possible until today—unless limited by statute—victims rarely exercised and exercise these rights because of costs, time and questionable benefits (Klerman 2001, 8). The right to private prosecution under common law is discussed in detail in Chapter 4.

Similar developments regarding the victims' role as described in the Australian context can be detected in colonial America.

2.3 USA

Elements of European legal traditions, including the English legal system, were introduced in the US with the first European settlers in the sixteenth and seventeenth centuries. As many colonies, especially those on the East Coast, were English, the English common law system soon became a major influence in the development of American law (Cardenas 1986, 366). As a consequence, in colonial America, as was the case in England at the time, crime was mainly understood as an offence against the individual victim and not against the community. This is why it was the private individual who was considered responsible for apprehending criminals and bringing prosecutions without great state involvement (Cardenas 1986, 366). Investigations and prosecutions often occurred with the help of officials who required payment for their services (McDonald 1975, 651). While private prosecutions may have been partially motivated by the victims' desire for vengeance, they also offered the victim an avenue to receive restitution from the offender. This can perhaps be seen as the most important factor driving private prosecutions at the time. During these early colonial times, police and prosecution services comparable to today's did not exist. Their establishment was viewed critically in society at the time, not the least due to questions of financing such services (McDonald 1975, 652–653).

During the nineteenth century, due to emerging inadequacies of the existing private prosecution system in a diversified urban setting in which private individuals were less willing to prosecute, the US criminal justice system was subject to major reforms. Shortly after the American revolution, for example, a public prosecution service was introduced and with that prosecutions, once reserved for private individuals, became public (McDonald 1975, 659). Some point out that the introduction of a public prosecution service in America was also influenced by similar developments in continental Europe (Cardenas 1986, 369). Generally, from that time onward, prosecutions were initiated by the public prosecutor who was also responsible for seeing them through in court. It has been suggested that the theoretical underpinning for this change is the idea that prosecutions need to serve public interests including deterrence of offenders and retribution for a breach of societal norms rather than the interests of private individuals such as redress. As a consequence, by the mid-nineteenth century, the American criminal procedure landscape had significantly been transformed into a system of public prosecutions in which the victim only played a marginal role (Tobolowsky et al. 2016, 6).

2.4 The General Role of Victims Under Common Law

The identified transformation from common law justice systems which were heavily dependent on private prosecutions to state-run criminal justice systems had the following implications for the role of victims.

Due to the establishment of public prosecution services sometime in the nineteenth century, the main role of the victim in England, the US and Australia became that of a witness for the prosecution. The adversarial trial no longer took place between the private individual and the accused but between the prosecution and the accused. The public prosecutor acting on behalf of the state naturally had and has significantly more resources available and much greater support when investigating a case against an accused than a private prosecutor had in past centuries. This was prone to create an imbalance of powers in the criminal trial between the state and the accused to the disadvantage of the latter. To counteract such imbalances, criminal procedure rules and policies were introduced in all jurisdictions. These focused on ensuring a fair trial for the accused and creating equality of arms between the accused and the state (Langbein 2003, 342–343). Thus, criminal trials, as well as law and policy, mainly focused on the accused and on measures taken to ensure that a wrongful conviction would not occur. The focus on the accused left little room for expansion of thought on the role of victims and their needs in criminal procedure until the 1970s and 1980s. Some commentators, therefore, refer to this period in time as the 'era of victim disenfranchisement' (Dignan 2005, 63).

The similar evolution of the victims' role in systems with a civil law tradition is discussed below.

3 The Role of the Victim in Civil Law Traditions Until the Twentieth Century

3.1 Germany

As was the case in common law jurisdictions, a shift away from the victim as the main actor in criminal proceedings is detectable under German law. Initially, criminal prosecutions in Germanic times during the Early Middle Ages (circa 476–900) were in private hands (Becker 2011, 13). Crime was perceived as an offence against the individual victim or their kinship group. The Germanic feuding rights allowed the victim 'to revenge injury to his person, honour, or property with the help of his family when he did not want to take the compensation ordered under the law' (Grimm 1899, 401 cited in Loeffelmann 2006, 31; see also Meder 2008, 120–121; Schmidt 1995, 6). Under Germanic law, no investigations into crimes by the state existed and the victim had to initiate proceedings against the offender to bring them to the state's attention (Deppenkemper 2004, 96). However, at the same time the victim was free to deal with the offender privately (Schmidt 1995, 37). If the victim chose to initiate a trial, the trial was conducted in public between the victim and the offender in front of a court, which was composed of members of the community (Lütz-Binder 2009, 31; Schmidt 1995, 38; Hubig 2008, 288). It was characteristic of courts at the time to refrain as much as possible from being involved in proceedings through investigations or other means. The trial was seen as a forum for parties to resolve their disputes (Schmidt 1995, 38). The limitation of state involvement is also expressed in the rule that judges at the time had no power to initiate proceedings on their own without a private prosecutor.[12] Similar to England, the view on crime changed with the establishment of the monarchy from the eighth century onwards. Charles the Great established rules he considered relevant for keeping the peace in his empire. A breach of these rules was at the same time a breach of the 'King's Peace' and demonstrated the disloyalty towards the king (Hubig 2008, 290; Becker 2011, 21).

In Germany, it was acknowledged early on that private prosecutions did not work efficiently or not at all in investigating offences and gathering evidence (Kade 1900, 1; Guthke 2009, 105). Consequently, a shift away from private to public prosecution occurred during the High Middle Ages, between the thirteenth and the fifteenth centuries (Langbein 2005, 152).[13] This brought about the development of the inquisitorial trial. In inquisitorial trials, no private prosecutor existed but the prosecution of crimes was the responsibility of an inquisitorial judge (Deppenkemper 2004, 164; Schmidt 1995, 86). The inquisitorial judge dominated proceedings (Langbein 1984, 216–217), while the victim had no role except that of a witness (Lütz-Binder 2009, 31). One of the first codifications of the state's obligation to carry out public prosecutions can be found in the Penal Code of 1532 (Peinliche Gerichtsordnung or

Constitutio Criminalis Carolina) introduced by the Emperor Charles V. The Code stated that the prosecution of serious crimes is a matter for the state.[14] Although private prosecutions were not directly forbidden with the introduction of the Penal Code of 1532, they subsequently decreased drastically. This is the case because the Code burdened private prosecutors with paying damages to an accused who was acquitted in order to compensate their shame (Deppenkemper 2004, 149). The payment had to be deposited before the trial commenced. If the victim was unable to deposit the amount, they were incarcerated.[15] Burdened with these risks, few victims dared to initiate private prosecutions.

The inquisitorial process carried out by an inquisitorial judge continued well into the nineteenth century. A problematic part of the process was that the same judge who had previously acted as a prosecutor was subsequently trying the defendant as the adjudicator. This created the appearance of prejudice in inquisitorial proceedings and was perceived as a weakness of the criminal trial (Mittermaier 1854 cited in Collin 2000, 47). To overcome this weakness, a public prosecution service, independent from the courts, was established in Germany in the first half of the nineteenth century.[16] The existence of a public prosecution service made private prosecutions largely superfluous. With the introduction of the Code of Criminal Procedure (*Strafprozessordnung, StPO*) in 1877, the State obtained a monopoly over prosecutions.[17] As a consequence, in Germany, the public prosecutor, and not the victim or the general public, has the exclusive right to prosecute criminal acts. However, as an exception to this monopoly, the victim has been granted the right to carry out private prosecutions in certain limited cases explicitly named in the legislation.[18] The intention behind the (re-)introduction of the right to private prosecution in the *StPO*, however, was not to give up the state's monopoly over public prosecutions but rather to decrease the prosecution's workload for less serious offences of a more private character (Ackermann 2006, 36). Such minor matters explicitly mentioned in the *StPO* include libel, threat and property damage. Due to the limited scope, private prosecutions can only be conducted in the few cases explicitly enshrined in legislation (StPO (Germany) s 374).

Public prosecution first by the inquisitorial judge and later by the public prosecution service essentially reduced the role of the victim to that of a witness in the process from the thirteenth century onward. Furthermore, most criminal policy and law reform in the nineteenth century was defendant-focused in an attempt to decrease the abuse of state power during criminal trials. During this time, important criminal principles and rules such as the presumption of innocence and equality of arms developed. The defence-focus in criminal law and procedure additionally contributed to the reduced role victims played during this time.

While French and German laws both originate in the Germanic legal tradition, differences in the role of victims in criminal procedure can be detected in the two jurisdictions as the below outlines.

3.2 France

The legal system in France is also based on the Germanic legal tradition which initially gave individual victims a strong role in the prosecution of offences. This is partially related to the fact that state justice in ancient times had no financial or personnel infrastructure (Zauberman 2011, 113), thus making victim involvement essential for its functioning. From the sixteenth century onwards, however, the role of victims in France, comparable to the developments taking place in other countries, was more and more reduced with the strengthening of the role of the public prosecution (Stehle 2007, 61). Some relate the gradual marginalisation of victims and the gain of state power in criminal trials to the emerging understanding that victims were driven by vengeance, which was considered undesirable in criminal proceedings (see Barbot and Dodier 2014, 23). With the introduction of the inquisitorial trial in 1539 via the *Ordonnance Sur le Fait De La Justice*, the prosecutor for the king initially became a party in criminal proceedings. Yet, in comparison with Germany, where the victims' role was almost entirely eliminated with the rise of the public prosecutor, in France victims continued to be able to participate in the criminal trial to a degree as civil claimants (*partie civile*) trying to recuperate their financial losses arising from the offence. The role of the French public prosecutor was further strengthened through law reform after the French Revolution. Yet, the *Code d'Instruction Criminelle* of 1808 explicitly enshrined the victims' right to act as a civil claimant during criminal proceedings. This right gained popularity in practice with the beginning of the industrial era from around the mid-nineteenth century (Stehle 2007, 62). In 1958, the Code of Criminal Procedure (*Code de Procédure Pénale, CCP*) was introduced in France replacing its predecessor, the *Code d'Instruction Criminelle*. The right for victims to act as civil claimants and to initiate proceedings this way continued to exist also under this new Code. Thus, although victims no longer held the strong role they once played in France, their involvement in criminal trials continued as *partie civile* to a much greater extent than, for example, in Germany, even after the introduction of a public prosecution service.

The below traces the historical development of the victims' role in the Scandinavian jurisdictions Denmark and Sweden.

3.3 Denmark

Ancient Nordic criminal justice, comparable to Germanic and early English systems, was accusatorial, and private individuals were responsible for carrying out prosecutions. In Denmark, in the medieval age, criminal prosecutions were carried out by the victim (Husabo 2010, 24). The first codified Danish criminal law was enshrined in Christian V's 'Danish Law' 1683 (*Danske Lov*), where it was contained in the sixth book (Langsted et al. 2014, 22). The codification, however, while unifying criminal laws from different Danish regions, failed to include a shift of power from the private prosecutor to the prosecution authority of the monarch. It was, therefore, based on the traditional system of private prosecutions by injured persons who sought to recuperate damages from offenders in this way. In this context, the victim as the injured party was responsible for outlining the facts of the case and providing sufficient evidence to establish an offence at their own cost. At the time, victims and defendants were considered equal parties in proceedings (Schmahl 1980, 16). On this basis, the codification has been described as being of consolidating rather than of reforming nature (Langsted et al. 2014, 22). Similar to the US, over time, the Danish population became generally less interested in conducting private prosecutions.

This development is often attributed to the costs associated with these proceedings as well as with the difficulties in satisfying the burden of proof (Schmahl 1980, 16). In 1751, an Ordinance (*Forordning om Deliquentager*) was issued separating criminal and civil proceedings. The party role previously held by the defendant was changed to that of a person responsible for truth finding by means of inquisitorial interview. This resulted in the subsequent development of an inquisitorial justice system in Denmark characterised by a court-dominated investigative phase in which the judge was responsible for gathering relevant evidence and a subsequent trial phase in front of a criminal court. Yet, even in this newly established inquisitorial system, in cases where defendants were indigent, the cost of proceedings fell onto the reporting victims who therefore became increasingly reluctant to report offences (Schmahl 1980, 17–18). As a consequence, public officials had to prosecute a growing number of cases.

The increased involvement of public officials in prosecutions led to a reduced role of the victim in Denmark in the eighteenth and early nineteenth centuries (Husabo 2010, 24). Their involvement consisted mainly of communicating the amount of compensation to the king's officials prior to proceedings as well as testifying during proceedings (Schmahl 1980, 21). The two-party criminal process between state and accused became better organised in 1916 with the introduction of the Danish Procedures Act. Comparable to Germany, the emphasis in criminal law and policy was largely on defendants and their fair trial rights. As such in Denmark, the defendant's right to be legally represented, although limited to serious offences, dates back to the eighteenth century (Husabo 2010, 25).

3.4 Sweden

Private prosecution in different forms was also common in early Swedish justice as crime and punishment were not considered state matters (Asp 2012, 145). Between 900 and 1100, for example, kin vengeance frequently occurred in case of murder. From the fourteenth century onward, the different Swedish provincial codes contained harsh punishments including outlawry, the forfeiture of personal property or public punishment for certain crimes. Yet, in case of other offences reparations could be made to the individual victim as well as to the ruler. In case of non-payment, outlawry could then be imposed (Orfield 1953, 280).

It was not until around 1600 that the Crown started to lay charges on behalf of some injured persons. This then stretched to cases where victims could not be identified, which ultimately led to the placing of prosecutions in the public hand (Asp 2012, 145). Yet, the National Law Code of 1734 still saw the right of the injured party to bring charges as prevailing over the right of the state to do so. Prior to 1948, the law treated private and public prosecutions equally, although in practice public prosecutions occurred more frequently. This changed with the introduction of the Swedish Code of Judicial Procedure (*Rättegångsbalken, RB*) on 1 January 1948 which set out a prosecution monopoly for the state affording the victim only a limited and subsidiary right to private prosecution. Explanatory memoranda to the Act stated that this shift away from private prosecution and towards public prosecution was undertaken to ensure that investigations were completed more holistically (Schmidt 1979, 849). As a consequence of this development, and comparable to the situation in the other analysed jurisdictions, the victims' role in proceedings became limited in Sweden. Accordingly, prior to the 1970s criminal policy in Sweden focused almost exclusively on offenders, including how to best eliminate circumstances potentially leading to offending and on how to best reintegrate offenders through treatment and support (Tham et al. 2011, 555–556). Implementing specific policies for crime victims was considered unnecessary, as it was assumed that the above measures would reduce crime rates and, respectively, reduce the number of crime victims (Tham et al. 2011, 556).

4 The Rediscovery of the Victim in the Mid-Twentieth Century

All of the analysed criminal justice systems have in common that the role of the victim changed from active participant and driving force in criminal justice to mainly that of a witness in criminal procedure with the rise of a public police and prosecution service. A limited exception to the diminished role of victims in criminal trials can perhaps be seen in France, where victims continued to be able to participate in criminal proceedings as civil claimants even after the formal separation of civil and criminal matters occurred. Hand in hand with the role reduction came the reduction of available procedural rights and the reduced focus on victims in criminal law and policy.

In what can be described as a global or, at least, a Western trend, victims and their plight were rediscovered in many criminal justice systems between the 1960s and 1980s. During this time, scholars and policy makers started to challenge the diminished role of victims in the justice process (see, in general, Ash 1972; McDonald 1976; Shapland et al. 1985). In particular, a study by Shapland et al. in 1985 on victims and their treatment in criminal proceedings received much attention (Shapland et al. 1985).[19] The researchers found that surveyed victims of violent crime in the United Kingdom often felt powerless as a result of not being able to participate in the criminal justice system. Consequently, many law and policy makers changed their focus from defendants and how to best reintegrate them into society after committing an offence to victims and their needs. Initial efforts frequently focused on establishing state-run victim compensation schemes. This strategy can perhaps be considered more of a welfare approach to dealing with victims (see, in general, Dignan 2005, 41–43). Yet, in subsequent decades, law and policy reform in the area of victims' rights also expanded into other arenas including support, information and respectful treatment.

In Germany, for example, the first exception to the general focus on defendants in criminal law and policy can be seen in the introduction of the Victim Compensation Act (*Opferentschädigungsgesetz*) in 1976. The Act allowed certain victims to receive compensation not under criminal law but under social law. Social law in Germany governs matters such as welfare and social assistance, social insurance as well as child and housing allowances (for an overview of social law in Germany, see Stolleis 2014). Subsequently, four major law reforms concerning victims of crime led to the current victims' rights situation. In 1986, the Victim Protection Act (*Opferschutzgesetz*) which amended and extended victims' rights in the *StPO* was passed. The Act, *inter alia*, introduced certain rights to information, including information on the outcome of proceedings, the right to inspect court files under certain circumstances and the right to be legally represented by a lawyer when participating at trial.[20] In 2004, the first Victims' Rights Reform Act (*Opferrechtsreformgesetz*) was passed amending sections of the *StPO* which dealt with the rights of aggrieved persons and witnesses.[21] The explanatory memorandum acknowledged that criminal proceedings could be an immense burden on the aggrieved person. It identified that the task of a democratic state was not only to prosecute crimes and watch over a fair criminal process that determines guilt or innocence of the offender but also to make sure that the interests of victims are safeguarded (Bundesregierung der Bundesrepublik Deutschland (*Bundesregierung*) 2003, 1). The Act increased victims' procedural and information rights in criminal proceedings and improved the possibility of claiming and collecting restitution from the defendant during the criminal trial. After passing the Act, the government was faced with ongoing demands from victim support organisations to expand victims' rights further (Bundesregierung 2009, 9; on this law reform, see also Safferling 2011). Additionally, potential voters were found to identify themselves more and more with being a victim than with being a defendant (Adam 2009). This pressure contributed to the passing of the Second Victims' Rights Reform Act (*Zweites Opferrechtsreformgesetz*) in 2009.[22] This new Act again strengthened the procedural rights of aggrieved persons in criminal proceedings, the rights of juvenile victims/witnesses and the rights of adult witnesses (for detailed analysis of the Act, see Peter 2010). Lastly, in 2015, the Third Victims' Rights Reform Act (*Drittes Opferrechtsreformgesetz*) was introduced again strengthening the role of victims and witnesses by, *inter alia*, expanding information rights and affording victims the assistance of a psycho-social court support person. The Third Reform Act was mainly motivated by the need to implement the 2012 EU Directive Establishing Minimum Standards on the Rights, Support and Protection of Victims of Crime into national law until 2015 (see Ferber 2016).

In comparison with Germany, in France victims never lost their role in criminal procedure entirely as they were continuously able to act as civil claimants in criminal proceedings. Yet, also in France, a significant emphasis on victims of crime is noticeable since the 1970s (Barbot and Dodier 2014, 23). The altered view of crime victims in France since the 1970s is associated with a growing feminist movement pointing out the shortfalls of the criminal justice system in relation to the treatment of rape victims (see Berard 2016). One of the first noticeable victim-related changes was the establishment of the Commission for the Compensation of Victims in the late 1970s (Meyer and Romanova 2014, 172). Subsequently in 1982, the Ministry of Justice introduced an office for victim protection and prevention which still exists today as the Office for Victim Support and Related Policies. Its role is to further develop and coordinate victim-related approaches. Furthermore, the National Council on Victim Support (*Conseil National d'Aide aux Victimes*) chaired by the Ministry of Justice was established in 1999 which is tasked with coordinating victim-related strategies between governmental and non-governmental bodies to promote victims' interests (Meyer and Romanova 2014, 16). The victims' role in criminal procedure was particularly strengthened by amendments to the CCP in 2000. Since then, Article 1(2) CCP calls upon judicial authorities to ensure 'that victims are informed and that their rights are respected throughout any criminal process'.

Similar developments are noticeable in the Scandinavian context. Tham et al. (2011, 555) explain that in Sweden prior to the 1970s the term crime victim (*brottsoffer*) as such did not exist. Yet, since then, in both Denmark and Sweden much emphasis has been placed on victims of crime (see for Sweden Ljungwald and Elias 2010, 170). For this reason, some contend that now in Scandinavia the 'central focus of crime policy is the crime victim' (Tham et al. 2011, 556). The newly gained focus on crime victims in Sweden is frequently associated with the feminist movement and its efforts to improve the position of female crime victims of male violence (see Kawesa 2014, 42). Ultimately, a strong victims' rights movement contributed to affording victims a prominent place on the public agenda (Heber 2014, 413). The increased focus on crime victims in Sweden *inter alia* led to the establishment of the Crime Victim Compensation and Support Authority in 1994, tasked with ensuring the compensation for criminal injuries and endorsing the interests of crime victims. In addition, numerous law reforms in the area of crime victims, their protection and rights, have occurred since the 1980s(Tham et al. 2011, 560, 594). In Denmark, in 1998, the victim support organisation Victim Support Denmark was established not the least due to the positive experiences Sweden had made with a victim support service (Joergensen and Badse 2014, 39). In both Denmark and Sweden, victims of certain offences, mostly victims of serious violent crime, have been afforded the right to be legally represented during proceedings at public expense since the 1980s. However, regarding the victims' role a divide exists between eastern Scandinavian criminal procedure models including Sweden and western Scandinavian models including Denmark. While victims in Denmark generally do not have party status, victims in Sweden are able to take on a formal party role during proceedings by joining the prosecution (Husabo 2010, 25; Tham et al. 2011, 579).

In England, the new focus on crime victims can be initially seen in the introduction of the first state victim compensation scheme in 1964, the Criminal Injuries Compensation Scheme, enabling victims of violent crime to recuperate their losses under certain circumstances. The 1970s saw the rise of the crime victims' rights movement in the UK with a focus on improving the situation for victims *inter alia* through compensation schemes, service rights and the enactment of statutory law containing victims' rights (Hall 2017, 51). Since then, victims have taken a prominent place in English criminal justice policy with governments pledging to focus on victims and their needs in the criminal justice system. Subsequent developments in England and Wales include the adoption of the first Victims' Charter in 1990, subtitled 'a statement of the rights of victims of crime'. The first charter was followed by a second modified charter in 1995 and the subsequent introduction of a Commissioner for Victims and Witnesses in 2010 (Hall 2017, 56). Furthermore, a Code of Practice for Victims of Crime was enacted in 2006 placing obligations towards victims on criminal justice agencies. One of the key aspects of the Code are so-called service rights. The Code was subject to major review and subsequent amendment by the Ministry of Justice in 2013 setting out specific entitlements and again in 2015, where it was modified to also make reference to victims of terrorism(Hall 2017, 83–84).

In the US, some commentators attribute the original initiation of victim-related discourse to the high crime rates in the 1960s and 1970s. The crime rates contributed to the formation of the President's Commission on Law Enforcement and Administration of Justice (Ivankovic and Altan 2017, 7). The Commission published its final report in 1967, which also examined issues surrounding crime victims and how to enhance possibilities for their participation with a focus on affording victims state-funded compensation for their losses (Tobolowsky et al. 2016, 7). Soon after, state-run victim compensation schemes were introduced in some US jurisdictions including California. Tobolowsky et al. (2016, 8) see the 1970s as the decade during which the victims' rights movement properly commenced in the US. In 1982, President at the time Ronald Reagan established the President's Task Force on Victims of Crime, which was asked to review how to best serve crime victims. The Task Force issued a final report with over 60 recommendations to law and policy makers as well as criminal justice authorities. Although perhaps not initially, over time, the Report had a significant impact at the federal and state level as it is estimated that currently more than 27,000 statutes are in place in the US concerning victims' rights to various degrees. On the federal level, for example, the Victim and Witness Protection Act 1982 contained norms relating to Victim Impact Statements as well as an independent restitution scheme. The 1990 Victims' Rights and Restitution Act contains a list of victims' rights and services (on all of the above see Tobolowsky et al. 2016, 9–12). Ultimately, in 2004 Congress passed the Crime Victims' Rights Act 2004 (US) (*CVRA*) with the aim of strengthening crime victims' rights in the federal criminal justice system. The Act enshrines certain rights for victims, for example, information obligations, as well as enforcement mechanisms. Research has found that within the first year of the Act's operation, the notifications victims received by criminal justice authorities doubled and almost tripled until 2010 (US Department of Justice cited in Spaelek 2017, 145). In 2008, relevant rights set out in the Act were included in the Federal Rules of Criminal Procedure. The CVRA has since been subject to further law reform amending, expanding and strengthening certain rights.

Many victim-related reforms have also occurred in Australia. Over the past 30 years, Australian states and territories have adopted legislation, charters and declarations on victims' rights which outline the treatment that victims can expect in the criminal justice system. The charters and declarations are often seen as recognition of victims as consumers of the criminal justice system rather than as parties to proceedings (Marsh and Melville 2004, 95 commenting on the UK situation; Williams 2005, 25). Zauberman (2000), for example, states that the introduction of victim charters in the UK is evidence of the development of a more service-oriented adversarial criminal justice system aiming to provide services to victims as consumers. The first administrative guideline setting out a declaration on the treatment of victims was introduced in the 1985 South Australian *Declaration of Rights for Victims of Crime*. The Declaration entailed 17 rights for victims of crime during criminal procedure.[23] These rights included the right to be informed about the trial process, to be dealt with at all times in a sympathetic manner and also to be entitled to have the full effects of the crime upon the victims made known to the sentencing court. Most states and territories followed the South Australian approach and introduced victims' charters or declarations in their own jurisdictions. Many charters focus on providing services to victims including information and respectful treatment (Garkawe 2005, 9). The major impact of victims' charters or declarations is seen to be mostly symbolic and a confirmation of the commitment of states to the improved treatment of victims (Booth and Carrington 2007, 348). Today, the majority of Australian states and territories have also enshrined these declarations and charters in legislation.[24]

Despite the fact that victims' rights are now predominantly enacted in statutory law, most victim-related legislation explicitly states that a violation of these rights by a public authority does not entitle victims to a remedy.[25] The South Australian victims' rights legislation, for example, explicitly sets out that no criminal or civil liability arises from a breach of charter/declaration rights.[26] Victims, however, may be able to file a complaint if their rights are not being honoured. In addition to victims' charters or declarations, which are mostly concerned with victims' treatment in the criminal justice system and available services, victims can exercise certain rights in Australian criminal trials.

Eligible victims in Australian jurisdictions have the right to receive compensation from a state-funded compensation scheme for the harm they have suffered. Victim compensation schemes have been operating in Australia for the last 40 years (for an overview, see Forster 2013; McCarthy 1990). For example, New South Wales introduced the first state-funded criminal injuries compensation scheme in 1967, which subsequently spread to the remaining states and territories. Under the schemes, victims can claim the reimbursement for expenses, such as, medical costs or specific payments for any purpose. The schemes, however, are typically limited to victims of violent crimes.

In order to ensure that victims are being treated in alignment with victims' charters and declarations and can exercise their rights adequately, some Australian jurisdictions have set up special government agencies to monitor the treatment of victims of crime and to assist them in their dealings with the criminal justice system. For example, New South Wales, Victoria, the Australian Capital Territory and South Australia have introduced commissioners for victims' rights.[27] They are *inter alia* tasked with ensuring that government agencies comply with victims' rights. In that regard, they act as specific complaint bodies for victim-related matters. The commissioners, for example, can recommend that agencies apologise to victims where charter/declaration obligations have been breached.[28] Their role also includes developing victims' rights legislation and promoting its implementation.

5 Concluding Remarks

In all of the analysed criminal justice systems, adversarial and non-adversarial, victims used to have a strong role in criminal justice as private prosecutors. Yet, this role diminished in all jurisdictions over time. One reason for the change in role is the separation of civil and criminal proceedings. Civil proceedings focus on harm done to the individual in the context of torts, and their main aim is providing compensation. Yet, criminal proceedings are concerned with a violation of the state's criminal laws, and the objectives of criminal law are typically seen in retribution, deterrence and restitution. As such, a changed understanding of criminal law emerged according to which a criminal act is most and foremost considered an offence against the state and not against the individual victim. In this context, the interests of the victim are subsumed by the interests of the state. Another but related reason for the diminished role is the introduction of public police and prosecution services which took over prosecutions on behalf of the state and made active victim involvement in the prosecution process largely superfluous. The emergence of state-run criminal processes also eventually set in motion the development of specific defendants' rights and trial guarantees to ensure that these proceedings were conducted fairly. All of this contributed to an increased emphasis on defendants and their rights in criminal law and policy and largely excluded victims and their needs from such discourse until the second half of the twentieth century. It becomes apparent that this state-run model of criminal procedure emerged through the intentional removal of victims from criminal proceedings. This holds true even though it is the victim, and not the state, who suffers the actual harm of an offence.

From the 1970s forward, similar victim-related developments occurred in the analysed jurisdictions once again. Based on various grounds, including the feminist movement, victims were rediscovered by national law and policy makers and debate commenced on how their situation could best be improved in national criminal justice systems. While contemporary victims' rights differ between jurisdictions, the underlying developments that led to their re-emergence are comparable as the above indicates.

Given the noticeable absence of crime victims from law and policy discourse during much of the nineteenth and early twentieth centuries, Chapter 3 explores which emphasis, if any, is placed on victims in traditional criminal theories. How these theories relate to crime victims is important to grasp, as they frequently shape domestic norms and policies and influence the understanding of crime and criminal justice in the national context. It is this underlying understanding of criminal justice which may particularly impact the perception of victims as well as their role and standing in different criminal justice systems.

Notes

1. Translated from German into English by the author.
2. Money to be paid for personal injury of another was called wer-gild or man-bot and was determined in accordance with the value of the person's life depending on their rank. See Forsyth (1875, 48).
3. For the differentiation between torts and criminal law in the history of English law. See Pollock and Maitland (1898, 43).
4. The Attorney General, for example, acted as public prosecutor in the case of *R v Holland* (1792) 4 TR 691, where the accused faced charges of corruption while holding a respectable position in the East India Company.
5. In 1819, the *London Metropolitan Police Act* was passed establishing a professional, paid police force for the first time. By 1850, the police had taken over the role as public prosecutors. Yet, for example, in England, in Black Country in 1836 still 80% of the offences were prosecuted by the victim, 10% by someone on behalf of the victim and only 7% by the police. See Shapland et al. (1985, 174).
6. In 1825 Van Diemen's Land later re-named Tasmania was established, followed on 21.01.1827 by Western Australia, on 28.12.1836 by South Australia, in 1851 by Victoria and on 10.12.1859 by Queensland.
7. See, for example, *Queensland Justices Act 1886*, 50 Vic. No. 17. Under s. 42 in Part IV dealing with the General Procedure, the Act stated that a complaint may be made by the complainant in person or a solicitor or other person authorised in that behalf. In order to emphasise that not only individuals but also police officers may prosecute apprehended person, s 35 of the Act stated explicitly that a police officer who may apprehend a person offending against the law by virtue of his office may lawfully take the person to and before any justice. Private prosecution is still generally possible for all citizens under common law today but may be limited in scope by statute.
8. Section 4 of the *Act for the Administration of Justice in New South Wales and Van Diemen's Land 1823* stated that all crimes, misdemeanors and offences cognizable in the Supreme Courts shall be prosecuted by information in the name of His Majesty's Attorney General. Reprinted in Bennett and Castle (1979, 42–53, 43, 44). Section 20 of the *Act to Amend the Constitution of the Supreme Court of Queensland and to Provide for the Better Administration of Justice* (07.08.1861) set out that

all treasons, felonies, misdemeanors and offences cognizable in the Supreme Courts shall be prosecuted by information in the name of Her Majesty's attorney-general or solicitor general. Reprinted in Bennett and Castle (1979, 198–205).

9. Colony police forces were established by the following acts: *Police Act 1844* (SA); *Police Act 1853* (Vic); *Police Act 1862* (WA); *Police Act 1863* (NSW) and *Police Act 1863* (Qld). See Edwards (2005, 32).
10. These were: Queensland, South Australia, Tasmania, Western Australia, New South Wales and Victoria.
11. Chapter 5 of the Commonwealth Constitution Act considers powers of the States. The former legislative powers of the colonies regarding criminal law and procedure remained within the states. Despite the Constitution limiting the powers of the federal government in relation to criminal law and procedure, the federal government has created criminal offences in accordance with legislative powers vested in it such as, external affairs, interstate trade, commerce, taxation and communications.
12. The main reason behind this was to stop judges from receiving financial benefits for initiating prosecutions. See Deppenkemper (2004, 97).
13. Becker (2011, 21) argues that this development is connected with an increase of church attention to the prosecution of heretics. These prosecution could not be conducted via private prosecution because the offences in question were not direct at another person but at the church and God.
14. Section 6 of the Penal Code 1532 sets out that the inquisitorial process is conducted by the authorities under certain circumstances.
15. Section 12 of the Penal Code 1532.
16. Public prosecution, for example, was made obligatory in all of Prussia with decree from 3 January 1849. At the time, Germany was not united but divided into different states after the end of the Holy Roman Empire of the German Nation in 1806. Some of the states were under the rule of Napoleon. Every state was responsible for the introduction of a public prosecution service. For a historical overview of the development of prosecution. See Frey (1850, 53–234).
17. Germany had been united as the German Empire (*Deutsches Reich*) since 1877.
18. Set out in the *RStPO*. These rights were kept on in the StPO after the legislation was amended and revised in 1950 after the break down of the German State under the Nazi regime.

19. For subsequent discussion of Shapland, Willmore and Duff's research, see, for example, Erez and Tontodonato (1990) and Bibas and Bierschback (2004, 138).
20. See *Erstes Gesetz zur Verbesserung der Stellung des Verletzten im Strafverfahren (Opferschutzgesetz - OpferSchG)* [Victim Protection Act] (Germany) 18.12.1986 entered into force 01.04.1987, BGBl I, 1986, 2496 ('OpferSchG') s 406 d.
21. See *Gesetz zur Verbesserung der Rechte von Verletzten im Strafverfahren (Opferrechtsreformgesetz – ORRG),* [Victims' Rights Reform Act (Germany) 24 June 2004 entered into force 9 September 2004, BGBl I, 2004, 1354 ('ORRG').
22. See *Gesetz zur Staerkung der Rechte von Verletzten und Zeugen im Strafverfahren (2. Opferrechtsreformgesetz - 2. ORRG)* [Second Victims' Rights Reform Act 2009] (Germany) 29 July 2009 entered into force 01 October 2009, BGBl I, 2009, 2280 (Nr. 48) ('2. ORRG').
23. A reprint of the South Australian document can be found in Gardner (1990, Appendix A, 66–67).
24. See, for example, *Victims of Crime Act* 1994 (WA) schedule 1; *Victims of Crime Act* 1994 (ACT) s 4; *Victims of Crime Assistance Act* 2009 (Qld) part 2, *Victims Rights Support Act* 2013 (NSW); *Victims of Crime Act* 2001 (SA) part 2, division 2; *Victims' Charter Act* 2006 (Vic). While Tasmania and the Northern Territory have enacted legislation stipulating financial assistance for victims, they have not implemented victims' charters into statutory legislation as such. The Northern Territory has a legal provision that allows the Minister to issue a Charter of Victims' Rights. See: *Victims of Crime Rights and Services Act* 2006 (NT) s 30. The Victims' Declaration in the Northern Territory, however, is an administrative statements published by the Director of Public Prosecutions. See also O'Connell (2011, 2). On the reasons for the transformation of the Declaration into statutory legislation in South Australia see Griffin (2000, 870). The developments in South Australia are the result of the review of policies on victims of crime by the Justice Strategy Unit and their recommendation 11: 'The government should reaffirm its commitment to improving the provision of information to victims of crime'. See South Australia Justice Strategy Unit (1999, 5). See also Kerin (2001, 2305).
25. In South Australia, it was stressed at the beginning of the discussion on implementation of the Victims' Declaration in legislation that the

legislation would not entitle victims to legal action against the state. See Griffin (2000, 870).
26. See *Victims of Crime Act* 2001 (SA) part 2, s 5 (3).
27. A Victims of Crime Co-ordinator was first appointed in 2001 in South Australia to assist victims to exercise their rights. In 2008, this position was terminated and replaced by the appointment of the Commissioner for Victims' Rights ('Commissioner') who has a broader role than the previous Victims of Crime Coordinator. The position of the Commissioner was established according to the *Victims of Crime (Commissioner for Victim's rights) Amendment Act* 2007 (SA). For the ACT and the appointment of a Victims of Crime Commissioner, see: *Victims of Crimes Act* 1994 (ACT) part 3, division 3.1. In NSW, a Commissioner for Victims' Rights has been appointed for the first time in June 2013. For further information on the Commissioner's duties, see: *Victims' Rights Act* 2013 (NSW) s 8. A *Victims of Crime Commissioner* has also been introduced in Victoria according to the *Victims of Crime Commissioner Act 2015* (Vic).
28. See, for example, *Victims of Crime Act* 2001 (SA) ss16 and 16 A; *Victims Rights and Support Act* 2013 (NSW) s 10.

Legislation and Related Sources

Code de Procédure Pénale (France), Code of Criminal Procedure
Crime Victims' Rights Act 2004 (US)
Drittes Opferrechtsreformgesetz (Germany) Gesetz zur Stärkung der Opferrechte im Strafverfahren, Third Victims' Rights Reform Act
European Union, Directive of the European Parliament and of the Council (2012). 2012/29/EU, 25 October 2012. Establishing Minimum Standards on the Rights, Support and Protection of Victims of Crime, and Replacing Council Framework Decision 2001/220/JHA
Opferentschädigungsgesetz (Germany), Victim Compensation Act
Opferrechtsreformgesetz (Germany) (Gesetz zur Verbesserung der Rechte von Verletzten im Strafverfahren), Victims' Rights Reform Act
Opferschutzgesetz (Germany) (Erstes Gesetz zur Verbesserung der Stellung des Verletzten im Strafverfahren), Victim Protection Act
Rättegångsbalken (Sweden), Code of Judicial Procedure

Strafprozessordnung (Germany), Code of Criminal Procedure
Victims' Rights and Restitution Act 1990 (US)
Victim and Witness Protection Act 1982 (US)
Zweites Opferrechtsreformgesetz (Germany) (Gesetz zur Stärkung der Rechte von Verletzten und Zeugen im Strafverfahren), Second Victims' Rights Reform Act
Victims of Crime Act 1994 (ACT)
Victims Rights Support Act 2013 (NSW)
Victims of Crime Rights and Services Act 2006 (NT)
Victims of Crime Assistance Act 2009 (Qld)
Victims of Crime Act 2001 (SA)
Victims of Crime (Commissioner for Victims' Rights) Amendment Act 2007 (SA)
Victims' Charter Act 2006 (Vic)
Victims of Crime Commissioner Act 2015 (Vic)
Victims of Crime Act 1994 (WA).

References

Ackermann, M. (2006). *Die Rechtsbehelfe des Verletzten gegen die negative Anklageentscheidung des Staatsanwaltes in den USA*. Munich: Herbert Utz Verlag.

Adam, K. (2009, April 12). Alle wollen Opfer sein. *Frankfurter Allgemeine Zeitung*.

Ash, M. (1972). On Witnesses: A Radical Critique of Criminal Court Procedures. *Notre Dame Lawyer, 48,* 386–425.

Asp, P. (2012). Prosecutor in Swedish Law. *Crime & Justice, 41,* 141–166.

Barbot, J., & Dodier, N. (2014). Repenser La Place des Victims au Process Penal. *Revue Francaise de Science Politique, 64*(3), 407–433. English translation by Railard, S.-L. Rethinking the Role of Victims in Criminal Proceedings, Lawyer's Normative Repertoire in France and the United States Revue. *Francaise de Science Politique, 64*(3), 23–49.

Becker, P. (2011). *Eine kurze Einfuehrung in die deutsche Rechtsgeschichte.* Munich: GRIN Verlag.

Bennett, J. M., & Castles, A. C. (1979). *A Source Book of Australian Legal History: Source Materials from the Eighteenth to the Twentieth Centuries.* Syndey: The Law Book Company.

Berard, J. (2016). Can a Patriarchal World Be Corrected by a Criminal Law? Feminist Struggles, Penal Justice and Legal Reform in France (1970–1980). *Laws, 5*(12), 1–14.
Bibas, S., & Bierschbach, R. A. (2004). Integrating Remorse and Apology into Criminal Procedure. *The Yale Law Journal, 114*(1), 85–148.
Blackstone, W. (1768). *Commentaries on the Laws of England* (Vol. 3). Oxford: Clarendon Press.
Booth, T., & Carrington, K. (2007). A Comparative Analysis of the Victim Policies Across the Anglo-Speaking World. In S. Walklate (Ed.), *Handbook of Victims and Victimology* (1st ed., pp. 380–416). Devon: Willan Publishing.
Bundesregierung der Bundesrepublik Deutschland. (2003, November 11). Entwurf eines Gesetzes zur Verbesserung der Rechte von Verletzten im Strafverfahren (Opferrechtsrefromgesetz- OpferRG) text identitical with Entwurf eines Gesetzes zur Verbesserung der Rechte von Verletzten im Strafverfahren (Opferrechtsreformgesetz-OpferRG) der Fraktionen der SPD und B90/GR, BT-Drucks 15/1976.
Bundesregierung der Bundesrepublik Deutschland. (2009, March 3). Entwurf eines Gesetzes zur Staerkung der Rechte von Verletzten und Zeugen im Strafverfahren (2. Opferrechtsreformgesetz) identical with Gesetzesentwurf der Fraktionen der CDU/CSU und SPD Entwurf eines Gesetzes zur Staerkung der Rechte von Verletzten und Zeugen im Strafverfahren (2. Opferrechtsreformgesetz) BT-Drucks 16/12098.
Burns, P. (1975). Private Prosecution in Canada: The Law and a Proposal for Change. *McGill Law Journal, 21*, 268–297.
Cardenas, J. (1986). The Crime Victim in the Prosecutorial Process. *Harvard Journal of Law and Public Policy, 9*, 357–398.
Castles, A. C. (1982). *An Australian Legal History*. Sydney: The Law Book Company.
Chesterman, M. (1999). Criminal Trial Juries in Australia: From Penal Colonies to a Federal Democracy. *Law and Contemporary Problems, 62*(2), 69–102.
Cooley, R. (1958). Predecessors of the Federal Attorney General: The Attorney General in England and the American Colonies. *The American Journal of Legal History, 2*(4), 304–312.
Corns, C. (2000). Police Summary Prosecutions in Australia and New Zealand: Some Comparisons. *University of Tasmania Law Review, 19*, 280–310.

Deppenkemper, G. (2004). Beweiswuerdigung als Mittel prozessualer Wahrheitserkenntnis: eine dogmengeschichtliche Studie zu Freiheit, Grenzen und revisionsgerichtlicher Kontrolle tatrichterlicher Ueberzeugungsbildung, para 261 StPO, para 286 ZPO. Osnabruecker Schriften zur Rechtsgeschichte (Universitaet Osnabrueck). Goettingen: V&R Unipress GmbH.
Dignan, J. (2005). *Understanding Victims and Restorative Justice*. Maidenhead: Open University Press.
Droysen, G. H. (1868). Grundriss der Historik, auf der Basis seiner Vorlesung ueber die Theorie der Geschichtswissenschaft in propaedeutischer Absicht, zwischen 1857 und 1882/83 quoted in Luederssen, K. (2002). Historische Erkenntnisinteressen moderner Kriminalpolitik. In K. Luederssen (Ed.), *Die Durchsetzung des Oeffentlichen Strafanspruchs: Systematisierung der Fragestellung* (pp. 21–38) Koeln: Boehlau.
Douglas, H., & Snyder, F. (1989). *Policing and Prosecution in Britain, 1750–1850*. Oxford: Clarendon Press.
Edwards, C. (2005). *Changing Policing Theories for 21st Century Societies* (2nd ed.). Annandale, NSW: Federation Press.
Erez, E., & Tontodonato, P. (1990). The Effect of Victim Participation in Sentencing on Sentencing Outcome. *Criminology, 28*(3), 451–474.
Ferber, S. (2016). Stärkung der Opferrechte im Strafverfahren – Das 3. Opferrechtsreformgesetz. *Neue Juristische Wochenschrift, 2016*(69), 279–282.
Forster, C. (2013). Victims of Crime Compensation Schemes: Compensating Victims of Family Violence. *Precedent, 116*, 40–44.
Forsyth, W. (1875). *History of Trial by Jury*. New York: James Cockcroft & Company.
Frey, L. (1850). *Die Staatsanwaltschaft in Deutschland und Frankreich*. Erlangen: Verlag von Ferdinand Ente.
Gardner, J. (1990). *Victims and Criminal Justice. Office of Crime Statistics*. Adelaide: South Australian Attorney-General's Department.
Garkawe, S. (2005). *Victims Rights Are Human Rights*. Paper Presented at the 20th Anniversary Celebration of the 1985 UN Victims Declaration, Canberra, November 16, 2005.
Griffin, K. T. (2000). Ministerial Statement on the Review on Victims of Crime and the Government's Response to it. Legislative Council Hansard, December 7, 2000, South Australian Parliament (pp. 869–873).
Grimm, J. (1899). *Deutsche Rechtsaltertümer* (Vol. 1., 4th ed.). Leipzig: Dieterich. cited in: Loeffelmann, M. (2006). The Victim in Criminal Proceedings: a Systematic Portrayal of Victim Protection under German

Criminal Procedure Law (Part 1: Rights of Participation and Victim Protection). In United Nations Asia and Far East Institute for the Prevention of Crime and Treatment of Offenders (Ed.), *The Use and Application of the United Nations Declaration of Basic Principles of Justice for Victims of Crime and Abuse of Power–Twenty Years After Its Adoption-Resource Material Series No. 70* (pp. 31–41). Fuchu, Japan: UNAFEI.

Guthke, T. (2009). *Die Herausbildung der Strafklage: Exemplarische Studien anhand, deutscher, franzoesischer und flaemischer Quellen*. Koeln: Boehlau Verlag.

Hall, M. (2017). *Victims of Crime, Construction, Governance and Policy*. Cham, Switzerland: Palgrave Macmillan.

Heber, A. (2014). Good Versus Bad? Victims, Offenders and Victim—Offenders in Swedish Crime Policy. *European Journal of Criminology, 11*(4), 410–428.

Hubig, S. (2008). Die historische Entwicklung des Opferschutzes im Strafverfahren. In F. Fastie (Ed.), *Opferschutz im Strafverfahren- Psychosoziale Prozessbegleitung bei Gewalt- und Sexualstraftaten* (2nd ed., pp. 285–302). Leverkusen, Opladen: Verlag Barbara Budrich.

Husabo, E. J. (2010). History and Tendencies in the Development of Criminal Procedure Law in the Scandinavian Countries, and in Norway in Particular. *Law & Justice Review, 1*(1), 19–34.

Ivankovic, A., & Altan, L. (2017). *Requirements and Recommendations for Support Services in Serbia-Establishing a National Victim Support Service*. Multi-Donar Trust Fund for Justice Sector Support in Serbia and Vicitm Support Europe. Retrieved from http://www.mdtfjss.org.rs/archive/file/Operating%20networks%20for%20Victim%20support%20services%20-%20EN.pdf.

Joergensen, L., & Badse, C. (2014). *FRANET: Victim Support Services in the EU: An Overview and Assessment of Victims' Rights in Practice*. Retrieved from http://fra.europa.eu/en/country-data/2016/country-studies-project-victim-support-services-eu-overview-and-assessment-victims.

Joutsen, M. (1987). *The Role of the Victim of Crime in European Criminal Justice Systems: A Cross-National Study of the Role of the Victim*. Helsinki: United Nations European Institute for Crime Prevention and Control (HEUNI) Finland.

Kade, C. (1900). *Die Privatklage in den Strafprozessordnungen der Jetztzeit, insebesondere in der deutschen R.Str.Pr.O.* Berlin: Heymann.

Kawese, V. (2014). *FRANET: Victim Support Services in the EU: An Overview and Assessment of Victims' Rights in Practice-Sweden*. Retrieved from http://

fra.europa.eu/en/country-data/2016/country-studies-project-victim-support-services-eu-overview-and-assessment-victims.
Kerin, R. G, Honourable (2001). Victims of Crime Bill, Second Reading Speech, South Australian House of Assembly, Hansard, September 27, 2001, 2305.
King, P. (1984). Decision-Makers and Decision-Making in the English Criminal Law 1750–1800. *Historical Journal, 27*(1), 25–28.
Kirchengast, T. (2006). *The Victim in Criminal Law and Justice*. New York: Palgrave Macmillan.
Klerman, D. (2001). Settlement and the Decline of Private Prosecution in Thirteenth-Century England. *Law and History Review, 19,* 1–65.
Kurland, P. B., & Waters, D. W. M. (1959). Public Prosecution in England, 1854–79: An Essay in English Legislative History. *Duke Law Journal, 1959*(4), 493–562.
Langbein, J. H. (1973). The Origins of Public Prosecution at Common Law. *American Journal of Legal History, 17,* 313–335.
Langbein, J. H. (1984). The Constitutio Criminalis Carolina in Comparative Perspective: An Anglo-American View. In P. Landau & F.-C. Schroeder (Eds.), *Strafrecht, Strafprozessrecht und Rezeption, Grundlagen, Entwicklungen und Wirkung der Constitutio Criminalis Carolina* (pp. 215–225). Frankfurt am Main: Klostermann.
Langbein, J. H. (2003). *The Origins of the Adversarial Criminal Trial*. Oxford: Oxford University Press.
Langbein, J. H. (2005). *Prosecuting Crime in the Renaissance: England, Germany, France*. Clark, NJ: The Lawbook Exchange.
Langsted, L. B., Garde, P., & Greve, V. (2014). *Criminal Law in Denmark* (4th ed.). Alphen aan den Rijn, The Netherlands: Kluwer Law International.
Ljungwald, C., & Elias, R. (2010). The Emergence of Crime Victims as a Target Group in the Swedish Social Services Act. *Journal of Scandinavian Studies in Criminology and Crime Prevention, 11*(2), 170–188.
Lütz-Binder, E. (2009). *Rechtswirklichkeit der Privatklage und Umgestaltung zu einem Aussoehungsverfahren: Untersuchung unter Auswertung der Privatklageverfahren der Jahre 1992–2002 aus den Amtsgerichtsbezirken Landau/Pfalz, Neustadt/Weinstrasse und Ludwigshafen/Rhein*. Frankfurt am Main: Peter Lang.
Laughlin, A. M. (2009). Learning From the Past? Or Destined to Repeat Past Mistakes? Lessons from the English Legal System and Its Impact on How We View the Role of Judges and Juries Today. *Widener Law Review, 14,* 357–382.

Marsh, I. J. C., & Melville, G. (2004). *Criminal Justice: An Introduction to Philosophies, Theories and Practice*. London: Routledge.
McCarthy, L. (1990). Victims of Crime. In J. Wallace and G. T. Pagone (Eds.), *Rights and Freedoms in Australia* (pp. 166–170). Annandale, NSW: Federation Press, 1992.
McDonald, W. F. (1975). Towards a Bicentennial Revolution in Criminal Justice: The Return of the Victim. *American Criminal Law Review, 13*, 649–673.
McDonald, W. F. (1976). *Criminal Justice and the Victim*. Beverly Hills: Sage.
Meder, S. (2008). *Rechtsgeschichte: Eine Einfuehrung* (3rd ed.). Stuttgart: Boehlau UTB.
Meyer, A., & Romanova, M. (2014) *FRANET Victim Support Services in the EU: An Overview and Assessment of Victims' Rights in Practice*. Retrieved from http://fra.europa.eu/en/country-data/2016/country-studies-project-victim-support-services-eu-overview-and-assessment-victims.
Mittermaier, C. J. (1854). *Die Muendlichkeit, das Anklageprinzip, die Offentlichkeit und das Geschworenengericht in ihrer Durchfuehrung in den verschiedenen Gesetzgebungen; dargestellt und nach den Forderungen des Rechts und der Zweckmassigkeit: mit Ruecksicht auf die Erfahrungen der verschiedenen Laender*. Stuttgart: Cotta. Cited in: Collin, P. (2000). '*Waechter der Gesetze' oder 'Organ der Staatsregierung'? Konzipierung, Einrichtung und Anleitung der Staatsanwaltschaft durch das preussische Justizministerium von den Anfaengen bis 1860*. Frankfurt am Main: Klostermann.
O'Connell, M. (2011). *Victim's Rights: Integrating Victims in Criminal Proceedings*. Retrieved from http://voc.sa.gov.au/sites/default/files/OConnell_Integrating%20Victims.pdf.
Orfield, L. B. (1953). *The Growth of Scandinavian Law*. Philadelphia: University of Pennsylvania Press for Temple University Publications.
Parkinson, P. (2010). *Tradition and Change in Australian Law* (4th ed.). Pyrmont, NSW: Thomson Reuters.
Peter, M. (2010). Measures to Protect Victims in German Criminal Proceedings. A Summary with Special Focus on the Key Points of the Second Victims' Rights Reform Act. In United Nations Asia and Far East Institute for the Prevention of Crime and Treatment of Offenders (Ed.), *The Enhancement of Appropriate Measures for Victims of Crime at Each Stage of the Criminal Justice Process—Resource Material Series No. 81* (pp. 125–137). Fuchu, Japan: UNAFEI.
Pollock, F., & Maitland, F. (1898). *The History of English Law Before the Time of Edward I* (Vol. 1., 2nd ed.). Cambridge: Cambridge University Press.

Rubin, E. L. (2003). Trial by Battle: Trial by Argument. *Arkansas Law Review, 56,* 261–294.

Safferling, C. (2011). The Role of the Victim in the Criminal Process—A Paradigm Shift in National German and International Law. *International Criminal Law Review, 11*(2), 183–215.

Schmahl, H. L. (1980). *Das Adhaesionsverfahren im Daenischen Recht.* Itzehoe: E.A George OHG.

Schmidt, G. (1979). Die Stellung des Verletzten im schwedischen Strafprozess. In A. Kaufmann, G. Bemmann, D. Krauss, & K. Volk (Eds.), *Festchrift fuer Paul Boeckelmann zum 70. Geburtstag am 7. Dezember 1987* (pp. 847–859) Munich: Beck.

Schmidt, E. (1995). *Einfuehrung in die Geschichte der deutschen Strafrechtspflege* (3rd ed.). Goettingen: Vandenhoeck & Ruprecht.

Seipp, D. J. (1996). The Distinction Between Crime and Tort in the Early Common Law. *Boston University Law Review, 76,* 59–87.

Shapland, J., Willmore, J., & Duff, P. (1985). *Victims in the Criminal Justice System.* London: Gower Publishing Company.

Sidman, A. (1976). The Outmoded Concept of Private Prosecution. *The American University Law Review, 25,* 754–794.

South Australia Justice Strategy Unit. (1999). *Victims of Crime Review-Report One.* Adelaide: Justice Strategy Unit, Attorney General's Department.

Stehle, S. (2007). *Das Strafverfahren als immaterielle Wiedergutmachung.* Hamburg: Verlag Dr Kovac.

Stephen, J. F. (1883). *A History of the Criminal Law in England* (Vol. 1). London: Macmillan.

Stolleis, M. (2014). *History of Social Law in Germany.* Berlin: Springer.

Strang, H. (2002). *Repair or Revenge: Victims and Restorative Justice.* Oxford: Oxford University Press.

Stubbs, W. (1870). *Selected Charters and Other Illustrations of English Constitutional History from the Earliest Times to the Reign of Edward the First.* Oxford: Clarendon Press Series.

Tham, H., Roenneling, A., & Rytterbro, L.-L. (2011). The Emergence of the Crime Victim: Sweden in a Scandinavian Context. *Crime and Justice, 40*(1), 555–611.

Tobolowsky, P. M., Beloof, D. E., Gaboury, M. T., Jackson; A. L., & Blackburn, A. G. (2016). *Crime Victim Rights and Remedies* (3rd ed.). Durham: Carolina Academic Press.

US Department of Justice cited in Spalek, B. (2017). *Crime Victims Theory, Policy & Practice* (2nd ed.). London: Palgrave.

Williams, B. (2005). *Victims of Crime and Community Justice*. London: Jessica Kingsley Publishers.
Zauberman, R. (2000). Victims as Consumers of the Criminal Justice System. In J. Goodey & A. Crawford (Eds.), *Integrating a Victim Perspective Within Criminal Justice: International Debates*. Aldershot: Ashgate.
Zauberman, R. (2011). Crime Victims and the Criminal Justice System: An Illustration from a French Regional Victimization Survey. In A. K. Mehra & R. Lévy (Eds.), *The Police, State, and Society: Perspectives from India and France* (pp. 109–130). Delhi: Pearson Education India.

3

Victim Perspectives and Criminal Justice

1 Introduction

Chapter 2 traced the role of victims in the selected criminal justice systems from the Middle Ages outlining the general change in position from key player in the prosecution of offences to mostly witness for the state—at least from around the early nineteenth century until the second half of the twentieth century. Accordingly, in the 1970s, some scholars started to refer to victims as forgotten persons in criminal procedure. Another noticeable consequence of the changed role of victims is the absence of victims' interests from pre-1970s policy making in many jurisdictions. At the time, law and policy initiatives largely focused on offenders, rehabilitation and punishment in general. After the so-called rediscovery of the victim, sometime between the 1960s and the 1980s, much national law and policy reform occurred in this area. In light of these changes, this chapter explores how the most common criminal theories conceptualise crime victims and their role in criminal justice. The theories *inter alia* aim to justify criminal law and criminal justice and to address the underlying questions of why, how and with what aim punishment is imposed. Understanding how these

K. Braun, *Victim Participation Rights*, Palgrave Studies in Victims and Victimology, https://doi.org/10.1007/978-3-030-04546-3_3

theories relate to victims is important as criminal theories frequently shape norms and policies in national systems and thus influence how these systems operate—also in relation to victims of crime.

Against this background, this chapter first examines the two main traditional criminal theories, non-consequentialist and consequentialist theories, sand how these theories conceptualise the role of victims. While the two schools of thought have been subject to much criticism from varying perspectives, the chapter does not directly enter this aspect of the debate. Instead, it focuses on whether and how the theories in their classical form relate to victims of crime. This is done with a view to examining the possible impact of said theories on the general role of victims in national criminal justice. Subsequent analysis turns to more contemporary criminal theories developed with victims and their role in criminal justice systems in mind. Finally, the chapter ponders what impact criminal theories could have on the understanding of and attitudes towards victims in national justice systems today.

2 Criminal Theories

Criminal theories were developed to explain the basic underpinnings of and reasons for criminal law and punishment. The theories aim to justify state-based criminal justice also in relation to the consequences for the defendant and for society on the whole (Schiemann 2015, 37). The below first analyses the two main traditional criminal theories, non-consequentialist and consequentialist theories, which have impacted the development of many domestic legal systems. This is done with a view to identifying what their approach is to the role of victims. On the importance of understanding the relationship between criminal theories and how they relate to victims in national criminal procedure, McGonigle Leyh (2011, 33) remarks that:

> the adopted attitude on the purpose (or goal) of a criminal justice system or institution reflects the mind-set of the community in which the system or institution serves. The primary and auxiliary goals of a criminal justice system in turn affect the procedures that system or institution will

implement in order to meet the purported aims. Therefore only once the proper aims and limits of criminal law within a specific system are understood can decisions about its internal structure be addressed and assessed.

Theories of criminal law seek to obtain, among other things, a better appreciation of the nature of law, legal systems and legal institutions. Theories help both to explain criminal justice systems and their purpose in societies and to shape criminal justice systems and how they actually operate in societies. In other words, theories attempt to clarify the philosophical motivations behind criminal justice practices and often inform the criminal procedures utilized by different justice systems. Generally the procedures applied by criminal justice systems are meant to further the overarching goals of that system.

What becomes apparent from the below analysis is the absence of victims and their needs for the most part from all theories in their classical sense. Subsequently, more contemporary theories are considered which have been developed to reflect the interests of crime victims in criminal procedure to a greater extent. The point of this exercise is to identify the theories' likely effect on the role of victims in national criminal law and procedure.

2.1 Traditional Criminal Justice Theories

Traditional criminal justice theories are frequently divided into two main categories: non-consequentialist and consequentialist theories, also referred to as retributivism and utilitarianism (for criticism on this differentiation see Hoernle 2017, 17–18). Non-consequentialist theories focus on retribution and are based on the assumption that any infringement of criminal law must be punished *per se*. An underlying reason for the punishment is not required in strictly non-consequentialist theories. In contrast, consequentialist criminal theories consider punishment only to be justified if it serves a specific purpose, for example, the prevention of future crime or the protection of the community. A general theoretical and philosophical distinction between non-consequentialist and consequentialist approaches can be found in Protagoras (Plato, 324a, 324b quoted in Niggli 2012):

> No one punishes a wrongdoer from the mere contemplation [324b] or on account of his wrongdoing, unless one takes unreasoning vengeance like a wild beast. But he who undertakes to punish with reason does not avenge himself for the past offence, since he cannot make what was done as though it had not come to pass; he looks rather to the future, and aims at preventing that particular person and others who see him punished from doing wrong again.

The below first considers non-consequentialist theories and consequentialist theories prior to concluding in detail on how they relate to victims.

2.1.1 Non-consequentialist Theories: Retributivism

Non-consequentialist theories, including retribution, revenge or atonement, have in common that they are not future-focused but concentrate on the criminal act which occurred in the past. Their classical theoretical underpinning is that a criminal deed requires (befitting) punishment *per se* as the punishment serves to balance out the harm done. The theory is based on the underlying understanding that punishment is necessary simply because a criminal offence has been committed (*poena est absoluta ab effectu*) and because the defendant has voluntarily violated the obligations contained in criminal norms, namely to respect the freedom of others (Sautner 2010, 44–45). As a consequence, deliberately harming a perpetrator 'tries to compensate the harm done by him and thereby tries to re-establish the balance of justice' (see Niggli 2012, 4).

Retributivism has been described 'as the most prominent and influential contemporary theory of punishment' (Galoob 2017, 466). The classical school of retributivism dates back to the eighteenth century with some of its most famous supporters being Immanuel Kant (1724–1804) and Georg Wilhelm Friedrich Hegel (1770–1831). Kant (translated by Gregor 1996, 105) describes the foundations of this perspective as follows:

> Punishment by a court (poena forensis) – that is distinct from natural punishment (poena naturalis), in which vice punishes itself and which

> the legislator does not take into account – can never be inflicted merely as a means to promote some other good for the criminal himself or for civil society. It must always be inflicted upon him only because he has committed a crime. For a human being can never be treated merely as a means to the purposes of another or be put among the objects of rights to things: his innate personality protects him from this, even though he can be condemned to lose his civil personality. He must previously have been found punishable before any thought can be given to drawing from his punishment something of use for himself or his fellow citizens.

To summarise, Kant sees criminal law as a categorical imperative meaning that where laws are broken, punishment must follow (Berndt 2017, 27). As per the theory, the punishment imposed should reflect the harm done in length as well as in impact and effect to restore justice (Peter 2014, 48). In this defendant-oriented criminal justice theory, there remains no room for individual victims or their interests. Due to its general aim, the theory is only relevant for those victims who seek retribution through the criminal process. McGonigle Leyh (2011, 39) notes the following on retributivism and its relationship with the individual victims:

> Therefore, although the entire process begins once an individual (the perpetrator) commits a wrong against another individual (the victim), as a whole, retributive theories are not victim-centered. Retributive theories view punishment as a response to a wrong and not a response to the harm experienced by the victim. [footnote omitted] Rather than focusing on the subjective suffering of the victim, the punishment focuses on the objective element of the act itself so as to avoid disparate sentencing of similarly situated defendants. This is also due, in part, because the victim's suffering is difficult to measure and can be disproportionate to the crime.

Similarly, Moore (1993, 15) comments on the objectives of retributivism as follows:

> Retributivism is the view that we ought to punish offenders because and only because they deserve to be punished. Punishment is justified, for a retributivist, solely by the fact that those receiving it deserve

> it. Punishment of deserving offenders may produce beneficial consequences other than giving offenders their just deserts. Punishment may deter future crime, incapacitate dangerous persons, educate citizens in the behavior required for a civilized society, reinforce social cohesion, prevent vigilante behavior, make victims of crime feel better, or satisfy the vengeful desires of citizens who are not themselves crime victims. Yet for a retributivist these are a happy surplus that punishment produces and form no part of what makes punishment just; for a retributivist, deserving offenders should be punished even if the punishment produces none of these other, surplus good effects.

Especially in relation to retributivism and criminal procedure, it has been explained that 'an infliction of punishment is just only if criminal justice institutions establish that there are good reasons for the adjudicator to believe that an offender deserves to be punished for a specific offense and these considerations actually cause the offender to be deemed liable to punishment' (Galoob 2017, 467).

Despite its origins in the eighteenth century, retributivism remains popular today especially in the Anglo-American setting. Flanders (2014, 310–311) notes on contemporary retributivism that '[r]etribution, no mere historical artifact, has also enjoyed a tremendous theoretical resurgence in the twentieth and twenty-first centuries as more and more philosophers and lawyers spend time articulating, defending, and elaborating versions of retributivism'. Some relate the regained popularity of retribution theory to the identified failure of other theories, including rehabilitation and deterrence, in reducing crime (Starkweather 1992, 854).

More recently, some calls have been made that victims and their plight need to be acknowledged to a greater extent under non-consequentialist theories in that these theories should pay 'attention to the place of victims in the analysis of responsibility or in the rationale for punishment' (Fletcher 1999, 51). In this context, it has been proposed that 'doing justice to victims should be part of the theory of retributive punishment' (Fletcher 1999, 55). Yet, this suggestion has been criticised in scholarship on the basis that 'victims should and must be ignored if you are claiming to be doing retributive theory' (Moore 1999, 67).

This is so because any procedural role for victims aimed at influencing the punishment of offenders is 'inconsistent with retributivism' (Moore 1999, 89). Proponents of classical retributivism thus maintain that victims should have no say in criminal procedure. This is based on the understanding that 'doing justice is the essence of retributive punishment and that victims have neither any moral right nor expertise to say how our legal institutions should achieve such justice' (Moore 1999, 89). Against this background, little 'in the retributive theories suggests that victims need to be given a central, procedural role in proceedings . . . ' (McGonigle Leyh 2011, 40). As a consequence, it appears plausible that criminal justice systems based on traditional retributivism are generally less likely to afford victims a key procedural role (McGonigle Leyh 2011, 41).

In the European context, Niggli (2012) explains that a 'pure retribution perspective, detached from all further social aims, is not frequent nowadays in Europe. Rather, governmental interventions in the realm of personal liberty and property are judged by their contribution to the common order'. This is the case as many scholars, especially in European countries, assume that punishment can only be justified where it intends to produce positive results (Hoernle 2006, 951). Traditional theories which do not exclusively focus on the criminal deed to justify punishment but, for example, on the community or the individual defendant, so-called consequentialist theories are analysed below.

2.1.2 Consequentialist Theories: Utilitarianism

In comparison with the school of retributivism, consequentialist theories, also referred to as utilitarian theories, do not focus on past criminal deeds but rather on how to prevent future criminal acts from occurring (Hoernle 2006, 951). Therefore, they justify the punishment of offenders in accordance with deterrence, prevention or reform (*punitur, ne peccetur* meaning punishment to avoid future sins). Utilitarianism has been defined as 'the view that the rightness of an action depends entirely on expected utility, that is on the sum of the utilities of its consequences weighted by their various probabilities'

(Smart 1991, 360). As a consequence, consequentialist theories do not promote punishment merely for the sake of punishment itself but argue that punishment is necessary to bring about a certain goal for society or the individual offender, for example, prevention and crime reduction. Therefore consequentialist theories see a social function in punishment which non-consequentialist theories do not acknowledge as a primary goal. The origins of utilitarian theory date back to the eighteenth century with one of the first mentions of such moral theory in Jeremy Bentham's *Introduction to the Principles of Morals and Legislation* published in 1780. The theory has since been described as continuing to hold its 'position as the centerpiece of Anglo-American moral, political, and legal philosophy' (see Sumner 1982, 701).

The below discusses the two main categories of this perspective: general deterrence and prevention as well as specific deterrence and prevention.

General Deterrence and General Prevention

General deterrence sees the purpose of criminal law and justice in influencing and controlling the conduct of society at large. Punishment, as the reaction of the state to an individual offence, is intended to deter members of society, who may be inclined to offend, from committing criminal acts in the future. The approach sees man 'as fundamentally hedonistic and therefore deterrable from crime only by swift, sure, and severe punishment' (Webb 1980, 23). Thus, as per the theory, the negative consequences criminal behaviour attracts in the form of punishment are intended to discourage other potential offenders. Kennedy (1983, 3) explains in this context that:

> persons are punished for violating the criminal law to serve as object lessons for the rest of society. Society, according to the theory, thus transmits the following message: It is wrong to behave in certain ways, and if a person behaves in one of those ways and fails to obey the law, society will punish him or her accordingly. The expression of society's disapprobation is punishment. Punishment, as a medium for communicating the deterrence message . . . results in habitual compliance by society as a whole.

On this basis, general deterrence uses the individual offender as a teaching tool for the rest of society (Buruma 2004, 2).

Similar to general deterrence, general prevention perspectives focus on influencing the conduct of society as a whole. However, the two approaches differ in that general prevention theory sees the aim of criminal justice and punishment in positively supporting society in the ongoing compliance with societal norms, including criminal norms, even after a breach of these norms has occurred (Schiemann 2015, 46). Society, so it has been explained, can build up trust in the criminal justice system by seeing that the law prevails even after a norm violation has occurred and that no one is allowed to breach said norms. As per the theory, 'punishment addresses everybody, but as law-abiding citizens who are confirmed in their common beliefs in the law, punishment here acts as a factor of integration' (Nigglie 2012). While general perspectives are concerned with influencing the behaviour of society as a whole or at least of other potential offenders, specific theories revolve around influencing the future conduct of the individual perpetrator.

Specific Deterrence and Specific Prevention

Specific or individual deterrence and prevention are concerned with the future conduct of the individual offender (Hoernle 2017, 22). The goal is, *inter alia*, to prevent their reoffending. This is attempted by educating and reintegrating perpetrators into society, by deterring them from the commission of future offences through strict sanctions or by incarcerating them, which *de facto* eliminates the commission of further offences outside of the detention facility (Hoernle 2006, 951). Specific deterrence is based on the assumption 'that the offender is a (sufficiently) rational actor to weigh the costs and benefits of committing crime and that the imposition of painful consequences such as imprisonment will tip his [footnote omitted] cost-benefit analysis against future offending' (Luna 2003, 209). In other words, specific deterrence is based on the assumption that offenders will consider the risks and benefits of future offending in the light of sanctions received for past offending and refrain from acting where the risk of future punishment appears too high.

The positive educational and rehabilitative measures are intended to strengthen the offender's belief in society's values in order to reduce the risk of future norm violations. This perspective ultimately 'views the criminal as suffering from a disorder that prevents him from conforming his behavior to the dictates of law. Through concerted treatment, it is argued that an offender can be rehabilitated and later released into society as a law-abiding citizen' (Luna 2003, 209).

All different variations of consequentialist theory, however, have not gone without significant criticism. It has been found that if applied in their purest form the theories can create unjust results for individual offenders and society at large. For example, the introduction of draconic sentences for minor offences to achieve a deterring effect for offenders can be unjust on the individual offender. The same goes for the interests of society in general where those perpetrators are not punished who have committed very serious offences but pose a minimal recidivism risk (Niggli 2012). Some scholars have pointed out that the concept of deterrence is in itself flawed, as much criminological research demonstrates that many in society are not deterred from committing criminal offences which seem important to them (Buruma 2004, 2).

Mixed or Hybrid Criminal Theories

Due to the harsh criticism of traditional criminal theories in their purest form, many jurisdictions rely on a combination of different theoretical approaches, some of retributive and some of utilitarian nature, in justifying criminal justice and punishment. These are frequently referred to as mixed or hybrid criminal theories defined as theories which 'treat crime reduction and retributive concerns as irreducibly important and so worthy of inclusion in a single justificatory framework' (Lippke 2006, 274). The aim of hybrid theories is to 'sidestep the mutual exclusivity of pure approaches to the criminal sanction' (Luna 2003, 225).

The perspective on victims in mixed theories, however, is equally as limited as in traditional theories.

2.2 Concluding Remarks: Victims in Traditional Criminal Theories

What all traditional theories have in common is that they see crime as a conflict between offender and state but not between victim and offender. Consequently, in their classical sense, criminal theories do not focus on victims of crime and their individual interests. Pure non-consequentialist theories especially do not take the consequences of punishment on anyone, including the perpetrator, society or the victim into account (Schiemann 2015, 38). They are non-consequentialist in the sense that they do not base the need for punishment on any specific purpose or motive. As such, non-consequentialist theories are not designed to accommodate victims' interests. Consequentialist theories focus mainly on prevention or deterrence and may therefore take the perpetrator and society but not the individual victim into account. While victims form part of society on the whole and are therefore also indirectly addressed by the general perspectives they are by no means a specific focus (Schiemann 2015, 46–47).

Nothing suggests that criminal theories envision a central role for victims in criminal procedure. National criminal justice systems heavily influenced by retributivism or utilitarianism may therefore be less likely to provide victims with a central role in proceedings based on the lack of theoretical underpinning and relatedly the more limited interpretation of the victims' role. Classical criminal theories have significantly influenced the development of criminal justice mechanisms and structures in many systems around the world and have shaped the national understanding of matters relating to criminal justice. The absence of victims from traditional criminal theories is perhaps unsurprising given the limited role victims played overall in criminal procedure in many justice systems until the second half of the twentieth century. Yet, with the refocus of criminal laws and policies on victims since the 1970s, a gap between victims' rights in practice and the theoretical underpinnings of such rights seems to have emerged. Against this background, more contemporary criminal justice theories have developed with a specific focus on victims and their role within and outside traditional criminal justice parameters.

3 Contemporary Criminal Theory

3.1 Expressive Criminal Theory

In light of the growing emphasis on victims in law and policy, calls have been made more recently to integrate victims further into criminal theory (Hoernle 2017, 61). On this basis, scholars have started to explore avenues in which victims' interests can feature to a greater extent (see Sautner 2010). Given the absence of victims from justice theories in their classical sense, part of the discourse has focused on so-called expressive or communication-oriented perspectives (on communicative elements of punishment see Murphy and Hampton 1988; Hampton 1992a; Duff 2005). Expressive or communicative theories see the main aim of criminal law and punishment not in influencing potential future criminal conduct but in communicating with certain persons or society on the whole through the values expressed in punishment (Duff 2005, 1182; Hoernle 2006, 954; 2017, 31). Wood (2010, 12–13) remarks that '[i]n examining such emotions, expression theorists drew upon, and in turn contributed to, a general awakening of interest in the emotions, a topic largely ignored in the western philosophical tradition . . . .'

Expressive theory understands criminal offences as expressive acts communicating to the victim that they have a lower standing than the offender. As such a person is considered to be 'morally injured when she is the target of behavior whose meaning, appropriately understood by members of the cultural community in which the behavior occurs, represents her value as less than the value she should be accorded' (Hampton 1992b, 1670). As a consequence, the 'state is required to respond to expressive wrongdoing by saying, "The victim and the wrongdoer are moral equals," and not just by imposing noncommunicative hard treatment upon the wrongdoer' (Adler 2000, 1424). Therefore, expressive theorists contend that the verdict communicates to the victim that they are not at fault as well as showing solidarity and acknowledging that they are worthy of state action on their behalf (see Hoernle 2017, 39–40). Bilz (2016, 358) elaborates further on the communicative function of punishment that

> Punishment sends a message—to victims, to offenders, to third parties—announcing that someone was wronged in a very particular way. It simultaneously corrects that wrong. Specifically, criminal punishment acknowledges that the victim was treated as "lower" in social standing than she deserved, and also asserts that the victim is not friendless, since the rest of us were collectively willing to step in to protect and affirm her in the face of such attacks. A *failure* to punish does the opposite of all of this.

He concludes that through the application of punishment 'we are telling the victim that she is valuable enough for us to expend resources to catch, prosecute, convict, and punish someone who has hurt her. Moreover, this message should be comprehensible to all who hear it' (Bilz 2016, 360). Duff (2005, 1183) elaborates further that the emphasis on communication in punishment

> is an attempt to turn the offender's punishment from a purely one-way process of communication from polity to offender into a two-way process in which there is then a communication back from the offender to the victim and the community: What is to be communicated is a kind of symbolic apology, which is given material and thus more forceful expression by the penal "hard treatment" that the offender undergoes. The hard treatment thus serves as a vehicle for the forceful communication of censure from polity to offender, as a way of focusing the offender's attention on his crime, and for the communication of formal apology from the offender to the victim and the wider polity . . . .

Expressive or communicative theory, in comparison with criminal theories in their classical sense, seems to focus on victims to a much greater extent. Yet, the theory has been heavily criticised and does not appear as widely supported in practice as its traditional alternatives (see also criticism discussed in Schiemann 2015, 60–63). One concern raised is that an expressive purpose alone is not appropriate to justify punishment. Ciocchetti (2003, 65) explains this point in the following words:

> Despite numerous attempts to formulate expressive justifications of punishment, they remain subject to a number of serious criticisms. The construal of expression as a matter of communication or as merely revealing

> a feeling of disapproval on the part of those who punish seems unable to justify the hard treatment involved in punishment. While many can acknowledge the need to censure criminal acts, the moral seriousness and apparent disvalue of the hard treatment involved in punishment requires that punishment serve a very significant moral purpose if it is to be worth imposing. If we have an urge to say something to the criminal, then we should satisfy that urge through speaking with the criminal.

The merits of the theory have also been questioned in relation to communication with victims and the underlying assumption that victims need to be told that the offender was not entitled to treat them in a certain way. It has been suggested that not all victims believe the perpetrator was entitled to treat them in the way they did and that while 'some people may be prone to believing that when others treat them poorly it is because they deserve poor treatment, . . . this psychological process is not universal' (Ciocchetti 2003, 69). As such, the victim may not be a suitable audience in this context. Furthermore, doubts have been raised whether communication really accounts for the most suitable government response and that 'government might more effectively achieve equality of status between victim and wrongdoer by coercing the payment of reparations from one to the other, or by bringing it about that the community learns of the victim's virtues and the wrongdoer's flaws, or by conferring upon the victim certain correlates of status, such as wealth and political power' (Adler 2000, 1424).

3.2 Restorative Justice

With the fresh focus on victims in domestic law and policy and the related question of what role victims should play in the national context, a more victim-focused restorative justice perspective emerged in Western justice systems (McGongile Leyh 2011, 51) concentrating on victims as well as on offenders and the community overall.[1] Restorative justice theories mainly developed in Anglo-American systems from which they spread into other legal systems including continental European ones. Some have classified the emergence of restorative justice as a shift in the aims and goals of punishment from retribution to reintegration (Gladfelter and Ruback 2017, 202). In contrast to the more traditional criminal theories, restorative justice does not focus on collective rights but on the individual rights of victims and offenders (Blagg 2017, 66). Thus, where retribution theories see crime primarily as an offence against the state and the victims' role reduced to that of a witness providing evidence on the harm done to the state, restorative perspectives view crime as an offence against the person and not the state itself. Restorative justice has therefore been described as seeking to return the dispute from the sphere of the state to its original victim and offender sphere (Pemberton and Aarten 2017, 316) and has thus been labelled as 'damage-centered' or 'conflict-centered' (Buruma 2004, 3).

There is no single accepted definition of restorative justice. Rather several sub-streams appear to exist. Some focus more on procedural aspects which may contribute to healing and reintegration, such as victim-offender mediation. Others see restorative justice in the creation of experiences which allow offenders to restore the victims' damages financially. Van Camp and Wemmers (2013, 118) comment that restorative practices include

> victim-offender mediation (VOM) (involving the victim and offender of a particular crime, brought together on a voluntary basis by a mediator who facilitates a face-to-face meeting or shuttle mediation), family group conferences (FGC) (used in cases involving juvenile offenders to facilitate communication between the victim and the offender, their relatives and a police representative in search for conciliation) and victim-offender encounters (VOE) (involving surrogate victims and surrogate offenders of similar types of crime who meet to share their experiences with one another in the presence of a facilitator).

Importantly, however, restorative justice generally does not focus on victims' procedural rights within the parameters of the criminal justice system itself but rather emphasises participation possibilities for victims and offenders outside of this traditional setting (McGonigle Leyh 2011, 46).

Restorative justice has been described as an 'empowering experience, because victims and offenders can identify their needs and actively participate in identifying, defining and actually constructing the way they want to meet their needs' (Bolivar 2017, 29). One of its main aims is to release victims from their passive position in traditional criminal justice and to provide them with an active role in which they can freely express their views and concerns (Achutti 2017, 18). One underlying assumption in this context is that victims need to be empowered to regain control by making them active participants in the process and allowing them to take up a role that goes beyond that of a witness (see Bolivar 2017, 30). Regarding its application in practice, 'restorative justice models often bring victims and offenders together to discuss the harm and to learn about each other's backgrounds' (McGonigle Leyh 2011, 55). However, it needs to be noted that restorative justice mechanisms remain heavily overshadowed by the traditional criminal justice system. Bolivar (2017, 39) explains that the traditional criminal justice authorities, namely prosecution and judges, make the decision as to who is eligible to partake in restorative justice processes such as mediation. In addition, restorative justice often serves as an alternative to traditional criminal justice which is why it can be perceived in society as subordinate to the traditional approach. For this reason some, perhaps more radical, proponents of restorative justice suggest the replacement of the formal criminal justice system altogether with other, more flexible ways of conflict management. This is ultimately intended to foster greater participation of victims and offenders in the respective dispute. The argument is based on the understanding that traditional criminal justice, due to its detachment from the views of the main stakeholders, is essentially incapable of resolving conflicts effectively (see discussion in Achutti 2017, 18–19). Furthermore, state interventions are seen to 'usurp the victims' decision-making power' leaving victims with 'no say' in the traditional criminal justice systems (Fattah 2004, 22).

While restorative justice concepts have been subject to wide criticism (see, e.g., discussion in Luna 2003) one main criticism relevant in the context of this book is that restorative justice is unsuitable to replace existing criminal justice mechanisms, especially in case of more severe offences (see discussion in McGonigle Leyh 2011, 57). For example, leaving serious violent offences, such as, homicide and sexual offences, to be settled between the parties involved in the conflict without the intervention of traditional criminal justice is problematic. Criminal norms are validated and upheld through criminal proceedings and verdicts. Thus specific norm violations, especially those relating to life and physical integrity, may require state intervention as private dispute settlement will likely not have the same degree of societal acceptance (see Buruma 2004, 5; Kaptein 2004, 80). Thus, as Groenhuijsen (2004, 77) puts it, there is a need for a

> punitive criminal justice system for the large number of cases where restorative justice does not work. The existing system of criminal justice is indispensable, for instance, in cases of 'victimless crime' . . . . Furthermore, we could not do without traditional criminal law in instances where a larger group of citizens is victimised, in such a way that individuals are not affected to an extent that justifies mediation or other types of restorative interventions. . . . And last but not least, some cases of hard-core crime are so serious that it would- for the time being- be inconceivable to consider them as a private affair between the offender and the victim.

As such, it is unlikely that restorative justice will replace classic criminal justice systems leaving open questions about the victims' role within these traditional parameters.

4 Concluding Remarks

Over the centuries, traditional theories have influenced the development of justice mechanisms in different jurisdictions and have shaped the national understanding of crime and criminal justice. Traditional theories originally developed with a focus on crime, offenders and society on the whole but without the individual victim in mind. According to these theories, punishment is imposed simply because a crime has been committed or to prevent the commission of future offences. Given the strong influence of retributivism on understanding criminal justice, some scholars even speak of a 'retributive paradigm' underlying many criminal justice systems (see Groenhuijsen 2004, 65). Jurisdictions heavily influenced by a classical understanding of criminal justice may be less likely to afford victims a central role in their criminal justice system due to the lack of theoretical and philosophical underpinning. Some scholars suggest that victims' rights in the traditional repressive system of criminal law sit uneasily because the system itself does not allow any additional perspectives to be taken seriously other than those relating to the conflict between prosecution and defence (see discussion in Groenhuijsen 2004, 65).

All traditional theories have been subject to substantial criticism, and many theorists appear to promote one theoretical approach over the other. Yet, they have in common that they are generally widely supported and applied in different jurisdictions. That is also the case for their (non-existent) stance on victims. While more contemporary theories take into account victims and their needs to a greater extent, they do not appear to attract the same level of support as the case of expressive theory demonstrates. In addition, restorative justice generally does not focus on the role of victims within the traditional justice system. Rather, it seeks to afford victims participation possibilities outside of this traditional arena. Accordingly, the actual victims' role in traditional criminal procedure remains unaffected by this approach.

In light of the above, the question arises what consequences the absence of victims from traditional criminal theories has for the role victims play in criminal procedure in national criminal justice systems today. Luna (2003, 250) points out that theories are important in practice as they 'inform legislative sentencing schemes, prosecutorial charging decisions, and judicial distributions of punishment'. In an attempt to identify whether national justice systems remain heavily dominated by a traditional understanding of crime and criminal justice and how this effects the role of victims, Chapters 4–6 provide a detailed analysis of victims' procedural rights at the pre-trial, trial and post-trial stage in the selected jurisdictions. Building upon these findings, Chapter 7 subsequently contains a comprehensive case study of how victims and their role in the criminal justice system are perceived by different actors in Germany, an inquisitorial system, and Australia, an adversarial system. This is done with a view to identifying what the theoretical underpinning of the enacted victims' participatory rights could be. The aim is to examine whether these rights can be understood as a new way of thinking about victims in criminal procedure apparently incompatible with traditional criminal theories in their classical sense or whether they should be seen as mere modifications of the traditional criminal justice system.

Note

1. The origins of the term 'restorative justice' are frequently attributed to Albert Eglash (1977). See, for example, discussion in Dignan (2005, 94).

References

Achuti, D. (2017). Is a Critical Model of Restorative Justice Possible? A Penal Abolitionist Approach. In I. Aertsen & B. Pali (Eds.), *Critical Restorative Justice* (pp. 14–28). Oxford: Hart Publishing.

Adler, M. D. (2000). Expressive Theories of Law: A Sceptical Overview. *University of Pennsylvania Law Review, 148*(5), 1363–1501.

Berndt, A. F. (2017). *Der Täter-Opfer-Ausgleich aus Sicht des Opfers: Theorie und Praxis einer alternativen strafrechtlichen Intervention unter Einbeziehung konsistenztheoretischer Annahmen*. Muenster: LIT Verlag.

Bilz, K. (2016). Testing the Expressive Theory of Punishment. *Journal of Empirical Legal Studies, 13*(2), 358–392.

Blagg, H. (2017). Doing Restorative Justice 'Otherwise': Decolonising Practices in the Global South. In I. Aertsen & B. Pali (Eds.), *Critical Restorative Justice* (pp. 61–78). Oxford: Hart Publishing.

Bolivar, D. (2017). Deconstructing Empowerment in Restorative Justice. In I. Aertsen & B. Pali (Eds.), *Critical Restorative Justice* (pp. 29–46). Oxford: Hart Publishing.

Buruma, Y. (2004). Doubt on the Upsurge of the Victims' Role in Criminal Law. In H. Kaptein & M. Malsch (Eds.), *Crime, Victims and Justice: Essays on Principles and Practice* (pp. 1–15). Aldershot: Ashgate.

Ciocchetti, C. (2003). Wrongdoing and Relationships: An Expressive Justification of Punishment. *Social Theory & Practice, 29*(1), 65–86.

Dignan, J. (2005). *Understanding Victims and Restorative Justice*. Berkshire, UK: McGraw-Hill Education.

Duff, R. A. (2005). Guidance and Guidelines. *Columbia Law Review, 105*, 1162–1189.

Eglash, A. (1977). Beyond Restitution: Creative Restitution. In J. Hudson & B. Galaway (Eds.), *Restitution in Criminal Justice* (pp. 91–129). Lexington, MA: D.C. Heath.

Fattah, E. (2004). Gearing Justice Action to Victim Satisfaction Contrasting Two Justice Philosophies: Retribution and Redress. In H. Kaptein & M. Malsch (Eds.), *Crime, Victims and Justice: Essays on Principles and Practice* (pp. 16–30). Aldershot: Ashgate.

Flanders, C. (2014). Can Retributivism Be Saved. *Brigham Young University Law Review, 2014*(2), 309–362.

Fletcher, G. P. (1999). The Place of Victims in the Theory of Retribution. *Buffalo Criminal Law Review, 3,* 51–64.

Galoob, S. R. (2017). Retributivism and Criminal Procedure. *New Criminal Law Review, 20*(3), 465–505.

Gladfelter, A., & Ruback, B. (2017). Victims' Needs and Restorative Justice. In C. Roberson (Ed.), *Routledge Handbook on Victims' Issues in Criminal Justice* (pp. 197–210). New York: Routledge.

Groenhuijsen, M. S. (2004). Victims' Rights and Restorative Justice: Piecemeal Reform of the Criminal Justice System or a Change of Paradigm? In H. Kaptein & M. Malsch (Eds.), *Crime, Victims and Justice: Essays on Principles and Practice* (pp. 63–79). Aldershot, Hampshire: Ashgate.

Hampton, J. (1992a). An Expressive Theory of Retribution. In W. Cragg (Ed.), *Retributivism and Its Critics* (pp. 1–25). Stuttgart, Germany: F. Steiner.

Hampton, J. (1992b). Correcting Harms Versus Righting Wrongs: The Goal of Retribution. *UCLA Law Review, 39,* 1659–1702.

Hoernle, T. (2006). Die Rolle des Opfers in der Straftheorie und im materiellen Strafrecht. *Justisten Zeitung, 19,* 950–958.

Hoernle, T. (2017). *Straftheorien* (2nd ed.). Tuebingen: Mohr Siebeck.

Kant, I. (1996). *The Metaphysics of Morals* (M. J Gregor, Ed. & Trans.). Cambridge: University Press.

Kaptein, H. (2004). Against the Pain of Punishment: Retribution as Reparation Through Penal Servitude. In H. Kaptein & M. Malsch (Eds.), *Crime, Victims and Justice: Essays on Principles and Practice* (pp. 80–111). Aldershot: Ashgate.

Kennedy, K. C. (1983). A Critical Appraisal of Criminal Deterrence Theory. *Dickinson Law Review, 88,* 1–13.

Lippke, R. L. (2006). Mixed Theories of Punishment and Mixed Offenders: Some Unresolved Tensions. *The Southern Journal of Philosophy, 44*(2), 273–295.

Luna, E. (2003). Punishment Theory, Holism, and the Procedural Conception of Restorative Justice. *Utah Law Review, 2003*, 205–302.
McGonigle Leyh, B. N. (2011). *Procedural Justice? Victim Participation in International Criminal Proceedings*. Antwerp: Intersentia.
Moore, M. (1993). Justifying Retributivism. *Israel Law Review, 27*(1–2), 15–49.
Moore, M. (1999). Victims and Retribution: A Reply to Professor Fletcher. *Buffalo Criminal Law Review, 3*(1), 65–89.
Murphy, J. G., & Hampton, J. (1988). *Forgiveness and Mercy—Cambridge Studies in Philosophy and Law*. Cambridge: Cambridge University Press.
Niggli, M. A. (2012, August 20–22). *Security as a Goal of Criminal Justice*. Presented at the Asian Criminological Society's 4th Annual Conference, Seoul/Korea. Retrieved from http://www.unifr.ch/ius/assets/files/chaires/CH_Straf_und_Rechtsphilo/files/PDFs/NiggliSeoulSecurity.pdf.
Pemberton, A., & Aarten, P. G. M. (2017). A Radical in Disguise: Judith Shklar's Victimology and Restorative Justice. In I. Aertsen & B. Pali (Eds.), *Critical Restorative Justice* (pp. 315–330). Oxford: Hart Publishing.
Peter, F. (2014). *Verbesserung der Stellung des Opfers im Strafverfahren*. Hamburg: Verlag Dr Kovac.
Plato, Protagoras. (1967). 324 a und b. In *Plato in Twelve Volumes* (W. R. M. Lamb, Trans.). Cambridge, MA: Harvard Universtiy Press; quoted in Niggli, M. A. (2012, August 20–22). *Security as a Goal of Criminal Justice*. Presented at the Asian Criminological Society's 4th Annual Conference, Seoul/Korea. Retrieved from http://www.unifr.ch/ius/assets/files/chaires/CH_Straf_und_Rechtsphilo/files/PDFs/NiggliSeoulSecurity.pdf.
Sautner, L. (2010). *Opferinteressen und Strafrechtstheorien, Zugleich ein Beitrag zum restorativen Umgang mit Straftaten*. Insbruck: Studienverlag.
Schiemann, C. F. (2015). *Die Beruecksichtigung von Opferinteressen in der Straftheorie*. Hamburg: Verlag Dr Kovac.
Smart, J. J. C. (1991). Utilitarianism and Punishment. *Israel Law Review, 25*(3), 360–375.
Starkweather, D. (1992). The Retributive Theory of 'Just Deserts' and Victim Participation in Plea Bargaining. *Indiana Law Journal, 67*(3), 853–878.
Sumner, L. W. (1982). Utilitarianism Reformed. *Michigan Law Review, 80*, 701–730.
Van Camp, T., & Wemmers, J.-A. (2013). Victim Satisfaction with Restorative Justice: More Than Simply Procedural Justice. *International Review of Victimology, 19*(2), 117–143.

Webb, S. D. (1980). Deterrence Theory: A Reconceptualization. *Canadian Journal of Criminology, 22*, 23–35.
Wood, D. A. R. (2010). *Punishment: Nonconsequentialism: Philosophy Compass* (Vol. 5/6, University of Melbourne Law School Research Series, Paper No. 487). Retrieved from https://papers.ssrn.com/sol3/papers.cfm?abstract_id=1659453.

4

Victim Participation: Investigation and Pre-trial Decisions

1 Introduction

Chapter 2 emphasised that the once strong role victims held in criminal procedure diminished with increased understanding of crime as an offence against the state and not against the individual victim. The introduction of public police and prosecution services led to the exclusion of victims in an active capacity from proceedings and mainly reduced them to witnesses if the system required their participation. The transition from key player to marginalised figure is mirrored by traditional criminal justice theories discussed in Chapter 3 which are largely characterised by the absence of any reference to victims.

Since the mid-twentieth century, much emphasis has been placed on victims, their needs and rights. On the international level, in 1985 the United Nations Declaration of Basic Principles of Justice for Victims of Crime and Abuse of Power stressed the importance of improving the treatment of victims by *inter alia* affording them opportunities to present views and concerns at relevant stages of the proceedings during which their interests are affected. The principle is based on the

K. Braun, *Victim Participation Rights*, Palgrave Studies in Victims and Victimology, https://doi.org/10.1007/978-3-030-04546-3_4

underlying assumption that participation during proceedings can be beneficial to those victims wishing to partake by giving them a voice.

Chapters 4–6 seek to identify to what extent victims have been afforded participation rights in the selected jurisdictions at distinct trial stages. This chapter focuses on the pre-trial stage and on four specific decision-making processes which may have a significant impact on victims: the non-investigation and non-prosecution decision, the decision to grant the accused pre-trial release from incarceration, as well as the decision to enter into a plea agreement. The analysis proceeds by tracing the possibilities for victim participation in detail in each of the selected jurisdictions. In so doing, the three chapters provide a holistic overview of existing victim participation rights in different legal systems with different legal traditions.

Much research relating to victim participation, especially in common law jurisdictions, focuses on the victims' possibility to be heard at the sentencing stage. This is often analysed through the use of Victim Impact Statements (VISs), statements describing how the crime has affected the victim. There has been less scholarly attention focused on victim involvement in decisions made during the pre-trial and post-trial phase. While victims' interests may be affected during the trial proper and at sentencing, it cannot be overlooked that their interests may also be significantly impacted by decisions taken before or after the trial. In fact, many cases may never proceed to the (full) trial stage for various reasons, rendering the pre-trial phase the only criminal justice space in which victims could potentially participate.[1]

Once notice of an alleged criminal act has come to the attention of relevant authorities, be it due to reporting by the victim, another informant or through other means, several subsequent decisions potentially impacting victims' interests can be made. For example, where criminal justice authorities decide not to investigate or not to bring public charges against an accused, the matter will likely not progress to trial and no verdict will be reached labelling the accused as guilty or innocent. Some victims may be left feeling frustrated that the offence they believe has been committed against them is not worth investigating by authorities or hearing in a public court. Additionally, scholars have noted that a large number of cases do not proceed to a (full) trial due to plea agreements negotiated during the pre-trial phase. Depending on the jurisdiction, in these often informal negotiations between prosecution and defence, a defendant pleads guilty to a specific offence in exchange for certain sentencing conditions. A plea agreement can therefore lead to the dismissal or reduction of certain charges, and the application of a lesser sentence than the accused would have likely received at the end of a trial. Where a plea agreement is made, victims may find that the charges agreed upon by prosecution and defence no longer reflect the reality of the offences they feel have been committed against them. Thus, although the defendant admits their guilt in relation to an offence against the victim in the context of the plea agreement, the victim may be dissatisfied with the specifics of the offence. Lastly, the decision to waive an accused's pre-trial detention can be very significant for victims from a safety perspective as the risk exists that they may encounter the defendant who awaits trial in the community.

For the above reasons, victims may have an interest in partaking in these decision-making processes. Whether and to what extent victims are able to do so depends on national laws. Edwards notes that victim participation can take four different forms, affording victims different levels of control over certain decisions (Edwards 2004, 975). Firstly, and most far-reaching, victims may be given the right to exercise complete decision-making control. That means victims' views must be provided and are binding on criminal justice authorities regarding a specific decision. Secondly, victims may have the right to consult with criminal justice authorities about a specific decision without having direct control over the outcome. Authorities would have to seek victims' views, if victims wish to give them, but are not bound to follow them. Thirdly, victims may be under a duty to provide certain information to criminal justice authorities. This means authorities must seek out victims and obtain information which, in turn, victims are obligated to provide. Fourthly, and lastly, victims may have a right to express whatever information they wish without any impact on the system. Wemmers (2017, 179) describes this as a 'one-directional flow of information from the victim to the court'.

The analysis in this chapter mainly focuses on participation which potentially allows victims to influence the decision made and to have some input in the process, even if it is in the form of requesting the review of a specific decision. The chapter assesses victims' statutory rights to participate while highlighting the structural differences of the investigation phase in the different legal systems where applicable.

2 Decision Not to Investigate

Criminal justice authorities in many of the jurisdictions examined, especially inquisitorial jurisdictions, are legally obligated to inquire whether there is sufficient cause to open a formal investigation into a matter which has come to their attention (see, e.g., the situation in Denmark: Administration of Justice Act, *Retsplejeloven*, *AJA* (Denmark) s 742(2)). In other words, where a credible allegation of an offence is brought to their attention, authorities cannot merely dismiss the case (see, e.g., German Code of Criminal Procedure *Strafprozessordnung*, *StPO* (Germany) ss 152(2), 170(1)).[2] However, after relevant inquiries, criminal justice authorities may refuse to open a formal investigation, for example, where no sufficient formal grounds for initiating an investigation can be identified. The question then arises, whether and how the individual victim can challenge said non-investigation decisions. The below first provides an overview of the main principles of the investigative stage in the relevant criminal justice systems. It proceeds with an analysis of adversarial jurisdictions before turning to inquisitorial and mixed criminal justice systems.

2.1 Adversarial Systems: England and Wales, Australia and the US

Criminal proceedings in most adversarial jurisdictions are characterised by their bipartisan nature. It is usually the parties, namely defendant and prosecution, who are responsible for gathering and introducing their own evidence at trial (De Meester et al. 2013, 206). In typical adversarial tradition, the prosecutor gathers evidence to build the case for the prosecution while the defendant also investigates the matter to build a defence and to improve their chances of an acquittal. Different to the situation in inquisitorial jurisdictions discussed below, the criminal investigation is carried out by police and the public prosecutor generally does not control the police during the investigation phase. The prosecution may, however, suggest that the police carry out certain investigations (Cape and Hodgson 2007, 61). The role of the public prosecution traditionally commences with the conclusion of the police investigative steps (McClelland 2002, 14).[3] The other party to the proceedings, the defendant, is able to carry out their own investigation. However, the right is limited in practice as public funding for these investigations is limited and few formal investigative powers are bestowed upon defendants.

Under common law, the police have no general duty to investigate all offences which come to their attention. For this reason, in Australia, in the absence of exceptional circumstances, authorities are under no duty to investigate every case (see *Taha v. Shaq Industries Pty Ltd & Ors* 2012). Rather, the police have broad discretion regarding the investigation of offences (Oxford Pro Bono Publico 2015a, 17). In England and Wales, however, the introduction of the *Human Rights Act 1998* (UK) incorporating the rights contained in the *European Convention on Human Rights* into UK law may have created such a duty for police in relation to specific serious offences (Oxford Pro Bono Publico 2015c, 8; see also *DSD & NBV v. Commissioner of Police for the Metropolis* 2018). Victims have no statutory rights to be consulted in relation to the non-investigation decision as such. Yet, in England and Wales, victims may be able to challenge a decision not to open a formal investigation in the court system in cases where this amounts to a human rights' violation (see, e.g., *DSD & NBV v. Commissioner of Police for the Metropolis* 2018). In order to do so, however, the victim must bring separate proceedings. A formal avenue to appeal the decision not to investigate to either a superior police officer or public prosecutor, as available in a number of inquisitorial and mixed systems, does not exist for victims in England and Wales. While it is possible to complain to the Independent Police Complaints Commission, the subject of the review is the conduct of the acting police officer and not the non-investigation decision as such (Oxford Pro Bono Publico 2015c, 8).

In Australia, victims have no right to be consulted in the context of the non-investigation decision and have not been afforded formal avenues to appeal said decision. Rather, different Australian jurisdictions have policies in place allowing victims to complain internally to the state police service to varying degrees (Oxford Pro Bono Publico 2015a, 18), or externally to victim service coordinators or commissioners for victims' rights, where available. These processes, however, do not amount to explicit statutory rights to request a formal review of the decision not to investigate.

In the US, on the federal level, authorities are under the obligation to carry out reasonable investigations or make a reasonable decision why the investigation will not be carried out (Oxford Pro Bono Publico 2015d, 6). A complaint against the decision not to investigate may be directed to the Department of Justice. This process, however, is not a review of the decision as such but focuses on possible misconduct of the acting police officer arising in the context of refusing the investigation (Oxford Pro Bono Publico 2015d, 7). As such, also in the US, no specific avenue designed for victims to complain against non-investigation decisions or to be heard in the process is in place.

The particulars of the investigation phase in the selected inquisitorial and mixed criminal justice systems and whether victims can participate in the non-investigation decision are analysed below.

2.2 Inquisitorial and Mixed Systems: Germany, France, Denmark, Sweden

The criminal investigation phase in countries with an inquisitorial tradition, such as Germany and France, differs greatly from adversarial jurisdictions. Generally, the pre-trial investigation phase is lengthy, state run and requires criminal justice authorities to act as impartial investigators (De Meester et al. 2013, 205; Hodgson 2005, 30). The investigation phase is designed for truth finding (Hodgson 2005, 30), which, so it is traditionally believed, cannot be achieved through a bipartisan investigation process as available in common law jurisdictions. Due to the official nature of the investigation phase in inquisitorial jurisdictions, the defendants' role is limited. The investigation authority is under an obligation to examine any incriminating but also exonerating facts (for Germany, see: StPO (Germany) s 160(2)). The public prosecution, acting through the police, carries out most investigations, at least initially.[4] In this capacity, the police act in the service of the public prosecutor and is bound by the public prosecutor's directions. In Germany, during the investigation phase police officers are referred to as the 'supporting force of the public prosecution' (*Hilfsbeamte der Staatsanwaltschaft*) (Court Organisation Act, *Gerichtsverfassungsgestz, GVG* (Germany) s 152(1)). The aim of the investigative phase is to enable the criminal justice authority's decision whether to bring charges or to dispense with proceedings (see StPO (Germany) s 160; Reinmann and Zekoll 2005, 423). This decision marks the end of the investigation phase.

Victims in Germany, France, Denmark and Sweden have all been afforded certain possibilities to participate in the context of the non-investigation decision.

2.2.1 Germany

In Germany, the public prosecution assisted by police is under a legal obligation to investigate an alleged offence brought to its attention where enough initial suspicion exists to support that an offence has been committed.[5] Where the required initial suspicion is missing, no formal investigation will be opened (StPO (Germany) s 152). While victims have no direct input into this decision-making process, they are able to request a review of the decision by complaining to a superior prosecutor (StPO (Germany) s 172(2)).[6] In cases where the non-investigation decision is not reversed by the prosecution authority, it seems settled case law that victims are able to initiate judicial proceedings to compel investigations.[7] These proceedings are not explicitly enshrined in German criminal procedure. Rather, the legislation on proceedings to compel prosecutions, discussed in detail below, is applied analogously in this context (StPO (Germany) s 172 analogue). In case of a successful application, the courts will direct the prosecution to commence the investigation and carry it out until there is enough information to reach a decision on whether the matter should be prosecuted.

While the nature of French pre-trial investigations can differ to those in Germany, victims in France have been afforded certain participation possibilities regarding the non-investigation decision.

2.2.2 France

Prior to considering victims' rights at the pre-trial phase, it needs to be pointed out that two different types of criminal investigations exist in France: (1) police investigation (*enquete policiere*) (see Code of Criminal Procedure, *Code de Procédure Pénale, CCP (France)* ss 53–78 CCP)[8] and (2) judicial investigation (*instruction or information judiciaire*) (see CCP (France) ss 92–121). The former is carried out by the French police under the supervision of the prosecution and informs the prosecutor's decision to commence judicial proceedings. The latter is undertaken under the supervision of an investigative magistrate (*juge d'instruction*) by the French police or, in some cases, by the magistrate themselves after a police investigation. As both investigations are essentially carried out by the police in practice, some have considered this distinction to be 'slightly artificial' (Elliott 2011, 214). Usually, it falls upon the prosecution to conduct an investigation in cases of less serious offences. The prosecution may call upon the investigative magistrate in these instances if the case appears particularly difficult. They must call upon the investigative magistrate in cases concerning serious criminal offences (Elliott 2011, 214; Pfuetzner et al. 2013, 87). Once an investigative magistrate becomes involved in proceedings, they remain in charge of the investigation until the charging decision has been reached. It is at this stage that the respective prosecution authority (*procureur* or *magistrat du parquet*) takes over the prosecution of the case. In France, in case of simple offences, it is generally discretionary whether an investigation will be carried out (Sulzer 2006, 135).

The French Code of Criminal Procedure enables victims to act as civil claimants (*partie civile*) during criminal proceedings. Their main objective during these proceedings is to claim compensation for their civil losses arising from the criminal offence. This is why they hold a special legal status with additional procedural rights which goes beyond that of a simple witness. These broad procedural rights allow civil claimants to directly file a criminal complaint with an investigative magistrate who subsequently investigates the matter (*plainte avec constitution de partie civile*, CCP (France) ss 85–91). In this context, the civil claimant must substantiate that they have suffered harm as the result of the offence in question. The investigating magistrate ultimately decides whether to refer the matter to trial or to dispense with proceedings. Hodgson (2005, 31) explains that the initiation of investigations through civil party claims has increased in recent decades and that sometimes up to 30% of the cases handled by an investigative judge are initiated by a civil claimant rather than a prosecutor. In addition, in cases of less serious offences, a civil claimant can submit their claim directly to the court, so-called *citation directe* (CCP (France) ss 390–392) in which case a suspect is summoned directly to court and matters commence (CCP (France) ss 392, 418, 536). This means that victims who act as civil claimants in France can activate investigations under certain circumstances with the investigating judge or with the court even against the will of the prosecution (Kühne 2010, 706). A victim who does not wish to participate as a civil claimant, however, or who is not eligible to do so, does not have these rights.

In comparison with the mostly inquisitorial jurisdictions Germany and France, Denmark and Sweden have been described as mixed inquisitorial and adversarial systems. Yet, also in these Scandinavian jurisdictions avenues for victims to be involved in the non-investigation decision can be detected.

2.2.3 Denmark and Sweden

The criminal justice systems in Sweden and Denmark are characterised by an inquisitorial investigation phase, which leads into a more adversarial trial phase. As a consequence, similar to the situation in France and Germany, the investigating authority in Denmark and Sweden acts with the obligation to remain objective and impartial (De Meester et al. 2013, 207; Wong 2013, 745). In typical inquisitorial tradition, the phase revolves around truth finding and the suspect is not considered a party to the pre-trial proceedings (Wong 2013, 745). This is expressed, for example, in s 96(2) AJA (Denmark) stating that the public prosecutor must 'not only ensure that the guilty are brought to justice, but also that prosecution of innocents does not take place' (translated in Oxford Pro Bono Publico 2015b, 6). The investigation phase ends with the decision to prosecute or to dispense with proceedings. In Scandinavia, criminal justice authorities are under an obligation to investigate where reasonable suspicion exists that an offence has occurred. The Swedish Code of Judicial Procedure (*Rättegångsbalken*, *RB*), for example, explicitly states in Ch 23 (1)(1) that investigations must be initiated 'as soon as a report is filed or there are other reasons to believe that an offense subject to public prosecution has been committed'.

In Denmark, preliminary judicial investigations in which suspects and witnesses were questioned in court were common until their abolition in 1978 (Langsted et al. 2014, 126). Since then, investigations are carried out by the public prosecution with the assistance of the police (AJA (Denmark) s 96(1)). As per the AJA, the purpose of an investigation is to identify whether the requirements of the offence can be established, to uncover relevant evidence and to ensure the preparation of the case for trial (AJA (Denmark) s 743). Generally, investigations will be triggered by a complaint to the police or through the power of their office, *ex officio*, where a reasonable suspicion exists that an indictable offence has been committed (AJA (Denmark) s 742). That means proceedings can continue even after an initial complaint has been withdrawn. Where no grounds for investigation or further investigation transpire, police may dismiss the complaint (AJA (Denmark) s 749). In this case, the victim has the right to complain to the regional prosecutor within four weeks of being notified of the decision (AJA (Denmark) ss 749(3); 102(1)).

In Sweden, initial investigations can be carried out either by police or by a public prosecutor with the assistance of the police (Wong 2013, 745). Less serious offences, including, for example, traffic offences, are usually investigated by police officers. Yet, the investigation can be taken over by the prosecution anytime should the need arise (Cornils 2013, 138). Investigations in more difficult cases are either investigated by the prosecution from the beginning or taken over by the prosecution as soon as a suspect can be identified (Cornils 2013, 138). In either case, the practical investigation is carried out by police officers. Victims have the right to request a review of the non-investigation decision by a more senior public prosecutor. In case of a successful application, the senior prosecutor may subsequently submit their own indictment in the case at hand.[9]

2.3 Concluding Remarks Concerning the Non-investigation Decision

The above shows that in most adversarial systems examined, victims have not been afforded specific avenues to request an official review of the decision not to open a formal investigation but can merely report their dissatisfaction with the outcome to certain entities. Victims' rights appear stronger in the analysed inquisitorial and mixed systems where victims have the right to request a review of the decision not to open an investigation by a superior police officer or a public prosecutor. In Germany, in case of a negative review outcome, victims can ultimately initiate court proceedings aimed at forcing authorities to open a formal investigation. In the case of civil party proceedings in France, eligible victims can activate investigations through application to the investigating judge or through direct submission to the courts under certain circumstances.

3 Decision Not to Prosecute

Closely linked to the decision not to open a formal investigation is the decision not to lay charges at the end of an investigation into an alleged offence. In some jurisdictions, such as Germany, charges must be laid where sufficient evidence exists that the accused is likely to be found guilty at trial. In this context, the prosecutor has no discretion (see, e.g., StPO (Germany) s 160). The obligation to prosecute without discretion is referred to in some jurisdictions including Germany as the 'principle of legality'. In other jurisdictions, the decision to prosecute is a discretionary decision even where sufficient evidence against the accused is available. In Australia, for example, a two-tier test is applied to identify whether charges will be brought. Initially, the question has to be addressed as to whether there is sufficient evidence to prosecute a case. To satisfy this tier, sufficient *prima facie* evidence concerning the elements of the respective offence and a reasonable prospect of obtaining a conviction must exist. If this is not the case, the prosecutor will not bring charges. Where sufficient evidence is available and a reasonable prospect of conviction can be affirmed, the question arises as to whether the prosecution is in the public interest. Matters to be taken into account in the context of public interest include the seriousness of the offence, any aggravating or mitigating circumstances, the background of the offender, the views of the victim as well as the time passed since the alleged offence (see, e.g., *Director of Public Prosecutions Guidelines (Qld)* Guideline 4).

Where a non-prosecution decision is made, the matter does not proceed to trial. Therefore, the guilt or innocence of an offender in relation to the alleged offence against the victim is never officially established by the court system through means of a verdict. For this reason, the decision not to bring charges may be of extreme significance to victims. Against this background, victims have been afforded possibilities to challenge the decision not to lay charges to varying degrees in adversarial, inquisitorial and mixed criminal justice systems.[10] The below first traces these developments in the European jurisdictions selected for analysis in this volume before considering the legal framework in Australia and the US.

3.1 European Jurisdictions

In relation to EU Member States, the 2012 EU Directive on Minimum Standards on the Rights, Support and Protection of Victims of Crime (*EU Directive on Victims*), a legally binding instrument which required implementation of its provisions in the national law of Member States until November 2015, enshrines in Article 11(1) a right to review of the decision not to prosecute. The article states that

> Member States shall ensure that victims, in accordance with their role in the relevant criminal justice system, have the right to a review of a decision not to prosecute. The procedural rules for such a review shall be determined by national law.

Official avenues for victims to seek a review of the non-prosecution decision are available in Germany, France, Sweden and Denmark as well as in England and Wales. The particulars of the right, however, differ between jurisdictions. Some states allow an internal review of the decision not to prosecute within the police or office of the prosecution, while others have enacted legislation allowing for a judicial review of the decision within the court system. Yet others allow both.

3.1.1 Denmark and Sweden

In Denmark, the investigation phase can end with the decision to prosecute, the decision to dispense with proceedings because a conviction at trial seems unlikely or with the decision to end proceedings for reasons of opportunity (Feldtmann and Reventlow 2013). While the AJA itself does not contain an explicit obligation to prosecute, it is generally accepted that prosecutors are under such duty where required by evidence if no discretionary provisions apply (Langsted et al. 2014, 185). In regard to discretionary provisions, law reform introduced in 1987 has empowered prosecutors in Denmark to dismiss a case on the basis that associated costs, length of proceedings or prosecutorial workload seem disproportionate to the prosecution (AJA (Denmark) s 721(1)(3); see Langsted et al. 2014, 184). Furthermore, prosecutions can be waived, for example, in case of minor offences, conditionally or unconditionally, providing the public prosecution with some discretion (AJA (Denmark) s 722(1)). Victims can initiate internal proceedings requesting a review of the non-prosecution decision by a more senior prosecutor irrespective of whether the decision is based on lack of evidence or on discretionary reasons (AJA (Denmark) s 724(1); see also European Judicial Network, n.d.). In Denmark, victims do not have the right to commence court proceedings with the aim of compelling charges after a non-prosecution decision has been made. As such, the victims' right to review is limited to an internal review within the office of public prosecution and does not extend to a court review of the non-prosecution decision.

Under Swedish law, a public prosecution must occur if, after the investigation, a conviction in court can be expected on reasonable grounds (Wong 2013). In other words, prosecutors in Sweden are under an obligation to prosecute (Carlsson 2010, 15). However, since 1985 (Jacobsson 1994, 507), similar to the situation in Denmark, prosecutions may be waived under certain circumstances even if sufficient evidence exists (RB (Sweden) Ch 20 ss 6–7(a)). This is the case, for example, where the offence is not a serious one and no private or public interest requires prosecution (*Åtalsunderlåtelse*), or where the prosecutorial workload and the expected outcome of proceedings (e.g. only monetary fines) seem disproportionate (RB (Sweden) Ch 20 ss (6)–(7), Ch 23 ss 4, 4a; Wergens 2002, 273; Zila 2012, 242). In any of these cases, prosecutions are closed with an official decision (*Beslut*). In case of non-prosecution, the victim has the right to request an internal review within the prosecution service (Wergens 2002, 273). The process only requires the victim to write to the public prosecutor with the request to reconsider the case and is not regulated in Swedish legislation (Carlsson 2010, 86). Wong (2012, 5) explains that the review process is based on the principle that an authority 'may re-examine its own decision and a superior administrative body may review the decisions of an inferior body within the same hierarchical structure'. Where a more senior prosecutor agrees that prosecution should be commenced, they take over the case and initiate proceedings themselves.

In comparison with the Scandinavian countries, victims in Germany have been afforded both internal and judicial avenues to complain against the non-prosecution decision under certain circumstances.

3.1.2 Germany

For a better understanding of victims' rights in relation to the decision not to bring charges, it is necessary to briefly outline the particulars of the German pre-trial process. German criminal procedure is threefold.

It consists of the initial investigation phase carried out by the prosecution with the assistance of the police, ending with the prosecutor's decision to prosecute or to drop the case. Where the prosecutor decides to file charges, they must do so by submitting an indictment to the relevant court (StPO (Germany) s 170). With few exceptions, prosecution is generally compulsory in Germany if sufficient suspicion exists that an offence has been committed (StPO (Germany) s 170). The submission of the indictment officially ends the investigation stage and commences the intermediate phase (*Zwischenverfahren*), which is controlled by the trial court (Bohlander 2012, 12). During this phase, a judge decides whether the case will actually proceed to trial proper by examining the indictment. In this context, the court carries out a preliminary investigation of all materials uncovered during the investigation phase. The aim of the intermediate phase is to prevent any cases from going to trial, which are unsupported by sufficient evidence against the accused (StPO (Germany) ss 201, 202; see also Hamm et al. 2007, 241). At the end of the intermediate phase, the judge can decide to commence the trial (StPO (Germany) s 203), not to commence a trial (StPO (Germany) s 204), or to temporary stay proceedings, for example, where certain witnesses are temporarily unavailable (StPO (Germany) s 205). Where the decision to commence the trial is made, the main trial phase begins, the particulars of which in relation to victims' participatory rights are discussed in detail in Chapter 5.

Under German law, victims are afforded certain rights to complain against the non-prosecution decision which differ depending on whether the decision was based on insufficient suspicion against the accused or on other discretionary reasons.

Remedies Against the Prosecutor's Decision to Dispense with Proceedings

Dispensing with Prosecutions Due to Insufficient Suspicion Against the Accused

In German criminal procedure, a victim has the right to complain against the prosecutor's decision not to bring charges to a more senior prosecutor within two weeks of the original decision (StPO (Germany) s 172(2)). Where the senior prosecutor is of the opinion that charges should be brought, for example, because they hold a different view on a legal or factual issue in question, they can direct the original prosecutor to file charges. In case the senior prosecutor finds that the facts of the case have not been investigated sufficiently, they can order the original prosecutor to recommence the investigation. Otherwise, they will dismiss the victim's complaint. It is important to note, however, that the review by a more senior prosecutor can only be sought if the decision of the initial prosecutor not to bring charges is based on the ground that no sufficient evidentiary basis for obtaining a conviction against the accused can be established (StPO (Germany) s 170(2)). Recent statistics for the year 2012 show that 32% of all investigation proceedings were dropped due to a lack of sufficient available evidence against the accused (Statistisches Bundesamt 2015, 13).

Where a more senior public prosecutor dismisses the complaint because they take the same view as the original prosecutor, victims have the right to initiate judicial proceedings to compel public charges (*Klageerzwingungsverfahren*) within one month of the dismissal (StPO (Germany) s 172(2)). During these proceedings, a court decides whether the non-prosecution decision was reasonable in light of the principle of legality enshrined in German criminal procedure (see Novokmet 2016, 92–93). Proceedings to compel can only be commenced through a lawyer, and legal representation for the complainant during these proceedings is mandatory (StPO (Germany) s 172(3)). Legal aid is available for victims who meet the usual eligibility criteria including insufficient financial means. In the court application, the complainant must set out why bringing public charges is justified in the case at hand and name supporting evidence for this claim. Subsequently, the court, exclusively based on the submitted materials, determines whether sufficient suspicion to initiate proceedings against the accused can be established (Schroth 2012, 105). Where the court is of the view that due to legal or factual reasons proceedings should not be commenced in the particular case, it will reject the application (StPO (Germany) s 174). Where the court finds that sufficient suspicion can be established, it will decide that charges must be brought. As the public prosecution is formally bound by the court decision, they must subsequently bring charges as a result of the verdict (StPO (Germany) s

175). The court's decision is not subject to any further review (StPO (Germany) s 304(4) sent. 2).

In practice, procedures to compel charges are extremely rare. According to some estimates, they occur in less than 0.2% of cases (Elsner 2008, 239). This is perhaps due to the fact that proceedings are costly and victims have to furnish security for the costs which are likely to be incurred by the Treasury and the accused at the beginning of the process (StPO (Germany) s 176). In addition, in case of an unsuccessful application, and most applications in practice remain unsuccessful (Meyer Krapp 2008, 103; Daimagueler 2016, 219), the procedural costs are imposed on the complainant (StPO (Germany) s 177).

Dispensing with Prosecutions Based on Discretion

The above may suggest that victims in Germany have ample internal as well as judicial avenues to specifically seek a review of the decision not to prosecute. However, in practice many victims are unable to seek either type of review for the following reasons.

While prosecutors in Germany are under a general obligation to prosecute where sufficient suspicion against the accused can be established, the law enshrines a number of cases in which prosecutors nevertheless have discretion to dispense with proceedings. For example, the prosecution can, in case of less serious offences, dispense with prosecutions on the grounds that the guilt of the offender is of minor nature and no public interest in the prosecution exists (StPO (Germany) s 153). Furthermore, a prosecution can be dismissed because the offence forms part of a number of offences and in light of the others appears to be of minor nature (StPO (Germany) s 154). In addition, the prosecution can conditionally drop an offence and order the accused to, for example, pay money to a charity organisation or do volunteer work in exchange (StPO (Germany) s 153a). Even though the accused is burdened with specific conditions, legally these do not amount to a conviction and the guilt or innocence of the accused is not determined. In the above three cases, prosecutors can dispense with a matter based on their discretion (*Einstellung aus Opportunitätsgründen*), which marks an exemption from the above described principle of legality in prosecutions. As statistics show, this avenue for termination occurs frequently in practice, namely in around 30%

of all cases Germany wide (Statistisches Bundesamt 2015).[11] Victims have no right to request an internal or judicial review of any of these discretionary prosecutorial decisions. The reasoning behind this is that proceedings to compel prosecutions were not introduced to provide victims with an avenue of participation. Rather, they serve to make the non-prosecution decision and relatedly, the question of whether the principle of legality has been observed correctly in the case at hand, subject to court review (Daimagueler 2016, 221). Where decisions are discretionary and the principle of legality therefore does not apply, it has been assumed that there is no need to allow for court review. The only remedy available to a victim in these cases is a disciplinary complaint against the individual prosecutor. This complaint, however, may be difficult to support as the proceedings only allow for review of the manner in which the case was handled. The complainant therefore has to establish, for example, that the prosecutor's termination of proceedings was arbitrary or discriminatory.

Moreover, in case of specific offences including trespass, defamation, violation of the privacy of correspondence, bodily injury, stalking or threat, where the public prosecutor feels that prosecution is not in the public interest, it will advise the victim that the offence can only be pursued via means of private prosecution (StPO (Germany) s 374). In the majority of all cases, this advice *de facto* ends proceedings. This is so because private prosecutions are associated with a great cost risk for the victim and investigations without police powers are difficult to undertake. As a consequence, private prosecutions are very rarely carried out. No complaint mechanism is available to victims against the prosecutorial decision advising them to pursue private prosecutions. Statistics show that in up to 11% of all cases Germany wide victims were directed to pursue private prosecutions in lieu of public prosecutions (Statistisches Bundesamt 2015).

The Court's Decision to Dispense with the Case During the Intermediate Phase

After the prosecution submits an indictment, the criminal process enters into the intermediate phase, which is controlled by the trial court. The court revisits all evidence uncovered during the investigation phase and decides whether it is likely that a trial will lead to a conviction. Where the court finds that the available evidence is not sufficient, it can terminate proceedings. In practice, however, most matters are committed to trial (Weigend 2013). Victims without a special role in proceedings, namely those who are not eligible or do not wish to act as a Private Accessory Prosecutor (*Nebenkläger*, PAP),[12] have no right to request a review of the court's decision not to commence the trial.

Proceedings to compel charges comparable to those available in Germany do not exist under French criminal procedure law. Yet, French victims have been afforded certain rights to participate in the non-prosecution decision as analysed below.

3.1.3 France

In France, in contrast to the situation in Germany, the principle of opportunity applies to the decision to prosecute (*Le principe de l'opportunité des poursuite*) (CCP (France) s 40; Novokmet 2016). This means that even where sufficient evidence against an accused is available, it is in the discretion of the prosecution to decide whether or not to prosecute based on public interest considerations.

In case of police investigations supervised by the public prosecution, victims without additional legal status are able to appeal the non-prosecution decision internally in writing to the Prosecutor General at the Court of Appeal within one month of the dismissal (CCP (France) s 40(3)). If the Prosecutor General agrees with the victim's request, they may order the original prosecutor to initiate proceedings or to carry out further investigations (CCP (France) s 40(3)). Otherwise, they will dismiss the complaint and inform the victim about the decision. In case of dismissal, the victim may contact a review committee comprised of different prosecutors (CCP (France) s 48). Where the committee agrees with the victim, they can order the public prosecutor to commence proceedings (CCP (France) s 48(4)).

In addition, as pointed out above, victims have the possibility to lodge an application as a civil claimant for compensation (crime report with compensation request) with the investigative judge. This can set in motion criminal investigation proceedings before the investigative court and is possible even in cases where the prosecutor has refused to commence proceedings (CCP (France) s 1(2)).[13] As such, the civil claimant has an indirect right to initiate criminal proceedings. Yet, as victims in France must choose whether they wish to pursue their claim in civil or criminal courts and are generally bound by that decision (Spiess 2008, 239), victims who pursue their claim in the civil courts may be unable to activate criminal proceedings this way. In case of judicial investigation, the investigative judge will decide whether to commence proceedings or dispose of them. A civil claimant can appeal the magistrate's decision not to continue proceedings to the investigation court (CCP (France) s 186). Lastly, victims can apply to the bailiff to have the alleged offender directly summoned before the court and commence proceedings this way. This last option, however, requires the payment of a deposit.

The right for victims to request an internal review of the non-prosecution decision in the adversarial system of England and Wales has been introduced much more recently than in the analysed inquisitorial and mixed criminal justice systems.

3.1.4 England and Wales

In England and Wales, the decision to prosecute is based on whether there is sufficient evidence against the accused and subsequently on whether the prosecution is in the public interest (Code for Crown Prosecutors (UK), para 4.1). As per the Crown Prosecution Service's (*CPS*) guidelines, prosecutors must take into account the consequences for the victim as well as any views expressed by the victim (Code for Crown Prosecutors (UK), para 4.12). This, however, does not give victims an explicit right to express their views in relation to the prosecution decision. Prosecutors may satisfy their obligations by examining the content of the police file in relation to the consequences of the crime on victims. Furthermore, where victims have not expressed any views, no specific obligations are placed on prosecutors to seek out such views (Wolhuter et al. 2009, 177–178).

Victims in England and Wales are now able to request a review of the decision not to prosecute within the CPS. Prior to 2013, the only avenue available to victims to seek a review of the non-prosecution decision was judicial review by an administrative court in the form of court proceedings. This process was often associated with financial and procedural burdens for victims. As per *R v. DPP Ex parte Chaudhary* (1995), in order for a judicial review to be successful, complainants must demonstrate to the court that the CPS failed to initiate a prosecution because of the application of unlawful policy or that they did not bring charges due to a failure to act in accordance with their 'own settled' policy as enshrined in the Code for Crown Prosecutors or that the decision not to prosecute was perverse and no reasonable prosecutor would have made that particular decision. Both questions of law[14] and questions relating to evidence can be examined by the reviewing court. While the reviewing court cannot compel a prosecution, they can nullify the decision and request the public prosecutor to reconsider their decision. They have, however, no control over the outcome of the prosecutor's decision after additional reconsideration and the prosecutor may reach the same decision as before, namely not to prosecute (see, e.g., *R v. DPP, Ex parte Manning and another* [2001]).[15]

While victims were able to seek a judicial review, an official internal review process within the CPS, similar to the ones available in the analysed continental European and Scandinavian jurisdictions, did not exist in England and Wales prior to 2013. In 2011, the Court of Appeal in *R v. Killick* (2011) dealt with a non-prosecution decision and internal and judicial review requests by victims. It found *inter alia* that the CPS is under the obligation to consider victims' requests for a review of the non-prosecution decision as that decision is final for victims. It also emphasised the importance of an internal review scheme in order to avoid victims having to seek a judicial review each time.[16] Perhaps partially due to this decision, since June 2013, the *Victims Right to Review Scheme* ('VRR Scheme') has been introduced in England and Wales. As per the scheme, victims can initiate internal proceedings by complaining to the CPS and asking for a case review. During the review, various actors within the prosecution service can reconsider whether there is sufficient evidence and whether the prosecution is in the public interest. Based on the review, CPS may decide to recommence proceedings. Within one year of the scheme's operation in 2014, 146 decisions not to prosecute were reportedly successfully reversed by the CPS. This equals a success rate for review applications of around 13% (Shaw 2014). Therefore, in the UK victims are now able to seek an official internal as well as a judicial review in an administrative court against the non-prosecution decision.

The below highlights that the possibilities for victims to be involved in the non-prosecution decision differ significantly between the selected European and non-European jurisdiction.

3.2 Non-European Jurisdictions: Australia and the US

Victim involvement in the non-prosecution decision is much more limited in Australia and the US which, as non-EU countries, are not bound by the EU Directive on Victims or other EU victims' rights legislation.

In Australia, victims in general have not been afforded statutory rights to be heard in relation to the non-prosecution decision. The *Victims of Crime Act 2001* (SA) in South Australia sets out that victims of serious offences should be consulted prior to the charging decision.[17] The section states:

> Section 9A Victim of serious offence entitled to be consulted in relation to certain decisions. A victim of a serious offence should be consulted before any decision is made: (a) to charge the alleged offender with a particular offence; or (b) to amend a charge; or (c) to not proceed with a charge; or (d) to apply under Part 8A of the Criminal Law Consolidation Act 1935 for an investigation into the alleged offender's mental competence to commit an offence or mental fitness to stand trial.

The obligation, however, is weakly worded by using 'should' instead of 'must'. Furthermore, as per the Act, the enshrined principles do not constitute enforceable rights for victims (*Victims of Crime Act 2001* (SA) s 5(3)). In other Australian jurisdictions, some prosecutorial guidelines and policy documents contain obligations to take the victims' views into account in the context of the charging decision.[18] Given the legal quality of these obligations, however, victims do not have a positive right to express their views in this context and cannot enforce the right to be heard where prosecutors fail to do so. Moreover, because the ultimate decision to prosecute is discretionary, formal review schemes allowing victims to request an internal review of the non-prosecution decision are not currently in place in Australia. In the context of Victoria, for example, the Victorian Law Reform Commission (2015, 45–47) highlights that an Office of Public Prosecution Complaints Policy exists which theoretically allows victims to complain against the non-prosecution decision. However, no information is provided to the public on how a complaint can be made. In addition, victims have limited possibilities to initiate a judicial review of the discretionary decision not to prosecute (see, e.g., *Maxwell v. The Queen* 1996). As a consequence, with few exceptions, victims in Australian jurisdictions do not have statutory rights to be consulted in relation to the prosecution decision, the right to request an internal review of said decision or to initiate a judicial review of the non-prosecution decision.

In the US, on the federal level, one US Attorney is appointed by the President for each federal judicial district and carries out their obligations under the supervision of the US Attorney General. The decision whether or not to charge a suspect is in the prosecutorial discretion of the Attorney (Pizzi 2012, 189). Relevant factors in the decision-making process include the seriousness of the crime, what deterring effect prosecution may have on the individual and society as well as the offender's past crimes (Boyles 2015, 129). The Crime Victims' Rights Act 2004 (US) (CVRA) sets out that the victim has a 'reasonable right to confer with the attorney for the Government in the case' (CVRA (US) s 3771(a)(5)). Whether this gives victims the right to be consulted before the charging decision is made, however, is unclear. The Senate sponsors of the section state that '[u]nder this provision, victims are able to confer with the Governments' attorney about proceedings <u>after</u> charging' (Kyl 2004, S4268; see also discussion Doyle 2008, 25).[19] This indicates that victims may not have the right to be consulted in relation to the non-prosecution decision but only after charges have been brought by the prosecution. However, some courts have interpreted the CVRA in the context of its obligation to treat victims with fairness and respect to include an obligation of the government to consult with the victim prior to dismissing charges.[20] While this may also extend to the non-prosecution decision, victims' rights in this context appear somewhat opaque.

The CVRA does not afford victims an explicit statutory right to request an internal review of the non-prosecution decision as such. In addition, courts have demonstrated some reluctance in reviewing discretionary prosecution decisions including the decision not to pursue criminal conduct. A judicial review of discretionary prosecutorial decisions appears therefore available only in exceptional circumstances (see, e.g., discussion in *Armstrong v. United States* 1996).

It may be suggested that victims have the right to act as private prosecutors, especially under common law, and thus have ample possibilities to participate and bring proceedings even where the public prosecutor fails to do so. The below explains why the availability of private prosecution cannot be considered an adequate avenue for victims to participate in criminal proceedings.

3.3 The Right to Private Prosecution

Victims in adversarial and non-adversarial systems have the right to pursue private prosecution of a criminal matter under certain circumstances. Where the public prosecutor refuses to investigate or to prosecute, victims may be able to initiate a private prosecution instead. It could therefore be argued that the right to private prosecution allows victims to actively participate during the pre-trial phase. This, however, is not the case as the right is frequently limited in scope and places legal and financial burdens on victims pursuing it. The below outlines the differences in the right to private prosecution in inquisitorial and adversarial jurisdictions by using Germany and Australia as examples prior to identifying why the right does not constitute an appropriate avenue for victim participation during proceedings.

The right to participate as a private prosecutor in Germany differs significantly from the right to private prosecution in common law jurisdictions. As outlined in Chapter 2, a public prosecution service, independent from the courts, was established in Germany for the first time in the first half of the nineteenth century (see overview in Frey 1850, 53–234). With the introduction of the StPO in 1877, the state was granted a monopoly over prosecutions. This means that in Germany the public prosecution, and not the victim or the general public, has the exclusive right to prosecute criminal acts. However, as an exception to this monopoly, the victim has been granted the right to carry out private prosecutions in certain, limited cases explicitly named in legislation. The intention behind this right, however, was not to give up the monopoly of public prosecution but rather to decrease the prosecution's workload in cases of less serious offences of a more private nature (Ackermann 2006, 36). Such minor matters explicitly mentioned in the StPO include libel, threat and property damage.

Private prosecution in Germany has proven difficult for victims in practice for the following reasons. Firstly, victims have to conduct their own investigation without assistance from state investigation authorities. As such, private prosecutors do not have any of the investigatory powers the police have when conducting an investigation. Thus, it may not be possible for many private prosecutors to investigate the criminal offence in a manner that will allow them to present sufficient evidence at trial (Lütz-Binder 2009, 136). Secondly, private prosecutors are obligated to finance the private prosecution by paying an advance on the trial fees, and possibly also a security deposit for the potential costs arising for the accused, before a trial can commence (Act on Court Costs and Fees, *Gerichtskostengesetz, GKG* (Germany) s 67). In case of unsuccessful prosecution, the costs of the proceedings as well as the costs for the defence of the accused, including legal costs, can be placed on the private prosecutor. Thus, a high cost risk exists (StPO (Germany) s 471(3)). The cost distribution in private prosecutions, despite the fact that legal aid is available for eligible private prosecutors, has been described as favouring financially able victims over victims without financial means (Lütz-Binder 2009, 136). Thirdly, the court can terminate private prosecutions at any stage if it finds the perpetrator's guilt to be negligible. This occurs frequently in practice (Schroth 2012, 212). As a consequence, private prosecutions in Germany occur rarely (Statistisches Bundesamt 2017).[21] In front of this background, scholars have voiced concerns that private prosecution in its current form is not worth maintaining (Schroth 2012, 212).

Private prosecutions in Australia differ to Germany in that a common law right to private prosecution for everyone, including victims, exists in all jurisdictions (Kirchengast 2006, 96–97; Gans 2011, 57). In some jurisdictions in Australia, the right to private prosecution is explicitly set out in legislation. According to legislation in New South Wales, for example, a 'common informer' (*Criminal Procedure Act 1986* (NSW) s 14) has the right to commence private prosecution. In that case, the defendant is summoned to court to answer the charges (*Criminal Procedure Act 1986* (NSW) s 54). Yet, victims as private prosecutors in Australia face similar problems to the ones outlined above for private prosecutors in Germany. Conducting private prosecutions in Australia is costly for victims, and legal aid is usually not accessible. Additionally, private prosecution is time intensive for victims, as it requires them to discover evidence and develop strategies to run the trial. Overall, it holds few benefits for the individual victim (Klerman 2001, 8). Furthermore, private prosecutions may be stayed, terminated or taken over by the state on various grounds (Kirchengast 2008, 8–9).[22] Finally, private prosecutors must have the right skill set and the evidence to prove a case 'beyond a reasonable doubt', which constitutes a high standard of proof. This may be a difficult undertaking for a private individual without police investigation powers. Consequently, comparable to the situation in Germany, the right to private prosecution is seldom exercised by victims in Australian jurisdictions (Kirchengast 2008, 11–12).

Even if private prosecutors did not face the above challenges, it is doubtful whether the right to private prosecution can be considered of any benefit to victims. Research by Wemmers and Cyr (2004) on crime victims in Canada has identified that where victims were given the choice of what kind of participation they preferred in proceedings, the majority stated that they wanted to be heard while not being responsible for the decisions taken.[23] This finding is in accordance with earlier research on crime victims and their perception of criminal justice in the Netherlands. Research there indicates that victims felt burdened when being held responsible for the decisions in the criminal justice system and that they did not want to be responsible for taking control of the case (Wemmers 1996, 208). In other words, both studies suggest that victims do not want to be burdened with being directly responsible for the conviction of the defendant and other decisions made. Rather, they want to be heard by decision makers. As private prosecutors, however, they are exclusively responsible for all decisions in addition to being responsible for collecting the evidence, conducting the trial and possibly being subject to trial costs in certain courts. As such, the benefits of private prosecutions for victims may be very limited.

While the above mainly focused on the victims' role in the non-investigation and non-prosecution decision, the below considers victim involvement in decisions relating to pre-trial release and plea agreements.

4 Decisions Relating to Pre-trial Detention and Release

Depending on the particulars of national law, once a person is charged a judge may decide whether the person shall be committed into custody and whether pre-trial release is possible under certain conditions. All of the jurisdictions analysed have enacted provisions relating to pre-trial detention although specific grounds for and the processes of pre-trial detention vary between jurisdictions. Common themes which warranted pre-trial detention in the analysed jurisdictions were flight risk of the accused, risks associated evidence tampering, as well as the risk of committing further offences while awaiting trial. In addition, all jurisdictions but for Sweden allowed for some form of conditional release from custody in exchange for a monetary deposit to court under certain circumstances. While the decisions to grant pre-trial release can significantly impact victims' interests, especially their safety, only a few jurisdictions have afforded victims the right to participate in the decision-making process and none of the analysed jurisdictions allows victims to request a review of the pre-trial release decisions.

England and Wales, Australia and the US all require that victims' interests should be taken into account in relation to bail decisions. This does not mean, however, that victims in these jurisdictions have the right to make direct submissions in relation to pre-trial detention and release as the below outlines.

Most Australian jurisdictions have enacted laws outlining that the interests of the victim for protection should be taken into account in relation to bail applications among other considerations.[24] Relevant obligations placed on criminal justice authorities in this context have further been enshrined in victims' rights legislation. For example, the *Victims of Crime Act 2001* (SA) states the following in relation to victims' views and pre-trial detention:

> Section 7 Right to have perceived need for protection taken into account in bail proceedings. If a police officer or a person representing the Crown in bail proceedings is made aware that the victim feels a need for protection from the alleged offender (a) the police officer or other person must ensure that the perceived need for protection is brought to the attention of the bail authority . . .

However, this does not go hand in hand with a right for victims to make direct submissions to the bail decision-making body. Instead, relevant information is brought to the attention of the court by state officials and not the individual victim.

In the UK, certain victims have the possibility to make a Victim Personal Statement (VPS) explaining how the crime has affected them, which the CPS must submit to the court in a timely manner (Code of Practice for Victims of Crime (UK) 2013 (*Code for Victims*) s 1.12). The right to make such a statement and related issues are discussed further in Chapter 5. An initial statement is made to the police at the same time a witness statement is made with the intent of allowing victims to express their concerns in relation to bail (Code for Victims (UK) s 1.11; Crown Prosecution Service, n.d.). Yet, no legislation is in place in England and Wales specifically allowing victims to present a submission in the context of the bail decision.

In the US, as per the CVRA applicable to federal offences, victims have been afforded the right to be 'reasonably heard at any public proceeding in the district court involving release' (CRVA (US) s 3771(a)(4) (1st alt.)), which concerns bail proceedings. Whether victims have the right to be heard verbally or only via a written submission is disputed in practice. Some courts have interpreted the right to mean that victims can make a verbal statement (see *US v. Degenhardt* 2005), while others limit it to written submissions (see *US v. Marcello* 2005; see discussion in Doyle 2015, 25). Furthermore, the legislation is unclear on the content of the victims' communication and relatedly what victims may comment on (Doyle 2015, 26). It appears that victims are able to provide information on whether release should be granted and if so, what the terms of release should be (Broyles 2015, 131).

None of the inquisitorial systems (Germany and France) or mixed criminal justice systems (Denmark and Sweden) afford victims any participation rights in relation to the pre-trial release decision.

5 Decision to Enter into a Plea Agreement

Even where a positive charging decision is made, it does not follow that a full criminal trial will occur. Scholars suggest that plea agreements, often negotiated informally between prosecution and defence, occur very frequently in practice.[25] Where such an agreement is made a main trial either becomes superfluous or is significantly shortened depending on the jurisdiction. In the US, for example, statistics for the federal level suggest that defendants in around 97% of all cases plead guilty (United States Sentencing Commission 2016), many likely due to plea agreements. While plea bargaining has traditionally been more prominent in the Anglo-American setting, different forms of the practice have found their way into many European legal systems. In the jurisdictions analysed, for example, plea agreements in different forms appeared unavailable only under Swedish law (Ervo 2014, 99; Fair Trials 2017). However, in all other jurisdictions varying models existed that allowed certain benefits for the accused, including a more lenient sentence, in exchange for a guilty plea and thus a waiver/reduction of the trial.[26] While plea bargaining, for example, had no formal basis in German criminal procedure until 2009 (StPO (Germany) s 257c), the practice has been frequently applied since the 1980s (Weigend 2013, 257–258). As a consequence, it has been suggested that in Germany the traditional main trial characterised by dispute is now the exception rather than the rule (Weigend 2017, 782). A confession in this context does not render a trial superfluous per se in Germany and other inquisitorial and mixed systems, and the court theoretically remains responsible for determining the relevant facts. Yet, in practice the specific sentence agreed upon will frequently be handed down by the court after a limited trial (Weigend 2013, 258). As a consequence of early plea bargains, a significant number of cases may never reach the trial stage or will not be subject to a proper full trial.

Despite the possibility to issue a trial waiver to varying degrees, most analysed jurisdictions do not afford victims active participation rights in the plea-bargaining process through consultation, nor do they provide them with the right to request a review of the concluded plea agreement.[27] Few statutory provisions exist in Australia regarding the victims' role in the context of plea/charge bargaining. An exception is the *Crimes (Sentencing Procedure) Act 1999* (NSW), which in Section 35A specifically mentions consultation of the victim and the police in regard to charge negotiations:

> 35A Consultation with Victim and Police in relation to Charge Negotiations. (1) In this section: "charge negotiations" means negotiations between the prosecution and an offender with respect to a plea of guilty in relation to an offence other than the principal offence concerned. "prosecution guidelines" means prosecution guidelines in relation to charge negotiations issued by the Director of Public Prosecutions. "requisite consultation" means consultation with the victim and the police officer in charge of investigating an offence that complies with the applicable prosecution guidelines. "victim" has the same meaning as it has in section 26. (2) A court must not take into account offences other than the principal offence, or any statement of agreed facts, that was the subject of charge negotiations unless the prosecutor has filed a certificate with the court verifying that: (a) the requisite consultation has taken place or, if consultation has not taken place, the reasons why it has not occurred, and (b) any statement of agreed facts arising from the negotiations tendered to the court constitutes a fair and accurate account of the objective criminality of the offender having regard to the relevant and provable facts or has otherwise been settled in accordance with the

applicable prosecution guidelines. (3) The certificate must be signed by or on behalf of the Director of Public Prosecutions or by a person, or a person belonging to a class of persons, prescribed by the regulations. (4) A certificate is taken to be signed on behalf of the Director of Public Prosecutions if it is signed by a person who is authorised to do so by means of a written order signed by the Director of Public Prosecutions or who belongs to a class of persons so authorised. (5) The court may require the prosecution to explain the reason for a failure to file a certificate when it is required by this section to do so.

While the provision speaks of a 'requisite' victim consultation, it allows the prosecutor to explain why the victim was not consulted as an alternative. This essentially makes the consultation non-enforceable for victims.

In the US, victims are afforded a statutory right to provide some input into plea agreements for federal offences under the CVRA. The Act sets out that victims have the right to be reasonably heard in relation to decisions involving pleas (CRVA (US) s 3771(a)(4)(2nd alt.)) and that they have a reasonable right to confer with the government attorney in federal cases (CRVA (US) s 3771(a)(5)). This usually occurs through submissions to the public prosecutor prior to the finalisation of a plea agreement and the approval of the trial judge.[28] The prosecutor, however, is not obligated to comply with the victims' views and wishes. In addition, victims are able to address the court prior to the finalisation of a plea agreement (Pugach and Tamir 2016, 49). Victims who believe their rights during plea negotiations have not been complied with by the trial court are able to file a mandamus writ in the appellate court with the possible consequence of voiding a sentence or a plea (Pugach and Tamir 2016, 45). This right does not mean, however, that victims are able to veto the terms of the plea agreement (see, e.g., *Reed v. Becka* 1999).

It is less clear whether the CVRA affords victims the right to participate in plea negotiations between defence and prosecution which occur prior to the filing of charges, or only after charges have been laid. A memorandum issued by the US Justice Department in 2010 states that the rights enshrined in the CRVA do not apply to victims prior to the filing of formal charges against an accused (United States Department of Justice 2010, 9–10). This would mean that victims have no right to be heard in the context of plea bargaining if this takes place before the prosecution makes a charging decision. As a consequence, many victims would be unable to participate in proceedings. For this reason, scholars, as well as some US courts,[29] have taken the view that the CVRA does afford victims' rights prior to the formal charging decision based on the Act's language and legislative history (Cassell et al. 2014, 62). The Act has subsequently been amended and extended to the pre-trial phase but only in relation to the provision of information on certain decisions.[30]

In Germany, only victims who act as Private Accessory Prosecutors (*Nebenkläger*, PAP)[31] and thus hold special legal status in proceedings, a role which will be discussed further in Chapter 5, have the right to comment on a proposed bargain (StPO (Germany) s 257c (3)) if such a deal is discussed during the main trial. However, they do not exercise any control over the final decision. Victims without this special role do not have any right to be involved in this process at all.

As a consequence of plea agreements, a large number of criminal matters may not be dealt with by way of a full trial. As many victims have not been afforded participation rights in relation to these agreements, their participation possibilities in proceedings overall may remain very limited.

6 Discussion

Statistics suggest that many criminal cases never progress to a (full) trial, either because they are disposed of for various reasons or because prosecution and defence negotiate an agreement. Therefore, the pre-trial stage will frequently be the only stage in criminal proceedings in which victims could potentially participate. Some suggest that victims' rights at the pre-trial stage are 'well developed' in some jurisdictions (van der Aa 2015, 240). Yet, the analysis of victims' participatory rights during the pre-trial stage in the selected adversarial, inquisitorial and mixed criminal justice systems in this chapter paints an overall non-harmonised and fragmented picture. Victim participation rights in relation to key decision-making processes are often limited in scope if they exist at all.

Victims in all of the analysed European jurisdictions, adversarial, inquisitorial and mixed, have the right to seek a review of the decision not to prosecute to some degree. Perhaps this is due to the introduction of Article 11 of the legally binding EU Directive on Victims requiring Member States to allow for such review within the context of their national criminal justice system. Since 2013, victims in England and Wales have the right to request an internal review of the decision not to prosecute within the CPS, a right which has long been available to victims in most other EU countries analysed. On closer inspection, the right to request a review, however, does not apply to every non-prosecution decision in every jurisdiction. In Germany, for example, a review is not available for discretionary non-prosecution decisions. Thus, depending on the type of non-prosecution decision (discretionary or non-discretionary), victims in Germany may not be able to ask for a review even though the consequences of the decision are *de facto* the same: the matter does not proceed to trial. No explicit statutory rights to request an internal or judicial review of the non-prosecution decision are available to victims in Australia and in the US on the federal level. In addition to the internal review process, victims in some jurisdictions, for example, Germany, are able to initiate court proceedings to compel prosecutions. The judicial procedure to compel prosecutions in Germany, however, has proven unpopular in practice perhaps due to its low success rate and the associated high financial risks for victims who are burdened with the procedural fees. In France, victims who are eligible and elect to act as civil claimants in criminal proceedings are able to activate proceedings this way even after the prosecution has made a non-charging decision. This, however, does not apply to victims without this special legal role.

The decision to (conditionally) release the accused from pre-trial detention while awaiting trial may significantly affect the victim's safety interests as the decision makes it more likely that the victim will encounter the accused in the community. Yet, only one jurisdiction analysed, the US (on the federal level), gives victims a specific statutory and enforceable right to be heard during district court proceedings relating to release.

Lastly, while almost all analysed jurisdictions allowed for some form of agreement regarding a defendant's confession in exchange for a lower charge or sentence, only the US (on the federal level) give victims in general an explicit and enforceable right to be heard in relation to plea agreements during public proceedings and arguably only after charges have been laid. In Germany, a right to comment in relation to plea agreements has recently been introduced but only for victims who hold the special legal status of PAP.

7 Concluding Remarks

By way of concluding, what becomes clear from the above analysis is that victims' participatory rights in relation to the four pre-trial decisions examined in this chapter are few and limited in scope in adversarial and non-adversarial systems alike. While victims have received the right to be consulted or heard at some point during the pre-trial stage in most jurisdictions, this typically does not translate into a holistic approach to pre-trial victim participation as such.

Some jurisdictions have provided victims with a statutory right to be heard in the form of consultation prior to certain decisions. This is the case in the US on the federal level, for example, in relation to the right to be heard regarding pre-trial release decisions and in the context of plea negotiations. Furthermore, victims can have some input at the pre-trial stage by requesting a review of certain decisions they disagree with. In the European context, for instance, victims in the analysed jurisdictions have the right to request an internal review of the non-prosecution decision. On the whole, however, the participation rights which do exist pretrial are not harmonised between jurisdictions. As proof, in non-European jurisdictions formal rights for victims to request a review of the non-investigation or non-prosecution decision are rare. Moreover, available victims' rights are partially fragmented even within jurisdictions. To illustrate this point, in Germany certain non-prosecution decisions can be subject to internal or court review if requested by the victim while comparable others, namely those which are in the prosecutor's discretion, cannot. In addition, especially in the analysed inquisitorial and mixed criminal justice systems, victims have very few, if any, participatory rights in relation to plea negotiations and pre-trial release decisions. It follows that the situation for many victims concerning participation at the pre-trial stage may be as limited today as it was 30 years ago. *De facto*, however, the pre-trial stage might be the only procedural stage in which victims could potentially participate given that many cases are unlikely to advance to the full trial stage.

It needs to be noted that the UK has introduced a new scheme in 2013 allowing victims to request an internal CPS review of the non-prosecution decision. This development at the pre-trial stage could be seen as a sign that more criminal justice systems are accepting victims as participants in pre-trial proceedings or, perhaps, that criminal procedure is morphing into a more victim-friendly procedure. However, in light of the largely piecemeal approach to pre-trial participation in most jurisdictions analysed in this chapter, this development may not translate into a general stance on victim involvement in national criminal procedure.

Notes

1. This is the case due to an increase in plea agreements as well as other deviation practices aimed at avoiding a full trial in many criminal justice systems.
2. An English translation of the German StPO is available on the German Ministry of Justice website: https://www.gesetze-im-internet.de/englisch_stpo/.
3. Some suggest that in the US prosecutors have taken on a great investigative role, see Little (1999, 728–729).
4. In France, the investigation can be taken over by the investigative judge, see Tricot (2013).
5. The necessary initial suspicion is called *Anfangsverdacht* in Germany, see StPO (Germany) s 152(2). Where this degree of suspicion is affirmed an investigation must be carried out, StPO (Germany) s 160. This is referred to as the principle of legality (*Legalitaetsprinzip*). Proceedings then move to the investigation stage (*Ermittlungsverfahren*).

6. For the particulars of the application process in practice, see *Verfassungsgerichtshof München* (2015).
7. The procedure is not enshrined in the SPO in its own right. Rather, the provisions relating to the proceedings to compel charges (*Klageerzwingungverfahren)*, s 172 StPO, are applied analogue. For case law on these proceedings, see Oberlandesgericht Karlsruhe (2002) and Oberlandesgericht Bremen (2017).
8. An unofficial 2006 English translation of the French Code of Criminal Procedure is available online: http://www.legislationline.org/documents/section/criminal-codes/country/30.
9. The matter is dealt with in the so-called prosecution development centre. See also the Swedish Prosecution Authority's website with additional information on the legal process and the right to review: https://www.aklagare.se/en/the-legal-process/the-role-of-the-prosecutor/decision-to-prosecute/review/.
10. Victim charters or guidelines in some jurisdictions set out that victims should be consulted prior to the decision not to prosecute. In most cases, however, the wording of the provisions makes clear that this does not amount to an enforceable victim's right. See, for example, Victims of Crime Act 2001 (SA) s 9a 'A victim of a serious offence should be consulted before any decision is made—(a) to charge the alleged offender with a particular offence'.
11. The report shows that in 2012 Germany wide only 26% of all investigations ended with the decision to prosecute and the presentation of an indictment (or similar), see Statistisches Bundesamt (2015, 12). In addition, 31% of cases were terminated for reason of opportunity, Statistisches Bundesamt (2015, 13).
12. Private Accessory Prosecution and its requirements are analysed in detail in Chapter 5.
13. The claim will be served upon the prosecutor to respond prior to proceedings being initiated, see CCP (France) s 86(1).
14. In *R v. DPP ex parte Chaudhary* (1995) the plaintiff sought judicial review of the prosecutor's decision not to prosecute a husband suspected of buggery. While the application was successful in this case, the court highlighted that the power to review the DPP's decision not to prosecute must be exercised sparingly.
15. In *R v. DPP, Ex parte Manning and another* (2001) the applicants sought judicial review of the CPS' non-prosecution decision relating to

the death of their brother in prison custody while under the restraint of prison officials. A prior Coroner's jury had found the death to constitute an unlawful killing. The court emphasised that 'the effect of this decision is not to require the Director to prosecute. It is to require reconsideration of the decision whether or not to prosecute. On the likely or proper outcome of that reconsideration we express no opinion at all' (at 42).

16. See *R v. Killick* (2011, 48).
17. Other Australian guidelines for the public prosecution set out that victims' attitudes should be taken into account when deciding whether the prosecution is in the public interest. See, for example, *DPP (NSW) Prosecution Guidelines*, Guideline 4.3.20.
18. See, for example, *Policy of the Director of Public Prosecutions for Victoria*, Chapter 3 Victims and Persons Adversely Affected by Crime (7–9).
19. Underlined by the author.
20. See, *U.S. v. Heaton* (2006, 1272), where the prosecution planned to withdraw charges after proceedings had already commenced and the court found that it was necessary to consult with the victim via the prosecutor first in order to preserve fairness: 'the only way to protect the victim's right to be treated fairly and with respect for her dignity is to consider the victim's views on the dismissal'. If a court is under the obligation to consult with the victim, the same obligation may apply to the prosecution. See also Smith (2010, 425).
21. Overall in Germany in 2016 out of 640,474 terminated criminal matters in the lower courts only 433 matters were private prosecution. See Statistisches Bundesamt (2017, Tables 1.3 and 2.1).
22. Possibilities to limit private prosecutions include the DPP taking over private prosecutions and terminating them or entering into a *nolle prosequi*.
23. The research focused on victims who participated in victim-offender mediation programmes.
24. See *Bail Act 1992* (ACT) s 23A; *Bail Act 2013* (NSW) ss 17(2)(c), 18(1)(n); *Bail Act 1980 (Qld)* s 16(1)(a)(ii)(B); *Bail Act 1985* (SA) s 10(4); *Bail Act 1977* (Vic) s 3AAA (j); *Bail Act* (NT) s 24(e)(i).
25. In the US, the Supreme Court noted in the decision of *Lafler v. Cooper* (2012) that 'criminal justice today is for the most part a system of pleas, not a system of trials'.

26. They are available to a degree in Denmark where they are not called plea agreements but trial waivers.
27. No statutory obligations setting out enforceable rights for victims to be able to participate in the process leading to a plea bargain exist in Australia. See Victorian Law Reform Commission (2015, 45–47). The policy guidelines for prosecutors set out that victims' views should be taken into account in the plea-bargaining process, see, for example, *Director of Public Prosecutions Victoria*, Director's Policy, 5. This is also the case in New South Wales, see *Office of the Director of Public Prosecutions for New South Wales*, Prosecution Guidelines, 37 stating that the victims' views should be taken into account at the beginning of negotiations. In addition, in New South Wales, a signed certificate by the prosecutor has to be filed with the court demonstrating that the victim has been consulted prior to finalising the plea bargain, see *Crimes (Sentencing Procedure) Act 1999* (NSW) s 35A. This right, however, is non-enforceable by the victim. Similar non-enforceable prosecutorial guidelines exist in the UK, see Code for Crown Prosecutors, s 9.3 (Accepting Guilty Pleas).
28. See, for example, *In re Dean* (2008, 394) dealing with the obligation of the prosecutor to allow victims' views in the plea agreement decision-making process: 'Logically, this includes the CVRA's establishment of victims' "reasonable right to confer with the attorney for the Government." …At least in the posture of this case (and we do not speculate on the applicability to other situations), the government should have fashioned a reasonable way to inform the victims of the likelihood of criminal charges and to ascertain the victims' views on the possible details of a plea bargain'.
29. See, for example, *Does v. United States* (2011, 1342) '[i]f the CVRA's rights may be enforced before a prosecution is underway, then, to avoid a strained reading of the statute, those rights must attach before a complaint or indictment formally charges the defendant with the crime'.
30. CRVA (US) s 3771(9) now states that the victim has the 'right to be informed in a timely manner of any plea bargain or deferred prosecution agreement'.
31. Referred to as Private Accessory Prosecutor in the English translation of the German Code of Criminal Procedure. Also translated as 'additional private prosecutor' or 'auxiliary private prosecutor' in comparative literature.

Legislation and Related Sources

Administration of Justice Act (Denmark), Retsplejeloven
Bail Act 1992 (ACT)
Bail Act 2013 (NSW)
Bail Act 1982 (NT)
Bail Act 1980 (Qld)
Bail Act 1985 (SA)
Bail Act 1977 (Vic)
Brottsbalken (Sweden), Penal Code
Code de Procédure Pénale (France), Code of Criminal Procedure
Code for Crown Prosecutors (UK) (version of January 2013)
Code of Practice for Victims of Crime 2013 (UK)
Crimes (Sentencing Procedure) Act 1999 (NSW)
Crime Victims' Rights Act 2004 (US)
Criminal Procedure Act 1986 (NSW)
Director of Public Prosecutions Guidelines (Qld) (version of 30 June 2016)
Director of Public Prosecutions Guidelines (NSW) (version of 1 June 2007)
Director of Public Prosecutions Victoria, Director's Policy (Vic)
European Union Directive of the European Parliament and of the Council (2012). 2012/29/EU, 25 October 2012. Establishing Minimum Standards on the Rights, Support and Protection of Victims of Crime, and Replacing Council Framework Decision 2001/220/JHA
Human Rights Act 1989 (UK)
Rättegångsbalken (Sweden), Code of Judicial Procedure
Strafprozessordnung (Germany), Code of Criminal Procedure
United Nations Declaration of Basic Principles of Justice for Victims of Crime and Abuse of Power, General Assembly Resolution 40/34 of the General Assembly 29 November 1985
Victims of Crime Act 2001 (SA)

References

Ackermann, M. (2006). *Die Rechtsbehelfe des Verletzten gegen die negative Anklageentscheidung des Staatsanwaltes in den USA*. Munich: Herbert Utz Verlag.

Bohlander, M. (2012). *Principles of German Criminal Procedure*. Oxford: Hart Publishing.

Broyles, S. (2015). *Criminal Law in the USA*. Alphen aan den Rijn, The Netherlands: Kluwer Law International.

Cape, E., & Hodgson, J. (2007). The Investigative Stage of the Criminal Process in England and Wales. In E. Cape, et al. (Eds.), *Suspects in Europe: Procedural Rights at the Investigative Stage of the Criminal Process in the European Union* (pp. 59–78). Antwerp: Intersentia.

Carlsson, J. (2010). *Right to Counsel for the Injured Party—A Comparative Study of Sexual Assault Victims' Rights in Sweden, Arizona & Massachusetts* (Master thesis). Lund University Libraries, Faculty of Law. Retrieved from http://lup.lub.lu.se/luur/download?func=downloadFile&recordOId=1628195&fileOId=16281.

Cassell, P., Mitchell, N., & Edwards, B. (2014). Crime Victims' Rights During Criminal Investigations? Applying the Crime Victims' Rights Act Before Criminal Charges Are Filed. *Journal of Criminal Law & Criminology, 104,* 59–103.

Cornils, K. (2013). Sweden. In U. Sieber, K. Jarvers, & E. Silvermann (Eds.), *National Criminal Law in a Comparative Legal Context, 1.1: Introduction to National Systems, Schriftenreihe des Max-Planck Instituts fuer Auslaendisches und Internationals Strafrecht* (pp. 133–204). Berlin: Duncker & Humboldt.

Crown Prosecution Service. (n.d.). *Victim Personal Statements—Legal Guidance*. Retrieved from https://www.cps.gov.uk/legal-guidance/victim-personal-statements.

Daimagueler, M. G. (2016). *Der Verletzte im Strafverfahren: Handbuch fuer die Praxis*. Munich: C.H. Beck.

De Meester, K., Pitcher, K., Rastan, R., & Sluiter, G. (2013). Investigation, Coercive Measures, Arrest, and Surrender. In G. Sluiter, H. Friman, S. Linton, S. Zappala, & S. Vasiliev (Eds.), *International Criminal Procedure: Rules and Principles* (pp. 171–380). Oxford: Oxford University Press.

Doyle, C. (2008). *Crime Victims' Rights Act*. New York: Novinka.

Doyle, C. (2015, December 9). *Crime Victims' Rights Act: A Summary and Legal Analysis of 18 USC 3771*. Washington, DC: Congressional Research Service. Retrieved from https://fas.org/sgp/crs/misc/RL33679.pdf.

Edwards, I. (2004). An Ambiguous Participant: The Crime Victim and Criminal Justice Decision Making. *British Journal of Criminology, 44,* 967–982.

Elliott, C. (2011). France. In K. J. Heller & M. Dubber (Eds.), *The Handbook of Comparative Criminal Law* (pp. 209–251). Stanford: Stanford University Press.

Elsner, B. (2008). *Entlastung der Staatsanwaltschaft durch mehr Kompetenzen für die Polizei?: eine Deutsch-Niederländisch vergleichende Analyse in Rechtlicher und Rechtstatsächlicher Hinsicht*. Göttingen: Universitätsverlag Göttingen.

Ervo, L. (2014). Plea Bargaining as an Example of the Recent Changes in the Finnish Criminal Procedural Paradigm. *Baltic Journal of Law and Politics, 7*(1), 97–112.

European Judicial Network. (n.d.). *The Danish Prosecution Service*. Retrieved from https://www.ejn-crimjust.europa.eu/ejnupload/InfoAbout/The_Danish_Prosecution_Service.pdf.

Fair Trials. (2017, April). *The Disappearing Trial: Towards a Rights-Based Approach to Trial Waiver Systems, Report*. Retrieved from https://www.fairtrials.org/sites/default/files/publication_pdf/Report-The-Disappearing-Trial.pdf.

Feldtmann, B., & Reventlow, S. K. (2013). Denmark. In K. Ligeti (Ed.), *Towards a Prosecutor for the European Union: A Comparative Analysis* (pp. 58–94). Oxford: Hart Publishing.

Frey, L. (1850). *Die Staatsanwaltschaft in Deutschland und Frankreich*. Erlangen: Verlag von Ferdinand Ente.

Gans, J. (2011). *Modern Criminal Law of Australia*. Cambridge: Cambridge University Press.

Hamm, R., Hassemer, W., & Pauly, J. (2007). *Beweisantragsrecht* (2nd ed.). Heidelberg: C.F. Mueller.

Hodgson, J. (2005). *French Criminal Justice: A Comparative Account of the Investigation and Prosecution of Crime in France*. Oxford: Hart Publishing.

Jacobsson, U. (1994). Procedure. In H. Tiberg, F. Sterzel, & P. Cornhult (Eds.), *Swedish Law: A Survey* (pp. 488–565). Stockholm: Juristenfoerlaget.

Kirchengast, T. (2006). *The Victim in Criminal Law and Justice*. New York: Palgrave Macmillan.

Kirchengast, T. (2008). *Private Prosecution and the Victim of Crime* (Macquarie Law Working Paper Series No 2008-17). Retrieved from https://ssrn.com/abstract=1126439.

Klerman, D. (2001). Settlement and the Decline of Private Prosecution in Thirteenth-Century England. *Law and History Review, 19*, 1–65.

Kühne, H.-H. (2010). *Strafprozessrecht: Eine Systematische Darstellung des deutschen und europaeischen Strafverfahrensrecht* (8th ed.). Heidelberg: C.F. Mueller.

Kyl, J. S. (2004). *Statement of Senator Kyl*. 150 Congressional Record, S4268 (daily ed. April 22, 2004).

Langsted, L. B., Garde, P., & Greve, V. (2014). *Criminal Law in Denmark* (4th ed.). Alphen aan den Rijn, The Netherlands: Kluwer Law International.

Little, R. K. (1999). Proportionality as an Ethical Percept for Prosecutor in Their Investigative Role. *Fordham Law Review, 68,* 723–770.

Lütz-Binder, E. (2009). Rechtswirklichkeit der Privatklage und Umgestaltung zu einem Aussoehungsverfahren: Untersuchung unter Auswertung der Privatklageverfahren der Jahre 1992–2002 aus den Amtsgerichtsbezirken Landau/Pfalz, Neustadt/Weinstrasse und Ludwigshafen/Rhein. Frankfurt a.M.: Peter Lang.

McClelland, G. A. (2002). Non-adversary Approach to International Criminal Tribunals. *Suffolk Transnational Law Review, 26*(1), 5–38.

Meyer Krapp, E. (2008). *Das Klageerzwingungsverfahren* (Doctoral dissertation). Georg-August-University Göttingen. Retrieved from https://d-nb.info/991096339/34.

Novokmet, A. (2016). The Right of a Victim to a Review of a Decision Not to Prosecute as Set Out in Article 11 of Directive 2012/29/EU and an Assessment of Its Transposition in Germany, Italy, France and Croatia. *Utrecht Law Review, 12*(1), 86–108.

Oxford Pro Bono Publico. (2015a, April). *Victim Participation in Criminal Procedures: A Report to Assist Redress.* University of Oxford. Appendix: Country Report Australia. Retrieved from http://ohrh.law.ox.ac.uk/opbp-makes-submissions-to-redress-on-victim-participation-in-criminal-procedures/.

Oxford Pro Bono Publico. (2015b, April). *Victim Participation in Criminal Procedures: A Report to Assist Redress.* University of Oxford. Appendix: Country Report Denmark. Retrieved from http://ohrh.law.ox.ac.uk/opbp-makes-submissions-to-redress-on-victim-participation-in-criminal-procedures/.

Oxford Pro Bono Publico. (2015c, April). *Victim Participation in Criminal Procedures: A Report to Assist Redress.* University of Oxford. Appendix: Country Report England and Wales. Retrieved from http://ohrh.law.ox.ac.uk/opbp-makes-submissions-to-redress-on-victim-participation-in-criminal-procedures/.

Oxford Pro Bono Publico. (2015d, April). *Victim Participation in Criminal Procedures: A Report to Assist Redress.* University of Oxford. Appendix: Country Report USA. Retrieved from http://ohrh.law.ox.ac.uk/opbp-makes-submissions-to-redress-on-victim-participation-in-criminal-procedures/.

Pfuetzner, P., Adams, S., Neumann, L., & Walther, J. (2013). France. In U. Sieber, K. Jarvers, & E. Silvermann (Eds.), *National Criminal Law in a Comparative Legal Context, 1.4: Introduction to National Systems, Schriftenreihe des Max-Planck Instituts fuer Auslaendisches und Internationals Strafrecht* (pp. 79–174). Berlin: Duncker & Humboldt.

Pizzi, W. (2012). A Perfect Storm: Prosecutorial Discretion in the United States. In E. Luna & M. Wade (Eds.), *The Prosecutor in Transnational Perspective* (pp. 189–199). Oxford: Oxford University Press.

Pugach, D., & Tamir, M. (2016). Nudging the Criminal Justice System into Listening to Crime Victims in Plea Agreements. *Hastings Women's Law Journal, 28*(1), 45–72.

Reinmann, M., & Zekoll, J. (2005). *Introduction to German Law*. The Hague, The Netherlands: Kluwer Law International.

Schroth, K. (2012). *Die Rechte des Opfers im Straprozess* (2nd ed.). Munich: C.F. Mueller.

Shaw, D. (2014, July 19). Victims' Right of Review Scheme Sees 146 Charged. *BBC News* (online). Retrieved from http://www.bbc.com/news/uk-28377445.

Smith, E. (2010). *Is There a Pre-charge Conferral Right in the CVRA?* University of Chicago Legal Forum, Article 15, 407–446. Retrieved from https://chicagounbound.uchicago.edu/cgi/viewcontent.cgi?article=1467&context=uclf.

Spiess, K. (2008). *Das Adhaesionsverfahren in der Rechtswirklichkeit*. Berlin: LIT Verlag.

Statistisches Bundesamt. (2015). *Justiz auf einen Blick*. Wiesbaden: Statistisches Bundesamt. Retrieved from https://www.destatis.de/DE/Publikationen/Thematisch/Rechtspflege/Querschnitt/BroschuereJustizBlick0100001159004.pdf?__blob=publicationFile.

Statistisches Bundesamt. (2017). *Fachserie 10: Rechtspflege Strafgerichte*. Wiesbaden: Statistisches Bundesamt. Retrieved from https://www.destatis.de/DE/Publikationen/Thematisch/Rechtspflege/GerichtePersonal/Strafgerichte2100230167004.pdf?__blob=publicationFile.

Sulzer, J. (2006). Implementing the Principle of Universal Jurisdiction in France. In W. Kaleck, M. Ratner, T. Singelnstein, & P. Weiss (Eds.), *International Prosecution of Human Rights Crimes* (pp. 125–137). Heidelberg: Springer.

Tricot, J. (2013). France. In K. Ligeti (Ed.), *Towards a Prosecutor for the European Union: A Comparative Analysis* (pp. 222–263). Oxford: Hart Publishing.

United States Department of Justice. (2010). *The Availability of Crime Victims' Rights Under the Crime Victims' Rights Act of 2004*. Retrieved from https://www.justice.gov/sites/default/files/olc/opinions/2010/12/31/availability-crime-victims-rights.pdf.

United States Sentencing Commission. (2016). *United States Sentencing Commission's 2016 Sourcebook of Federal Sentencing Statistics*. Retrieved from http://www.ussc.gov/research/sourcebook-2016.

van der Aa, S. (2015). Post-trial Victims' Rights in the EU: Do Law Enforcement Motives Still Reign Supreme? *European Law Journal, 21*(2), 239–256.

Victorian Law Reform Commission. (2015, July). *Victims of Crime* (Consultation Paper). Retrieved from http://www.lawreform.vic.gov.au/sites/default/files/VLRC_Victims_of_Crime_consultation_paper_for_web_0.pdf.

Weigend, T. (2011). Germany. In K. Heller & M. Dubber (Eds.), *The Handbook of Comparative Criminal Law* (pp. 252–287). Stanford, CA: Stanford University Press.

Weigend, T. (2013). Germany. In K. Ligeti (Ed.), *Towards a Prosecutor for the European Union: A Comparative Analysis* (pp. 264–306). Oxford: Hart Publishing.

Weigend, T. (2017). Alle sind sich einig-und das Opfer? In C. Safferling, G. Kett-Straub, C. Jaeger, H. Kudlich, & F. Streng (Eds.), *Festschrift fuer Franz Streng zum 70. Geburtstag* (pp. 781–798). Heidelberg: Mueller.

Wemmers, J.-A. (1996). *Victims in the Criminal Justice System*. Amsterdam: Kugler Publications.

Wemmers, J.-A. (2017). *Victimology: A Canadian Perspective*. New York: University of Toronto Press.

Wemmers, J.-A., & Cyr, K. (2004). Victims' Perspective on Restorative Justice: How Much Involvement Are Victims Looking For? *International Review of Victimology, 11*, 259–274.

Wergens, A. (2002). The Role and Standing of the Victim in the Face of Criminal Procedure Sweden. *Revue internationale de droit pénal/International Review of Penal Law, 73*(1), 259–300.

Wolhuter, L., Olley, N., & Denham, D. (2009). *Victimology and Victims' Rights*. London: Routledge.

Wong, C. (2012). *Overview of Swedish Criminal Procedure.* Lund University Faculty of Law: From the Selected Works of Christoffer Wong. Retrieved from http://www.congreso.es/docu/docum/ddocum/dosieres/sleg/legislatura_10/spl_85/pdfs/24.pdf.

Wong, C. (2013). Sweden. In K. Ligeti (Ed.), *Towards a Prosecutor for the European Union: A Comparative Analysis* (pp. 742–778) Oxford: Hart Publishing.

Zila, J. (2012). Prosecutorial Power and Policy Making in Sweden and the Other Nordic Countries. In E. Luna & M. Wade (Eds.), *The Prosecutor in Transnational Perspective* (pp. 235–249). Oxford: Oxford University Press.

Cases

Armstrong v. United States, 517 U.S. 456 (1996) (US).

Does v. United States, 817 F. Supp. 2d 1337 (SD Florida 2011) (US).

DSD & NBV v. Commissioner of Police for the Metropolis [2018] UKSC 11 (UK).

Lafler v. Cooper, 566 U.S. 156 (2012) (US).

Maxwell v. The Queen, (1996) 184 CLR 501; [1996] HCA 46 (Australia).

Oberlandesgericht Karlsruhe, 16 December 2002—1 Ws 85/02 (Germany).

Oberlandesgericht Bremen, 21 September 2017—1 Ws 55/17 (Germany).

R v. Christopher Killick [2011] EWCA Crim 1608 (UK).

R v. DPP, Ex parte Chaudhary [1995] 1 Cr App R 136 (UK).

R v. DPP, Ex parte Manning and another [2001] QB 330 (UK).

Re Dean, 527 F. 3d 391 (5th Cir May 7, 2008) (US).

Reed v. Becka, 333 S.C. 676, 511 S.E.2d 396 (Ct.App.1999) (US).

Taha v. Shaq Industries Pty Ltd & Ors [2012] VSC 30 (Victoria).

US v. Degenhardt, 405 F. Supp.2d 1341 (D. Utah 2005) (US).

U.S. v. Heaton, 458 F. Supp. 2d 1271 (D. Utah 2006) (US).

US v. Marcello, 370 F. Supp. 2d 745 (N.D. III. 2005) (US).

Verfassungsgerichtshof München, 25 August 2015—Vf. 48-VI-14 (Germany).

5

Victim Participation: The Trial and Sentencing Process

1 Introduction

Chapter 4 highlighted that numerous criminal cases do not proceed to a full main trial due to the availability of trial waivers and plea bargains at the pre-trial stage in most of the jurisdictions analysed. Nevertheless, cases remain in which criminal courts are called upon to decide on the fate of a defendant after a criminal trial. The right to be heard during the trial may be particularly important to victims as the guilt or innocence of the defendant by means of a verdict is determined at this stage of proceedings. Whether and to what extent victims are able to participate during the trial phase depends on the national justice system and its legal traditions. The victims' role in common law systems has conventionally been that of a witness without additional legal status and respective participation rights. Yet, some civil law countries afford certain victims greater participation rights depending on their legal status in proceedings. After providing a brief overview of the trial structure in the respective jurisdiction, this chapter systematically assesses the right to victim participation at the trial stage in the selected adversarial and non-adversarial systems. Subsequently, it focuses

K. Braun, *Victim Participation Rights*, Palgrave Studies in Victims and Victimology, https://doi.org/10.1007/978-3-030-04546-3_5

on the possibility to participate during the sentencing stage in those jurisdictions which have such a separate phase.

2 Participation at Trial

Possibilities for victim participation at trial vary between adversarial jurisdictions in which participation has traditionally been very limited and non-adversarial jurisdictions where participation for some victims is possible to a greater extent. Although modes of operation vary between jurisdictions, four primary forms of victim participation can be identified in the chosen jurisdictions. Victims can participate as a Private Accessory Prosecutor or as a support for the prosecution next to the public prosecutor during the main trial (Germany and Sweden), they can participate as an applicant to the adhesion procedure where they seek civil compensation for financial losses during the criminal trial (Germany, Denmark, Sweden, France), they can participate by making a Victim Impact or Victim Personal Statement, which is submitted to the court during sentencing (UK, US and Australia) and finally by making (limited) submissions through their legal representative when acting as a witness at trial (Germany, Denmark, Sweden, US).

The below analyses victims' participation possibilities at trial commencing with Germany and Sweden, the two systems which feature the broadest participation possibilities for (certain) victims. It subsequently considers the situation for victims in Denmark and France which allow for more limited participation possibilities at trial. Lastly, it outlines the few participation possibilities available for victims in the analysed common law jurisdictions.

2.1 Germany

2.1.1 The Inquisitorial Trial Structure in Germany

The structure of the German criminal justice system is of inquisitorial nature, which has several implications for victims and their role in the system (Weigend 2011, 257; Hermann 1987, 123).[1] In Germany, the judge is responsible for conducting the criminal trial and not prosecution or defence. The trial judge has a very active role and conducts judicial inquiries (German Code of Criminal Procedure, (*Strafprozessordnung, StPO*) (Germany) s 244(2)).[2] Judges are generally responsible for initiating criminal proceedings, collecting all the evidence the court finds necessary and for deciding how to resolve the issues of the case (Kessler 2004, 1188). In relation to evidence examined at trial, prosecution and defence only have the right to request that additional evidence be introduced at trial if admissible under the rules of criminal procedure (StPO (Germany) s 244(3)). During proceedings, the judge undertakes most of the questioning of witnesses. Defence counsel and prosecution can only subsequently ask additional questions (Joachminski 1999). The duty of the court to examine the facts of the case includes gathering evidence that is exculpating for the accused, even against the accused's will. The court is furthermore obligated to find facts that are incriminating, even if the public prosecutor has no interest in relying on these facts. This means that, even where the prosecution and defence agree not to collect any further evidence, the court cannot *per se* refrain from further clarifying the facts of the case (Siegesmund 2000, 103). Thus the parties in the German criminal justice system play a subsidiary role, while the judge dominates proceedings and has primary control over the questioning of the parties and the collection of evidence (Doak 2008, 283). The system has been described as 'vertically structured', meaning that the judge keeps firm control over the trial participants compared to the adversarial system as the 'horizontal courtroom action' of prosecution and defence (Kury and Kilchling 2011, 48). For this reason, witnesses for the prosecution or defence do not exist and proper cross-examination as standard procedure in common law systems is not available. No separate trial and sentencing stage are in place. Some suggest that due to the German trial structure, it may be easier to accommodate the victim as a participant without offsetting the balance of the trial (Pizzi and Perron 1996, 41).

In Germany, not all victims can participate at trial in the same way. That means there is no general right to victim participation as such. Active participation is only possible for victims who are eligible to act in the role of a Private Accessory Prosecutor (*Nebenklaeger, PAP*)[3] and those who are able to participate as applicants to the adhesion procedure (*Adhäsionsverfahren*) relating to a civil claim. All other victims can participate only to a very limited degree. Therefore, Germany applies a multi-level system of victim participation analysed in detail below.

2.1.2 Victims with a Formal Role

The StPO allows certain victims to take up an active role at trial and to present views and concerns by joining the prosecution as a PAP or to participate in relation to their civil claim through the adhesion procedure. The below first analyses PAP participation prior to assessing participation in the context of the adhesion procedure.

Participation as a PAP

As outlined in Chapter 2, and comparable to many other criminal justice systems, no differentiation between criminal and civil law originally existed under Germanic law. It was not until the Middle Ages that this division started to become significant. At the same time, however, this did not mean that victims were barred from bringing criminal proceedings. It was not until 1848 that the German state introduced the accusation principle (*Anklageprinzip*), according to which criminal matters can only proceed where an individual is formally charged. This shifted the power to accuse someone from the individual citizen to the public prosecutor (Hoelzel 1980, 15). This power shift occurred rather abruptly in Germany and was perhaps undertaken to be in line with legal developments in France, where a public prosecution service was established around the same time. The reform was carried out without prior assessment of its suitability in the German context (Hoelzel 1980, 15). Overall, it was viewed negatively by the German population at the time and soon lobbying commenced for a stronger involvement of the citizen, including the victim, in criminal proceedings. When the drafting for the first Reichs Code of Criminal Procedure (*Reichsstrafprozessordnung, RStPO*) began in 1873, it included a rather general section on private accessory prosecution, a role private individuals could exercise next to the prosecutor. When the finalised RStPO came into force in 1877, the right to act as a PAP was included—although to a very limited degree. According to the Code, PAP participation was only possible in cases of minor crimes that generally allowed for private prosecution. That meant that victims could only act as PAPs in rare cases where the public prosecutor commenced public proceedings for an offence intended for private prosecution (Barton and Flotho 2010, 15). Although this extremely limited right was considered neither practical nor particularly systematic in its application, decades saw the legislation live on unchanged in German procedural law (Barton and Flotho 2010, 17).

Over the centuries, through amendments and restructure, the RStPO morphed into the StPO, still in force in Germany today, although heavily amended since its first introduction. The StPO sets out PAP participation in Sections 395–402. The rationale of PAP participation is often described twofold: firstly, to increase victim satisfaction of those victims deemed particularly worthy of protection by allowing them to participate in the prosecution of the offender and secondly, to control the prosecution and to ensure that they act appropriately in the case at hand (Huesing 1983, 9). The rights relating to PAP participation as they currently stand are the result of ongoing law reform in this area commencing with the Victims Protection Act 1986 (*Opferschutzgesetz*) which holistically transformed private accessory prosecution for the first time (Riess 2007, 752).[4] The reform separated private prosecution and private accessory prosecution with the aim of singling out specific victims, namely those of serious violent and sexual offences, and giving them a special legal status with far-reaching procedural rights (Barton and Flotho 2010, 17). Some attribute the development of this strengthened form of PAP participation to the growth of legal feminism in the 1980s and the related lobbying for better treatment of female sexual violence victims in the German court system (Anders 2012, 380). Subsequent victims' rights law reforms have amended aspects of this form of participation creating the following status quo of PAP rights in Germany.

PAP participation is only possible for victims and, where the victim is deceased, close family members including parents, children, siblings and spouses under the strict requirements of Section 395 StPO.

The number of victims who can act in this role is limited and includes victims of offences explicitly named in legislation. These are, for example, sexual offences, including rape and sexual assault, homicide offences, including attempts, intentional assault offences as well as offences concerning the deprivation of liberty and stalking. Additionally, victims of other offences not explicitly stipulated in the StPO may be eligible to participate where the courts find their participation indispensable to safeguard their interests—particularly in light of the consequences of the crime on the victim (StPO (Germany) s 395(3)).[5] The right for victims of other than the explicitly named offences to participate was introduced in 2009. Ultimately, it expands the right to participate to victims of any offence as long as 'special reasons' for their participation in the case at hand are recognised by the courts. This development is discussed further in Chapter 7. It is unclear and undefined when these 'special reasons' exist. What is clear is that the impact of the crime on the victim, including the psychological consequences, has to be taken into account in the context of this assessment (Weiner 2018, 23–27). The burden of proof to establish 'special reasons' falls onto the individual victim. This shows that while courts may find victims of other offences eligible to participate as a PAP in a particular case no general right to victim participation at trial exists in Germany.[6] Victims who wish to participate as PAPs, regardless of whether their participation is derived from an explicitly named offence or is due to special reasons, must declare their participation in writing to the respective court (StPO (Germany), s 396). This can occur at any stage even during the investigation before the actual trial commences.

During the criminal trial, PAPs are not part of the public prosecution and can therefore exercise their rights completely independently. That means they are not bound by prosecutorial directions. A victim who is acting as a PAP, or their legal representative, has a number of rights, which victims without such a formal role cannot exercise. Unlike victims who only act as witnesses in Germany, the PAP has the right to be present during the main trial even if they still have to testify at a later stage of the proceedings (StPO (Germany) s 397(2)). Yet, if they do not wish to be present, their attendance cannot be forced. The PAP has the right to be legally represented and their legal representative has the right to be present during the entire proceedings (StPO (Germany) s 397(2)).

In addition, the PAP or their legal representative has the following rights: to be heard at trial whenever the prosecution is heard (StPO (Germany) s 397), to request the introduction of evidence (StPO (Germany) ss 397(1), 244(3)-(6)), to refuse judges and expert witnesses in case of partiality (StPO (Germany) ss 397(1), 24, 31 (for judges), s 74 (for expert witnesses)), to question the accused, witnesses and experts (StPO (Germany) ss 397(1), 240(2)), to object to court orders and questions of the trial parties (StPO (Germany) ss 397(1), 242, 238(2)) and to make statements including a final pleading in which they can comment on the factual and legal findings of the main trial in an attempt to influence the court's decision (StPO (Germany) ss 397(1), ss 257, 258). The final pleading occurs after the summing up of the prosecution and before the final pleading of the defendant. In addition, the victim's legal representative can request the inspection of court files; a right which has the same scope as the defendant's right to inspect court files (StPO (Germany) s 406e). The PAP therefore has very broad rights during the criminal trial to participate and to present views and concerns.[7] The rights PAPs have been afforded are described as a combination of active rights (*status activus*), which allow them to actively influence proceedings, as well as defensive rights, which afford them protection during proceedings (*status negativus*) (Tumanishvili 2008, 113).

Research on PAP participation in practice is very limited and many existing studies stem from the early 1980s before victim-related law reform changed the particulars of PAP participation (for an overview on existing research studies see Barton and Flotho 2010, 40–43). One exception is a study by Barton and Flotho (2010) examining PAP participation and the role of their legal representatives in one German district court jurisdiction. The study found that PAP participation had increased from 10% in 1982 to around 22.3% in 2007 and that in more than 70% of cases PAP participation was exercised by victims of sexual offences (Barton and Flotho 2010, 78, 235).

In addition to PAP participation, victims in Germany are also able to participate during the criminal trial as applicants to the adhesion procedure in an attempt to recuperate their financial losses stemming from the criminal act.

Participation as an Applicant to the Adhesion Procedure

Under German law, victims can participate during the criminal trial to some extent by initiating an adhesion procedure. Every person who can 'claim that they have directly suffered financial loss resulting from a criminal act committed' or who can claim that 'they are the heir of such person' can make an application for an adhesion procedure during the criminal trial (StPO (Germany) ss 403–406c). The application must generally contain the exact monetary amount sought. Exceptions apply where the amount is to be evaluated by an expert witness during proceedings or where the monetary amount falls into the courts' sphere of determination, for example, in case of damages for pain and suffering (Dauer 2018, 6). The court, in an adhesion procedure, decides whether the victim, as the applicant, has a valid civil law claim for damages or compensation against the defendant. This determination occurs during the criminal trial.

An applicant to the adhesion procedure is not considered a main party to proceedings such as defendant or prosecutor. Rather they are seen as a special procedural participant, who can partake due to their civil claim (Spiess 2008, 234). As such, applicants to the adhesion procedure have not been afforded any rights to influence the criminal side of proceedings. Although not explicitly regulated in legislation, consensus exists in German scholarship and jurisprudence that the applicant has the following rights: the right to be heard during the main trial in relation to the civil claim, to ask questions and make requests for additional evidence to be introduced—if the requested evidence holds relevance for the outcome of the civil claim—and, arguably, to make a closing statement (Siegismund 2000, 106; Wemmers 2005, 126; Brienen and Hoegen 2000a, 284; on the argument that there is no right to make a closing statement see Stoffers and Moeckel 2013, 831). The applicant also has the right to be legally represented. How these rights are exercised in individual proceedings is for the respective trial court to decide (Zander 2011, 30). Due to their subsidiary role, the participation of the applicant is not obligatory. That means that the criminal trial is run and the adhesion decision reached with or without the presence of the applicant.

The adhesion procedure has been described as 'a bit of civil law tied onto the criminal justice process' (Wemmers 2005, 125). However, according to German law, victims who have not experienced any financial loss through the criminal act, for example in case of an attempted offence, or who do not want to 'put a price tag' (Wemmers 2005, 125) on any harm suffered, are not eligible to participate in an adhesion procedure. Furthermore, in complex cases with many evidential or legal difficulties, victims would usually commence proceedings in civil courts which are more specialised in this area rather than initiating adhesion proceedings in courts which specialise in criminal law. It follows that in these instances, victims are not able to participate as applicants to an adhesion procedure in the criminal trial.

The adhesion procedure was originally introduced in German law in 1943 during the Nazi reign. No explanatory memorandum to the introductory bill exists making it difficult to pinpoint the precise reasons for its introduction (Zander 2011, 36). Yet, it is commonly assumed that the introduction was largely related due to financial restrictions and the need to save administrative expenses during the Second World War (Stoffers and Moeckel 2013, 830; Hermann 2010, 236). The adhesion procedure held the advantage that civil and criminal trials could be combined and was therefore expected to save administrative costs. This was considered one of the main agendas in the public service sector during wartime (Kilchling 1992, 75). In comparison with many other criminal law and criminal procedure rules introduced during the Nazi regime, the adhesion procedure rules outlasted the end of the war largely because no Nazi ideology was associated with these norms (Zander 2011, 37). Despite the fact that the adhesion procedure allows victims, to some extent, to present views and concerns about their civil claim, its original introduction was largely based on financial considerations and not necessarily on the desire to give victims a voice (Spiess 2008, 12). The legislative motives may have differed when the first reform of adhesion procedure rules was undertaken in the context of the *Victims Protection Act* 1986 (Germany), *inter alia* providing the possibility to receive legal aid for these proceedings. Some suggest that this reform was based on the desire to improve the role of victims in criminal procedure (Zander 2011, 39–41).

Notwithstanding the fact that the adhesion procedure has existed since the first half of the twentieth century in Germany, in the past it has been used sparingly and has therefore sometimes been referred to as a 'stillbirth' (Weigend 1984, 765; see also Kaiser 1991, 561). Its limited use was perhaps based on the fact that conducting an adhesion procedure required the criminal judge's consent to do so. It appeared, however, that criminal courts frequently withheld their consent because they had little interest in dealing with and deciding on questions of civil law (see discussion in Kilchling 1992, 76; Hermann 2010, 243). For these reasons, applications were frequently dismissed on the basis that the adhesion procedure 'would lengthen the criminal trial' this being one of the reasons contained in legislation that allowed for a dismissal (Kilchling 1992, 76). The legal situation changed in 2004 and judges are no longer able to categorically dismiss an application solely based on the ground that proceedings could be increased in length. A dismissal now requires an expected 'significant' increase in trial length (Haller 2011, 970; StPO (Germany) s 406(1) sents 4–6). Whether a greater number of adhesion procedures will now occur in German criminal trials is uncertain. Figures published in 2011 still suggest that the adhesion procedure is seldom used (Haller 2011, 971). Some hypothesise that adhesion procedures in Germany will continue to remain underutilised not the least due to the relatively low fees lawyers can charge for representing their clients within the context of an adhesion procedure. Legal representatives will likely prefer raising their client's claim in front of civil courts with the associated higher fee schedule and advise their clients accordingly (Duenkel 2001, 182).

2.1.3 Victims Without a Formal Role

In Germany, victims without a formal role in proceedings are restricted to presenting views and concerns at trial exclusively in the role of a witness. German victims, who testify as witnesses, have the right to testify without interruption by questions and remarks from the court, public prosecution and defence (StPO (Germany) s 69(1)).[8] This means that victims can testify in an uninterrupted narrative form. Yet, at the same time this does not mean that the victim can freely present views and concerns as a witness about any possible issue they wish to bring up. In Germany, the role of a victim witness is to testify on the matter relevant to the criminal trial, for example how the crime has occurred (StPO (Germany) s 69(1)). Since law reform in 2013, the section also highlights that victims should be given an opportunity to comment on how the crime has affected them (StPO (Germany) s 69(2) sent. 2). The victim witness has no explicit right to address other issues they wish to raise in order to bring them to the court's attention. Furthermore, the possibility for victims to participate is different to mere witness participation. Victim participation is voluntary participation that allows victims to communicate their views and concerns, by comparison with witness participation which is obligatory, serves the interests of the court and consists of testifying on a particular matter in question (Mouthaan 2013, 620). Thus being able to testify as a witness cannot in itself constitute an active participation right for victims.

Victims who are required to testify as witnesses have the possibility to present views and concerns through their legal representative to a very limited degree (StPO (Germany) s 68b). In Germany, the victim's legal representative can be present when the victim is being questioned as a witness at trial. Prior to questioning, the legal representative can make applications on behalf of the victim, including the exclusion of the public (GVG (Germany) s 171b) and the defendant (StPO (Germany) s 247(1)) during examination of the victim witness. Furthermore an application can be made to allow victims to testify using video technology (StPO (Germany) s 247a). The task of the legal representative during examination is to object to abusive, compromising, disrespectful, suggestive or leading questions thereby ensuring compliance with existing witness protection legislation (StPO (Germany) ss 68a, 241(2)). Yet, German law generally does not grant the victim witness' legal representative the right to ask questions and thereby present the victim's views and concerns during the trial and sentencing stage. In 2004, the

German Federal Court of Justice (*Bundesgerichtshof*)[9] had to decide upon appeal whether a trial judge's decision to grant the victim's legal representative the right to ask occasional questions during criminal proceedings constituted a ground of appeal based on an error of law (Bundesgerichtshof 2004). The appeal, however, was ultimately unsuccessful. The Federal Court held that while a victim's legal representative generally has no explicit right to ask questions during criminal proceedings, it is in the trial court's discretion to grant them such a right on occasion during the trial. The fact that the Federal Court explicitly pointed out the absence of a general right for a victim's legal representative to ask questions suggests that victim witnesses only have limited opportunities to present views and concerns at trial. Their input is mostly related to issues concerning protection when testifying as a witness. Legal representation for victims and victim witnesses and related issues are discussed further in Chapter 8. No opportunities for victims to present views and concerns during the trial exist, where victims are not required to testify as a witness (Hanloser 2010, 146).

Victims in Sweden have the right to join proceedings and support the public prosecutor during the trial. This, in essence, is a role which gives Swedish victims a legal status comparable to that of a German PAP. The particulars of this, as well as other victim participation opportunities in Sweden, are discussed below after a brief introduction to the nature of the main trial.

2.2 Sweden

2.2.1 The Adversarial Trial Structure in Sweden

While the investigation phase in Scandinavian jurisdictions is generally described as inquisitorial, the trial phase has adversarial elements. In Sweden, these adversarial elements were introduced in the 1940s when the Swedish Code of Judicial Procedure was holistically reformed (Carlsson 2010, 15). The trial itself is party-centred (Wolhuter 2010, 9) and based on the principles of orality and immediateness (Carlsson 2010, 10). After the reading of charges and the subsequent pleading of the defendant, the trial enters the stage where oral testimony is presented (Wolhuter et al. 2009, 192). Witnesses are questioned by the prosecutor, defence lawyer and the trial judge and cross-examination is possible (Wolhuter et al. 2009, 192). In that context, Swedish criminal procedure shows similarities to the Anglo-American trial and differs significantly from German criminal procedure where the trial judge is almost exclusively responsible for examining the evidence and questioning witnesses. After the trial concludes the verdict is either announced immediately by the judge or is available within two weeks for collection by the parties (Carlsson 2010, 17). No separate sentencing stage exists. Despite the difference in the nature of the criminal process itself, the way in which some victims are able to participate at trial is comparable in Germany and Sweden.

2.2.2 Victims with a Formal Role

Participation as a Supporting Prosecutor

In Sweden, the victim or injured party is called 'målsägande'. It has been suggested that the term originates from the word 'mal' meaning speech, as historically the victim had to present their accusations during proceedings in free speech, and the term 'aga' meaning to have or to own. As a consequence, målsägande refers to the person who is capable of presenting their accusation in the required form (Schmidt 1979, 848).

Similar to the German situation, victims in Sweden can act in a party role comparable to that of the PAP with legal representation (målsägandebiträde) after the prosecution has initiated proceedings (Code of Judicial Procedure, *Rättegångsbalken, RB* (Sweden) Ch 20, s 8). The basis for this form of participation can be found in Chapter 20, Section 8 of the RB stating that '[w]hen a prosecutor has instituted a prosecution, the aggrieved person may support the prosecution'. Where a victim declares that they will be supporting the prosecution they become a party to the proceedings and cannot be questioned as a witness but only in a special role to clarify certain facts (*Upplysningsvis*) which are relevant for the evaluation of subsequent evidence (Schmidt 1979, 853). In comparison with Germany, the role is not limited to specific categories of victims and can thus be exercised by victims of any offence which is subject to prosecution. Supporting victims and their legal representatives in Sweden can exercise participation rights including the right to be present during the entire criminal proceedings. It has been reported that prior to the 1970s some courts excluded victims from proceedings while the indictment was being read out by the prosecution in order to avoid unduly influencing them. Yet, a ruling by the Justice Ombudsman put an end to this practice. It was explained that victims have the right to be present during the reading of the indictment to make an informed decision about whether they wish to join the prosecution (Schmidt 1979, 854). After the defendant has been given the opportunity, the participating victim can outline to the court what criminal act has occurred in their opinion. While they may not base their assessment on a different criminal act than the one relied upon by the public prosecutor, they can attribute a different legal appraisal to the action in question (Schmidt 1979, 854). This is described in the Code of Judicial Procedure in the following words (RB (Sweden) Ch 46, s 6(1)):

> At the main hearing the prosecutor shall state the charges. The defendant shall be requested to state briefly his position and the basis for it. Thereafter, the prosecutor shall introduce his action. The aggrieved person and the defendant shall, to the extent required, be furnished with an opportunity each to present his action.

Additionally, the supporting victim can pose questions during the main trial (Brienen and Hoegen 2000b, 891), object to certain questions asked by prosecution and defence, cross-examine the defendant and request the introduction of additional evidence (Wolhuter et al. 2009, 193). Furthermore, a victim supporting the prosecution has the right to give a final speech (European Justice 2012). Little information is available in languages other than Swedish on what the impact of such victim participation is on criminal procedure. Yet, a 2013 official report by the Swedish Government Official Committee Service, a temporarily-formed agency to provide a basis for governmental decisions—in this case on how to improve the functioning of the Swedish criminal justice system—takes a negative view on this form of victim involvement in criminal justice (Staten Offentliga Utredningar 2013, 48).[10] The Report (2013, 48) comments that 'when the prosecutor brings an action concerning criminal liability, the prosecutor should be solely responsible for this action. The provision entitling the aggrieved party to assist with the prosecutor's prosecution should be revoked'. This suggests that providing victims with a special procedural role in Sweden is not seen entirely uncritically. Rather than allowing for such prosecution support the Report suggests the improvement of procedures relating to claiming civil compensation in criminal proceedings discussed below..

Participation as an Applicant to the Adhesion Procedure

In Sweden, victims are also able to participate as parties in criminal trials when they bring a civil claim aimed at recouping any financial losses arising from the criminal act in the context of an adhesion procedure.[11] Chapter 22, Section 1 RB (Sweden) states that an 'action against the suspect or a third person for a private claim in consequence of an offence may be conducted in conjunction with the prosecution of the offence'. The right to pursue civil claims in Swedish criminal procedure was introduced for reasons of procedural economy as well as due to the desire to prevent the victim from being subjected to two separate proceedings, one civil and one criminal (Carlson 2009, 147). When bringing such a civil claim, victims have the right to be legally represented (*Lag om Målsägandebiträde*, Counsel for the Inured Party Act (Sweden) s 3). Where a victim elects to be legally represented their lawyer is tasked with pursuing the civil claim during criminal proceedings. That means that the representative for the victim can question witnesses with the aim of supporting the victim's claim for compensation during the criminal trial (Carlsson 2010, 17). Where the victim elects not to have a legal representative, the public prosecutor is to present the civil claim on the victim's behalf during the trial if this does not amount to a 'major inconvenience' for the prosecution or the claim is 'manifestly devoid of merit' (RB (Sweden) Ch 22, s 2). A civil action during the criminal trial may be terminated by the court if it feels that 'joint adjudication would cause major inconvenience' (RB (Sweden) Ch 22, s 5).

When the right to legal representation for applicants to the adhesion procedure was first introduced it was assumed that it would receive very little use in practice (Carlsson 2010, 60). However, a 1996 study by a

Swedish government agency responsible for court administration issues showed that in 85% of all cases analysed in the study victims brought a private claim during criminal trials and that in 95% of these cases the claim was submitted by a legal representative (study discussed in Carlsson 2010, 60). This indicates that the adhesion procedure is used more frequently in Sweden than in Germany and that most victims are legally represented when initiating such proceedings. Yet, in practice 'inadequacies in the support received by aggrieved parties on matters relating to private claims and the way in which these claims are dealt with within the current procedure' have been identified in a 2003 official Swedish report on the functioning of the criminal justice system (Staten Offentliga Utredningar 2013, 60). One problematic issue the committee acknowledged was the unclear distribution of roles between the prosecution and the victim's legal counsel in relation to the civil claim. It notes (2013, 61) *inter alia* that the

> division of responsibility between prosecutor and the aggrieved party counsel appointed should be clarified so that it is prescribed by statute that such counsel should always bring the aggrieved party's actions for private claims if such a claim has been presented by the aggrieved party.

While the adhesion procedure may work more effectively in Sweden than in Germany it seems to have problems in its practical application. Apart from the above-described forms of participation victims without a special role in Sweden can participate to a limited degree through their legal representative.

2.2.3 Victims Without a Formal Role

In Sweden, since the late 1980s certain victims who do not elect to become parties to proceedings and thus remain witnesses without additional legal status have the right to a state-funded legal representative ('Målsägandebiträde') (Counsel for the Inured Party Act (Sweden) s 1). This is the case for victims of serious offences including sexual offences, homicide, assault, kidnapping, coercion and robbery if victims do not 'lack the need for such counsel' (Counsel for the Injured Party Act

(Sweden) s 1). In addition, a legal counsel is available for other offences punishable with imprisonment if the court believes this to be necessary based on the particular circumstances of the victim (Counsel for the Injured Party Act (Sweden) s 1 (1)-(3)). The act enshrining the right to legal representation in Sweden in 1989, the Counsel for the Injured Party Act, was originally introduced to improve the situation of victims of sexual violence before and during court proceedings. That was because several victim surveys in Sweden in the early and mid-1980s found that victim witnesses who testified on sexual violence offences were often treated harshly by actors in the criminal justice system and that sexual offences were underreported due to victims' fear of the system (Carlsson 2010, 51). One of the main aims of the act was to decrease victims' anxiety in regard to the criminal justice process including the investigation of the offence (Carlsson 2010, 53). Since the introduction of legal representation for witnesses in Sweden, the lawyers' role is to pursue the victims' interests throughout the pre-trial and trial phase (Counsel for the Injured Party Act (Sweden) s 3). While the lawyer has the right to be present during the trial they cannot exercise independent participation rights during this stage. Rather their rights are derived from the rights of the victim witness. As such they can make an application that the victim is questioned without the defendant present or that the public is excluded from proceedings (Carlsson 2010, 60). In addition, during questioning they can make the court aware of offensive questions in case the court did not notice (CJP (Sweden) Ch 36, s 17).

Although the Danish and Swedish legal systems are closely related, they differ significantly in regard to the victims' role in proceedings. Particularly the active participation in support of the public prosecutor available to victims in Swedish trials does not exist under Danish law as the below details.

2.3 Denmark

The Danish criminal justice system is mainly inquisitorial in the investigation phase and is of adversarial nature in the trial phase. As a consequence, judges have a more passive role during the actual trial and the parties are able to examine and cross-examine the evidence. Although

Denmark and Sweden are both Scandinavian justice systems, the role victims have been afforded in either jurisdiction differs significantly. While Sweden grants victims a party status in proceedings with the ability to support the public prosecution, the role of victims in Denmark is mainly that of a witness with only the state and defendant constituting parties (Tham et al. 2011, 579). As such, victims have no comparable right to support the prosecution and to become a party to proceedings (Greve 1991, 11). In Denmark, certain offences which allow private prosecution by the victim but which, due to public policy considerations, are pursued by the public prosecutor instead enable victims to join the prosecution (Administration of Justice Act, *Retsplejeloven*, *AJA* (Denmark) s 727(3)). However, in this role Danish victims do not receive any additional rights. This is why Brienen and Hoegen (2000b, 218) describe joining the prosecution in Denmark as having no practical value. Tham et al. (2011, 579) explain that in Denmark no desire can be identified to expand the role of the victim to that of a party in proceedings. This is why their role is generally defined as that of a witness (Oxford Pro Bono Publico 2015).

While Danish victims are unable to support the prosecution they have the right to become applicants to the adhesion procedure (*Adhaesionsproces*) in order to reclaim damages or losses arising from the criminal act during the trial. Proceedings are wider than their German counterpart. While aggrieved persons can claim losses arising from the criminal act in question it is also possible to recoup additional losses, such as rent costs or court costs, associated with the criminal act (Schmahl 1980, 10, 71).

A written right of the injured person to link criminal and civil proceedings to reclaim damages can be traced back to the *Danske Lov*, the Danish Legal Code of 1683, which also dealt with crimes in its sixth book (Schmahl 1980, 13). At the time, however, differences between civil and criminal proceedings were not yet dominant in Denmark and victims were generally responsible for accusations. The final separation of civil and criminal proceedings occurred with a decree on 21 May 1751 which ultimately led to the changed role of the victim to that of a witness and the state as prosecutor (Schmahl 1980, 17). Much of the background to allowing adhesion procedures in Denmark, especially in the twentieth century, relates to motor vehicle accidents and the belief that the lower socio-economic classes were unable to recoup damages against motor vehicle owners in civil courts due to financial restrictions. It was suggested that these victims could at least receive restitution through criminal proceedings to which their claim could be attached (Schmahl 1980, 24). Therefore, adhesion procedures have a long-standing tradition in Danish traffic law. The particulars of the adhesion procedure are set out in Chapter 89 of the AJA titled 'enforcement of civil claims in criminal procedure'.[12] Section 991 AJA (Denmark) allows for the decision on civil claims in criminal proceedings where an application is made. The application can be made until the last day of proceedings. Victims who take part in an adhesion procedure are afforded additional rights (AJA (Denmark) ss 685, 991(1–2); Brienen and Hoegen 2000b, 217; Schmahl 1980, 112). In their role, they can introduce evidence and in actuality it is mostly their responsibility or that of their legal representative to provide evidence which supports the amount of compensation requested. The victim's legal counsel can furthermore provide a closing statement relevant to the civil claim.

Where courts consider the civil claim as a significant inconvenience to the criminal proceedings they can dismiss it, leaving victims to pursue their claim in civil courts (AJA (Denmark) s 991(4)). In practice, such a rejection has mainly occurred in cases, where the amount of compensation is disputed between the parties and the gathering and introduction of a large volume of evidence would be required to determine the matter (Schmahl 1980, 32). In Denmark, if the accused is acquitted of the criminal charges, the criminal court is no longer able to decide on the civil claim (AJA (Denmark) s 992). Brienen and Hoegen (2000b, 237) remark that adhesion procedures in Denmark are largely unsuccessful in practice due to lack of sufficient evidential support. In comparison, however, and despite their limitations, adhesion procedures appear more broadly accepted and more generally used in Denmark and Sweden than in Germany (Dauer 2018, 101; Schmahl 1980, 117).

Furthermore, victim witnesses without additional legal status have the right to be legally represented during proceedings. Denmark was the first jurisdiction to allow victims to be legally represented in the 1980s (Brienen and Hoegen 2000b, 218). In case of sexual offences and certain violent offences including homicide, assault and robbery, victims have the right to have a legal representative appointed for them through the courts (AJA (Denmark) s 741a(1)). Where certain sexual offences have been committed a legal representative is usually appointed automatically by the courts (AJA (Denmark) s 741a(2)), while in other cases a representative will only be appointed if the victim actively requests such representation (AJA (Denmark) s 741a(1)). Courts can refuse the request for legal representation if a representative is considered unnecessary and the offence of minor nature (AJA (Denmark) s 741a(3)). Where the legal representative is court appointed the state covers the legal fees for the representation. Victims of other offences, that is non-violent offences, have the right to employ a legal representative but are generally under the obligation to cover the fees themselves. Traditionally, the legal representative has no active participation rights but is mostly appointed to provide legal guidance and support. However, in certain limited cases the victim's legal counsel may cross-examine the alleged offender and object to the introduction of evidence relating to the victim's sexual record (AJA (Denmark) s 741c(1); Oxford Pro Bono Publico 2015, 47). Additional cross-examination of witnesses through the victim's legal counsel as well as submissions in relation to specific procedural matters are possible if allowed by the court on a case by case basis (Oxford Pro Bono Publico 2015, 47).

Victims in France, comparable to victims in Denmark, are unable to actively participate during proceedings as PAPs or as victims supporting the prosecution. Yet, similar to the other three jurisdictions analysed above, French victims are able to participate in criminal trials with the aim of reclaiming financial losses arising from the criminal act.

2.4 France

French criminal procedure is largely inquisitorial and dominated by judges. As pointed out in Chapter 3, the investigating judge examines the evidence and questions witnesses prior to the trial. The parties are generally not seen as adversaries. However, prosecution and defence are able to present oral arguments (Terrill 2015, 163).

While Germany and Sweden allow certain victims to become PAPs or victims supporting the prosecution, which provides them with broad participation rights, this form of participation is not available to victims in France. The only way victims are able to participate in criminal trials in a role other than a witness is as civil claimants (*partie civile*) seeking compensation for the offence committed against them. Section 2 of the Code of Criminal Procedure (*Code de Procédure Pénale*, CCP (France))[13] states that:

> Civil action aimed at the reparation of the damage suffered because of a felony, a misdemeanour or a petty offence is open to all those who have personally suffered damage directly caused by the offence.

In order to be eligible to participate victims must therefore have suffered harm caused directly by the offence. The harm suffered can be material, moral or both (CCP (France) s 2). The aim of these proceedings is comparable to the above-discussed adhesion procedure in Germany, Sweden and Denmark.

As pointed out in Chapter 4, victims can activate proceedings by applying to an investigating judge as civil claimants or they can join matters which have already been initiated by the prosecution anytime during the pre-trial or trial stage up until close of argument. The joinder can occur by submitting a declaration containing the relevant facts of the claim and the losses they are trying to recoup (Brienen and Hoegen 2000b, 319). In contrast to Germany, the French judge has to decide on the civil claim and cannot reject such an application on the same grounds as their German counterpart. After joining proceedings as a civil claimant, the victim is considered a party to the proceedings with special legal status and additional participation rights. In their role, civil claimants have the right to be legally represented (CCP (France) s 424). During the investigation, the legal representative can file a request with the judge asking for the introduction of expert evidence but only in so far as it relates to their civil claim. These requests may relate to, for example, the introduction of medical or psychological reports (CCP (France) s 82). While judges may reject requests for the introduction of additional evidence they must provide reasons for doing so

(CCP (France) s 329). In addition, the civil party may apply to hear certain witnesses and to have a crime scene inspected. They may also file a request with the investigating judge to order the parties to disclose elements useful to the investigation (CCP (France) s 82). During the trial, the legal representative can question witnesses and experts in order to establish the amount of compensation, ask for certain investigative actions which they believe necessary for truth finding, and apply for the disqualification of a judge under certain circumstances (CCP (France) ss 120, 156, 312, 442–1, 662, 665). The legal counsel generally does not have the right to object to questions put to the victim by defence and prosecution (Bacik et al. 1998, 218). Yet, they can make remarks in writing about issue arising at trial, for example, questions of law or fact, which the judge must subsequently address (French Ministry of Justice 2013, 38). Due to the inquisitorial nature of the trial, civil claimants are under no obligation to actively contribute to proceedings. That is because it is the role of the prosecution and investigating magistrate and not the civil claimant to uncover relevant evidence for the trial (Brienen and Hoegen 2000b, 320). Although empirical research on matters relating to adhesion procedures is limited, it is generally assumed that they play an important role in French criminal trials (Spiess 2008, 229).

Victims who act as witnesses without additional legal status generally do not have the right to present views and concerns through a legal representative during proceedings. Assistance of a lawyer, either elected or court appointed, is available to civil parties at their request. The legal costs generally have to be covered by the civil party unless they qualify for legal aid. Legal representation schemes for victims are discussed in detail in Chapter 8.

The role of victims at trial in traditional adversarial systems, as well as similarities and differences to the analysed inquisitorial and mixed criminal justice systems, is assessed below.

2.5 Adversarial Jurisdictions

Australia, England and Wales and the US are common law jurisdictions which have an adversarial criminal justice system. The adversarial system has been described as a system in which 'the parties, and not the judge have the primary responsibility for defining the issues in dispute and for investigating and advancing the case' (Australian Law Reform Commission 2000, [1.117]). The system accentuates the control of the contesting parties, prosecution and defence, over the legal proceedings (Block et al. 2000, 171). The judge is mainly responsible for ensuring procedural fairness to the parties by, for example, deciding on questions of law and admissibility of evidence (Erez and Roberts 2010, 600–601). The bipartite structure of the adversarial system is often considered the reason why giving victims an individual role in the adversarial trial is impossible without offsetting the existing trial balance (see Doak 2005, 294). Therefore, victims in the adversarial system usually have no standing in criminal trials. In general, victims have very limited opportunities to present views and concerns during the trial stage in the analysed common law jurisdictions. They are potential witnesses, who may be called—usually by the prosecution—to present their account of the facts in relation to a particular criminal act (Wilson 2005, 261). Victims in Australia, England and Wales and the US, however, have no opportunities to present views and concerns in relation to the crime as such and can only be heard in regard to answering the particular questions they are asked as witnesses (Erez 1991; Victim Support Agency 2009, 16). For this reason, their role has been described as 'reactive' rather than 'active' (Bibas and Bierschbach 2004, 136). For reasons pointed out above, being questioned as a witness and the related obligation to provide information does not qualify as an active victim participation right for the purposes of this book.

Only in few of the analysed common law jurisdictions do victims have standing in relation to certain trial-related matters and the possibility to be heard in a role other than a witness providing testimony. For example, under New South Wales law, a sexual assault communications privilege exists. The privilege includes any counselling communication made by, to or about a victim of a sexual offence (*Criminal Procedure Act 1986* (NSW) s 296(1)). Defence planning to subpoena such privileged evidence at trial must make an application and seek leave from court. In the context of this application, since 2011, victims in New South Wales have received standing to respond to the application and have the right to be legally represented when doing so (*Criminal Procedure Act 1986* (NSW) s 299A). Legal aid is available for qualifying victims and victims are referred to private lawyers specifically trained in this area.[14] Yet, apart from few very isolated instances which do not necessarily form part of the trial proper, victims in Australia have not received a general right to be legally represented.

Victims in Australia, as well as other non-parties, have on occasion been permitted to appear in court, so-called non-party participation. This occurs mostly in cases where they can contribute to factual or legal information and thus assist the court. Regarding this form of participation Brennan CJ (*Levy v. Victoria* 1997, [39]) stated that

> where a person having the necessary legal interest to apply for leave to intervene can show that the parties to the particular proceeding may not present fully the submissions on a particular issue, being submissions which the Court should have to assist it to reach a correct determination, the Court may exercise its jurisdiction by granting leave to intervene. The grant may be limited, if appropriate, to particular issues and subject to such conditions, as to costs or otherwise, as will do justice as between all parties. In that situation, intervention may prevent an error that would affect the interests of the intervener. Of course, if the intervener's submission is merely repetitive of the submission of one or other of the parties, efficiency would require that intervention be denied.

Furthermore, participation is possible as an *amicus curiae*, a friend of the court, which may be 'when the Court is of the opinion that it will be significantly assisted thereby, provided that any cost to the parties or any delay consequent on agreeing to hear the amicus is not disproportionate to the assistance that is expected' (*Levy v. Victoria* 1997, [45]). The above non-party participation possibilities, however, do not afford victims participatory rights. Rather, the participation is placed in the discretion of the court making it dependent on whether the court finds the victim's involvement useful and of interest.

In the US, victims have standing where their private records are being subpoenaed by prosecution or defence. That means that victims can oppose such requests and can be legally represented when doing so (Garvin and Beloof 2015, 77). In addition, victims can object to the introduction of certain evidence at trial relating to their prior sexual activity (Garvin and Beloof 2015, 77). The victims' right to legal representation as well as associated benefits and risks in different jurisdictions is discussed further in Chapter 8.

Moreover, in the US, victims have the rights established by the *Crime Victims' Rights Act 2004* (US) (CVRA), especially the right to be heard in relation to release and plea agreements after charges have been filed. These rights have been discussed in the pre-trial context in Chapter 4 and are not subject to further analysis in this chapter. The CVRA also gives victims the right to confer with the prosecution in a reasonable way. After the consultation, however, the decision is in the discretion of the prosecution. That victims may confer with the prosecution and have a right to be heard but do not have the right to intervene in prosecutions was clarified in the appellate decision of *In re Bustos* (2010). In this decision, the court had to review the trial court's denial of a victim's motion to intervene in a security fraud prosecution. The court explained that '[t]he function of §3771(a) is to ensure that victims are heard out. Giving victims a *voice* in the criminal process differs from giving them a *veto power*, which often is both the goal and the effect of intervention' (*In re Bustos* 2010, 1–2).

While all inquisitorial and mixed systems analysed above only have one combined trial and sentencing stage, England and Wales, the US and Australia differentiate between a trial and sentencing phase. For this reason, the below considers to what extent victims can participate during the separate sentencing phase.

3 Participation at Sentencing

Due to the limited role victims have been afforded at trial in common law jurisdictions, much academic debate has arisen as to how victims' views could be considered during these bipartite adversarial proceedings. This has led to the introduction of Victim Impact Statements (VISs) or Victim Personal Statements (VPSs) in all of the common law systems analysed.

3.1 Australia

In order to allow victims to present their views in the criminal justice system, VISs were introduced in Australian jurisdictions from the mid-1980s. Wemmers (2005, 124) asserts that VISs were originally introduced in adversarial criminal justice systems as a response to the generally passive role victims had in adversarial criminal trials. This is in accordance with the justification for the introduction of the first VIS scheme in South Australia in 1989. The Attorney General at the time of their introduction, Sumner, explained that VISs were introduced in South Australia, *inter alia*, to minimise victims' feelings of alienation from, but also dissatisfaction with, the criminal justice system due to their role (see Erez et al. 1994, 206). Similarly, in the Queensland case of *R v. Singh* (2006, 8), Fryberg J. explained that the introduction of VISs was meant to have a 'primarily therapeutic' purpose for victims. That means that these schemes are predominantly designed to provide the individual victim with certain benefits. Furthermore, the rationale for the introduction of VISs in Victoria has been described as giving victims the opportunity to have a 'voice' in proceedings, providing therapeutic benefits for victims and increasing victim satisfaction with the criminal justice system (Victim Support Agency 2009, 4; Victorian Parliamentary Debates 1994, 778).

VISs can be defined as statements that are submitted to the sentencing judge (orally or in writing, also sometimes in the form of drawings, pictures and poems) after a guilty verdict and before the sentence is determined. The statements outline the consequences the crime has had on the victim (Garkawe 2007, 91). The first VIS pilot scheme was introduced in South Australia in the 1980s (Philips 2003, 52). After the pilot scheme, the right to submit a VIS was enshrined for the first time in Australia in South Australian legislation (*Criminal Law (Sentencing Act) 1988* (SA) s 7). Today all Australian states and territories have enacted statutory legislation allowing victims to submit VISs. Generally, these are to be taken into account by the court according to its discretion and the rules of evidence when formulating the penalty.[15] Prescribed content and form of VISs vary between Australian jurisdictions. Victoria, Western Australia and the Northern

Territory, for example, generally allow victims of all criminal acts to submit a VIS.[16] In South Australia, the Australian Capital Territory and Tasmania, VISs can only be made for indictable offences and some other offences specified in legislation.[17] According to New South Wales legislation, VISs can be submitted for offences that result in death or actual bodily harm, as well as for actual or threatened violence or certain prescribed sexual offences (*Crimes (Sentencing Procedure) Act* 1999 (NSW) s 27). Queensland law stipulates that a VIS can be submitted for offences committed or attempted against the person (*Penalties and Sentences Act*1992 (Qld) s 179J; *Victims of Crime Assistance Act* 2009 (Qld) s 5). In some jurisdictions, relatives or other persons authorised by the court are allowed to submit a VIS on behalf of the victim if the victim is no longer alive or if the victims are unable to prepare and tender the statement themselves.[18] As a consequence, in some Australian jurisdictions only victims of certain criminal offences have the right to be heard through the use of VISs. In others, all victims and even some family members are eligible to communicate what harm they have suffered through the use of a VIS at the sentencing stage. Also legislation stipulating how VISs must be submitted to the relevant authorities upon completion varies between the different Australian jurisdictions. In most jurisdictions, VISs can be submitted in written form and can also be read out during the sentencing stage.[19] In all Australian jurisdictions, VISs can contain an expression of how the crime has affected the victim. However, with few exceptions, for example, the Northern Territory, the VIS cannot contain an expression of what sentence the victim finds appropriate for the defendant.[20] The defendant is further generally accorded the right to cross-examine victims on the content of their VISs (South Australia Justice Strategy Unit 1999, 134).[21] Also, in some jurisdictions such as Queensland, prosecutors may edit the victim's statement in order to remove any information that may be contested by the defence. That means that the public prosecution has the power to decide what information from the VIS, if any at all, will be presented to the sentencing judge.[22] Ultimately, in all Australian states, it is in the court's discretion whether, and to what extent, they will consider the content of the VIS in their sentencing decision.[23]

3.2 England and Wales

In England and Wales, victims have been able to submit a VPS demonstrating how the crime has affected them since 2001. The scheme derived from the commitments made to victims in the Victims' Charter issued by the Home Office in 1996 (Roberts and Manikis 2013, 247). Particulars of these statements are enunciated in the Code of Practice for Victims of Crime (UK) 2013 (*Code for Victims*). While the Code for Victims is enshrined in statute, the provisions are not legally binding and cannot be enforced by victims (Doak 2015, 148). In general, VPSs are written statements which may contain a description of the physical, psychological, emotional but also financial impact of a crime on victims. They must, comparable to a witness statement, meet the formal requirements set out in Section 9 *Criminal Justice Act* 1967 (UK), which includes being true to the best of the victim's knowledge. The process of making a VPS is twofold with an initial statement being made to the police. The initial statement is not completed by the victim but taken down in writing by the police at the time the victim is reporting the victimisation (Roberts and Manikis 2013, 248). A subsequent statement can be made during the criminal process (Wolhuter et al. 2009, 179). VPSs and supporting evidence must be considered by the courts prior to the sentencing decision. No instructions are available, however, on how and to what extent judges should take these statements into account (Doak 2015, 149). The statements must not contain victims' opinions and suggestions on sentencing and any such recommendations will not be considered by the courts (Wolhuter et al. 2009, 179–180). Some victims, mostly victims of more serious offences, are afforded the possibility to read out a VPS in court (Code for Victims (UK) s 1.21). Studies on the use of VPS suggest that they are underutilised in England and Wales (Mastrocinque 2014, 219). In a study published in 2014, Mastrocinque (2014, 227) found that only a small number of victims were informed of the possibility to make a statement by police. The lack of information may explain the overall low participation rates in VPS schemes.

3.3 USA

VISs were first introduced in the US in the 1970s in California and have since been implemented in all US jurisdictions (Wemmers 2017, 170, 217). On the federal level, there appears to be some controversy on what content and form a VIS can take. In other words, it is unclear whether VISs are limited to written submissions or whether victims have the right to make oral statements. In *US v. Degenhardt* (2005), for example, the CVRA was interpreted to give victims the right to make written but also verbal submissions at sentencing and to speak directly to the judge. This interpretation of the CVRA was also confirmed by the appellate court in *Kenna v. United States District Court* (2006). When making such statements, victims have the right to be legally represented (CVRA (US) s 3771 (2)(d)). While victims have the right to present their statement to the court, they do not have the right to have the statement form part of the pre-sentence report, a report investigating the history of the convicted person to identify any information relevant to sentencing (Doyle 2015, 31). Similar to the situation in Australia and England, it is unclear what evidential value such statements hold and to what degree courts are meant to consider them.

3.4 Germany, Sweden, France, Denmark

Traditionally, VISs were available only in common law jurisdictions with a distinct trial and separate sentencing phase. In these bipartite settings, the trial stage focuses on determining the defendant's guilt and the sentencing stage on finding an appropriate sentence where a guilty verdict has been reached. The use of VISs in common law jurisdictions is usually limited to the sentencing stage as they cannot be tendered and introduced during the trial proper. As a consequence, a jury, for example, cannot be influenced by the content of such statements. Most continental European jurisdictions, including the ones selected for analysis in this volume, do not differentiate between trial and sentencing phases but rather announce the verdict and sentence after a singular trial has been conducted. Victim participation exclusively at the sentencing stage is therefore unavailable. Perhaps due to the lack of a distinct sentencing phase, VISs, as available in common law jurisdictions, have not been introduced in Germany, France, Denmark and Sweden.[24] European jurisdictions which have allowed the use of VISs, such as, for example, the Netherlands, must do so at a stage of the proceedings where the defendant has not yet been found guilty due to the singular nature of proceedings.

4 Discussion

The analysis in this chapter shows that the opportunities for victims to participate during trial and sentencing are most limited in common law jurisdictions with the right to submit a VIS/VPS as one of the only exceptions. Yet, VISs do not give victims party status or provide them with opportunities to express views and concerns during the trial. Essentially through VIS schemes victims only gain the right to make a submission to court (in writing or orally) outlining what losses they have suffered or what harm has been done to them. The statements are designed to inform sentencing judges prior to imposing a sentence. In all of the analysed jurisdictions which allow for such statements, however, it appears unclear what evidential value these submissions have and to what extent courts should consider the statements in their decision making. Ultimately, with few exceptions, victims remain largely excluded from the trial but also sentencing phase in the analysed adversarial jurisdictions.

Some victims have been afforded broader participation rights in inquisitorial and mixed criminal justice systems. For example, eligible victims in Germany and Sweden who take up participation as a PAP (Germany) or as a victim supporting the prosecution (Sweden) have numerous active procedural rights and thus opportunities to be heard at trial. While this role is available for victims of all types of offences subject to prosecution in Sweden, German law generally limits the possibilities to participate as a PAP to victims of certain offences. The role is mostly reserved for victims of serious violent offences, such as, homicide and sexual offences. Other victims have fewer opportunities to participate during proceedings. To illustrate this point, victims who participate as applicants to the adhesion procedure/civil party procedure, as permitted under German, Danish, Swedish and French law, can make submissions only in regard to their financial claim. This is why their participation is mostly reduced to the civil aspects of the criminal case. Ultimately, in order to qualify for this kind of participation, victims must have a civil claim arising from the criminal act and must be willing to assert this claim during criminal proceedings.

Victims who have no additional legal status but who are involved in the criminal justice process exclusively as witnesses have the right to be legally represented to varying degrees in some jurisdictions, for example, in Germany, Denmark, Sweden and the US. In that role they can present views and concerns to a very limited degree mostly in regard to matters relating to their protection when giving testimony.

5 Concluding Remarks

It becomes apparent that adversarial trials afford victims the fewest opportunities to participate in proceedings. The victim's role essentially remains that of a witness with the exception that they are able to tender and possibly read out a VIS/VPS at certain designated procedural stages. This may be due to the nature of the adversarial justice system, which is considered less flexible in accommodating third parties including victims. However, it is important to note that most other systems analysed, except perhaps Sweden, have not afforded victims a general participation role during criminal proceedings. Germany applies a multi-tier strategy in identifying what rights victims can exercise at trial. As a consequence, victims of certain offences are privileged over others when it comes to active participation in proceedings. No active participatory role for victims in criminal trials, except for those acting as *partie civile* or applicants to the adhesion procedure in pursuit of a civil claim, is envisioned in French and Danish criminal procedure. The reluctance to modify existing national trial structures in adversarial, inquisitorial and mixed criminal justice systems alike to afford victims a greater participatory role may be largely related to two aspects: the legal traditions of a particular country as well as the underlying understanding of crime and criminal justice as a conflict between state and offender from which the victim has been intentionally removed. These limitations and their possible consequences for law reform in this area are discussed further in Chapter 7.

Notes

1. For explanations on why no criminal justice system today remains purely inquisitorial or adversarial, see Freiberg (2011).
2. An English translation of the German StPO is available on the German Ministry of Justice website: https://www.gesetze-im-internet.de/englisch_stpo/.
3. Referred to as Private Accessory Prosecutor in the English translation of the German Code of Criminal Procedure. Also translated as 'additional private prosecutor' or 'auxiliary private prosecutor' in comparative legal literature.
4. Erstes Gesetz zur Verbesserung der Stellung des Verletzten im Strafverfahren (*Opferschutzgesetz - OpferSchG*) (Germany) December 18, 1986 entered into force April 1, 1987, BGBl I, 1986, 2496 ('OpferSchG').
5. The introductory bill's explanatory memorandum remains rather vague in regard to when victims should be able to participate in other than the named cases. It states that in order to determine whether victims should participate or not the overall situation of the victim has to be taken into consideration, see Bundesregierung der Bundesrepublik Deutschland (2009, 31).
6. For criticism that the discretion of the court may lead to the unequal treatment of similar cases see (Celebi 2009, 111). The German Federal Court of Justice (*Bundesgerichtshof*) held in a case concerning the offence of 'breach of trust' where the losses amounted to more than 13 million Euro that the amount of losses as such was not sufficient to satisfy the criteria of s 395(3) StPO and give rise to PAP participation. The Court, however, clarified that the trial court's decision to allow PAP participation could not be overturned on appeal as this discretionary power of the court was not subject to judicial review. (See Bundesgerichtshof 2012). Arguing for a restricted use of PAP

participation under this section are Jahn and Bung (2012, 758). In regard to the question of whether the introduction of such a right has led to a 'paradigm shift' in German criminal procedure, see Chapter 7.

7. For an overview of the *Nebenklage* in English, see in general Kury and Kilchling (2011, 4), Browne (2004, 29–37).
8. Victims in Germany without a formal role have received certain rights, such as, the right to receive information on particular events, StPO (Germany) ss 406d, 406h; the right to inspect court files under certain circumstances, StPO (Germany) s 406e; the right to be legally represented either as a witness when testifying, StPO (Germany) s 406f, or as a victim eligible to participate as a Private Accessory Prosecutor but refusing to do so, StPO (Germany) s 406g. The right to legal representation for different victims is analysed in detail in Chapter 8.
9. The *Bundesgerichtshof* is Germany's highest court of civil and criminal jurisdiction.
10. In Sweden, the law making process usually commences with the government appointing a legislative committee to investigate a specific issue. The committee subsequently produces a report on the issue published in the Swedish Government Official Reports, SOU (*Statens Offentliga Utredningar*). The report is subsequently circulated for comment to governmental and non-governmental bodies (Carlsson 2010, 12). Many of the reports are available with an English summary at http://www.sou.gov.se/.
11. Under the provisions of CJP (Sweden) Ch 22, s 2 the prosecutor has an obligation to present the victim's claim for compensation if this can be done without marked inconvenience and the claim is not manifestly unfounded.
12. Particular regulations for the adhesion procedure can be found in the Danish Traffic Act and the Dog-Owner Act, which will not be considered in this book.
13. An unofficial 2006 English translation of the French Code of Criminal Procedure is available online: http://www.legislationline.org/documents/section/criminal-codes/country/30.
14. For details on the Sexual Assault Communications Privilege Service see information provided on the Legal Aid (NSW) website: https://www.legalaid.nsw.gov.au/what-we-do/civil-law/sexual-assault-communications-privilege-service.
15. See the following state legislation: *Crimes (Sentencing) Act* 2005 (ACT) ss 47–53; *Crimes (Sentencing Procedure) Act* 1999 (NSW) ss 26–30A;

Penalties and Sentences Act 1992 (Qld) ss 179I–179N; *Sentencing Act* 2017 (SA) s 14*Sentencing Act* (NT) ss 106A, 106B *Sentencing Act* 1997 (Tas) s 81A, *Sentencing Act* 1991 (Vic) ss 8K–8S; *Sentencing Act* 1995 (WA) ss 24–26.

16. See *Sentencing Act* (NT) s 106A; *Sentencing Act* 1991 (Vic) s 8k; *Sentencing Act* 1995 (WA) s 24.
17. See *Crimes Sentencing Act* 2005 (ACT) s 48; *Sentencing Act* 2017 (SA) s 14; *Sentencing Act* 1997 (Tas) s 81A.
18. For example, *Crimes (Sentencing Procedure) Act* 1999 (NSW) s 30(2).
19. *Crimes (Sentencing) Act* 2005 (ACT) s 50; *Crimes (Sentencing Procedure) Act* 1999 (NSW) s 30A; *Penalties and Sentences Act* 1992 (Qld) s 197M; *Sentencing Act* 1995 (NT) s 106A; *Sentencing Act* 2017 (SA) s 14(2); *Sentencing Act* 1997 (Tasmania) s 81A; *Sentencing Act* 1995 (WA) s 25; *Sentencing Act* 1991 (Vic) s 8.
20. *Sentencing Act* (NT) s 106B (5A). A sentencing recommendation is specifically prohibited in WA see *Sentencing Act* 1995 (WA) s 25(2).
21. For explicit reference in legislation see *Sentencing Act* 1991 (Vic) s 8o(2); *Crimes (Sentencing) Act* (ACT) 2005s 53(3).
22. See, for example, *Penalties and Sentencing Act* (Qld) 1992 s 197k (3).
23. The NSW cases of *R v. Previtera* (1997), for example, held that it was not appropriate for courts to take a VIS by a family member of a deceased victim into account in determining an offender's sentence. For analysis of the decision and its consequences, see Kirchengast (2008, 615), Booth (2012, 214). The decision has since been overturned by law reform in NSW making it possible to take into account such family VISs.
24. On the problems of introducing VISs in Germany, see Braun (2013).

Legislation and Related Sources

Administration of Justice Act (Denmark), Retsplejeloven
Code de Procédure Pénale (France), Code of Criminal Procedure
Code of Practice for Victims of Crime 2013 (UK)
Crimes (Sentencing) Act 2005 (ACT)
Crimes (Sentencing Procedure) Act 1999 (NSW)
Criminal Law (Sentencing Act) 1988 (SA)

Criminal Procedure Act 1986 (NSW)
Criminal Justice Act 1967 (UK)
Crime Victims' Rights Act 2004 (US)
Lag om Målsägandebiträde (Sweden), Counsel for the Inured Party Act
Opferschutzgesetz (Germany) (Erstes Gesetz zur Verbesserung der Stellung des Verletzten im Strafverfahren), Victim Protection Act
Penalties and Sentences Act 1992 (Qld)
Rättegångsbalken (Sweden), Code of Judicial Procedure
Sentencing Act (NT)
Sentencing Act 2017 (SA)
Sentencing Act 1997 (Tas)
Sentencing Act 1991 (Vic)
Sentencing Act 1995 (WA)
Strafprozessordnung (Germany), Code of Criminal Procedure
Victims of Crime Act 2001 (SA)
Victims of Crime Assistance Act 2009 (Qld).

References

Anders, R. P. (2012). Straftheoretische Anmerkungen zur Verletztenorientierung im Strafverfahren. *Zeitschrift fuer die gesamte Strafrechtswissenschaft, 124*(2), 374–410.

Australian Law Reform Commission. (2000). *Managing Justice: A Review of the Federal Civil Justice System*. Sydney: Australian Law Reform Commission.

Bacik, I., Maunsell, C., & Gogan, S. (1998). *The Legal Process and Victims of Rape*. Dublin: Dublin Rape Crisis Centre.

Barton, S., & Flotho, C. (2010). *Opferanwaelte im Strafverfahren*. Baden-Baden: Nomos.

Bibas, S. & Bierschbach, R. A. (2004). Integrating Remorse and Apology into Criminal Procedure. *The Yale Law Journal, 114*(1), 85–148.

Block, M., Parker, K., Jeffrey, S., & Vyborna, O. (2000). An Experimental Comparison of Adversarial Versus Inquisitorial Procedural Regimes. *American Law and Economics Review, 2*(1), 170–194.

Booth, T. (2012). 'Cooling Out' Victims of Crime: Managing Victim Participation in the Sentencing Process in a Superior Sentencing Court. *Australian & New Zealand Journal of Criminology, 45*(2), 214–230.

Braun, K. (2013). Giving Victims a Voice: On the Problems of Introducing Victim Impact Statements in German Criminal Procedure. *German Law Journal, 14,* 819–837.

Brienen, M. E. I., & Hoegen, E. H. (2000a). Compensation Across Europe: A Quest for Best Practice. *International Review of Victimology, 7*(4), 281–304.

Brienen, M. E. I., & Hoegen, E. H. (2000b). *Victims of Crime in 22 European Criminal Justice Systems: The Implementation of Recommendation (85) 11 of the Council of Europe on the Position of the Victim in the Framework of Criminal Law and Procedure.* Nijmegen: Wolf Legal.

Browne, M. K. (2004). International Victims' Rights Law: What Can Be Gleaned from the Victims' Empowerment Procedures in Germany as the United States Prepares to Consider the Adoption of a "Victim's Rights Amendment" to Its Constitution? *Hamline Law Review, 27,* 15–44.

Bundesregierung der Bundesrepublik Deutschland. (2009, March 3). Entwurf eines Gesetzes zur Staerkung der Rechte von Verletzten und Zeugen im Strafverfahren (2. Opferrechtsreformgesetz) identical with Gesetzesentwurf der Fraktionen der CDU/CSU und SPD Entwurf eines Gesetzes zur Staerkung der Rechte von Verletzten und Zeugen im Strafverfahren (2. Opferrechtsreformgesetz), BT-Drucks 16/12098.

Carlson, L. (2009). *The Fundamentals of Swedish Law: A Guide for Foreign Lawyers and Students.* Lund: Studentlitteratur.

Carlsson, J. (2010). *Right to Counsel for the Injured Party—A Comparative Study of Sexual Assault Victims' Rights in Sweden, Arizona & Massachusetts* (Master thesis). Lund University Libraries, Faculty of Law. Retrieved from http://lup.lub.lu.se/luur/download?func=downloadFile&recordOId=1628195&fileOId=16281.

Celebi, G. (2009). *Kritische Wuerdigung des Opferrechtsreformgesetzes' Zeitschrift fuer Rechtspolitik, 42*(4), 110–111.

Dauer, M. (2018). *Das Adhaesionsverfahren im Rechtsvergleich.* Hamburg: Verlag Dr Kovac.

Doak, J. (2005). Victims' Rights in Criminal Trials: Prospects for Participation. *Journal of Law and Society, 32*(2), 294–316.

Doak, J. (2008). *Victims' Rights, Human Rights and Criminal Justice: Reconceiving the Role of Third Parties.* Portland: Hart Publishing.

Doak, J. (2015). Enriching Trial Justice for Crime Victims in Common Law Systems: Lessons from Transitional Environments. *International Review of Victimology, 21*(2), 139–160.

Doyle, C. (2015). *Crime Victims' Rights Act: A Summary and Legal Analysis of 18 USC 3771.* Washington, DC: Congressional Research Service (December 9, 2015). Retrieved from https://fas.org/sgp/crs/misc/RL33679.pdf.

Duenkel, F. (2001). The Victim in Criminal Law—On the Way from Offender-Related to Victim Related Criminal Justice. In E. A. Fattah, S. Parmentier, & T. Peters (Eds.), *Victim Policies and Criminal Justice on the Road to Restorative Justice: A Collection of Essays in Honour of Tony Peters* (pp. 167–211). Leuven: Leuven University Press.

Erez, E. (1991). *Victim Impact Statements.* Canberra: Australian Institute of Criminology.

Erez, E., & Roberts, J. (2010). Victim Participation in the Criminal Justice System: Normative Dilemmas and Practical Responses. In S. G. Shoham, P. Knepper, & M. Kett (Eds.), *International Handbook of Criminology* (pp. 599–618). Boca Raton, FL: CRC Press.

Erez, E., Roeger, L., & Morgan, F. (1994). *Victim Impact Statements in South Australia: An Evaluation.* Adelaide: Office of Crime Statistics of the South Australian Attorney General's Department.

European Justice. (2012, May 2). *Sweden-My Rights During the Trial.* Retrieved from https://e-justice.europa.eu/content_rights_of_victims_of_crime_in_criminal_proceedings-171-SE-maximizeMS-en.do?clang=en&idSubpage=2&member=1.

Freiberg, A. (2011). Post-adversarial and Post-inquisitorial Justice: Transcending Traditional Penological Paradigms. *European Journal of Criminology, 8*(2), 82–101.

French Ministry of Justice. (2013). *EVVI: Evaluation of Victims Project.* (Document No. JUST/2013/JPEN/AG/4602). Retrieved from http://www.justice.gouv.fr/publication/evvi_guide_en.pdf.

Garkawe, S. (2007). Victim Impact Statements and Sentencing. *Monash University Law Review, 33,* 90–114.

Garvin, M., & Beloof, D. E. (2015). Crime Victim Agency: Independent Lawyers for Sexual Assault Victims. *Ohio State Journal of Criminal Law, 13,* 67–88.

Greve, V. (1991). *Criminal Procedure in Denmark-An Outline.* Copenhagen: Kriminalistik Institut.

Haller, K. (2011). Das „kraenkelnde" Adhaesionsverfahren- Indikator struktureller Probleme der Strafjustiz. *Neue Juristische Wochenschrift, 64*(14), 970–974.

Hanloser, M. (2010). Das Recht des Opfers auf Gehör im Strafverfahren: ein Vorschlag zur Umsetzung des EU-Rahmenbeschlusses über die Stellung des Opfers im Strafverfahren auf der Grundlage einer Betrachtung des Victim Impact Statement im US-amerikanischen Recht. Frankfurt am Main: Peter Lang.

Hermann, J. (1987). The Federal Republic of Germany. In G. F. Cole, S. Frankowski, & M. G. Gertz (Eds.), *Major Criminal Justice Systems: a Comparative Survey* (2nd ed., pp. 106–133). Newbury Park: Sage.

Hermann, J. (2010). Die Entwicklung des Opferschutzes im Deutschen Strafrecht und Strafprozessrecht- eine unendliche Geschichte. *Zeitschrift fuer Internationale Strafrechtsdogmatik, 3*, 236–245.

Hoelzel, U. (1980). *Das Institut der Nebenklage-eine Betrachtung unter rechtshistorischen, rechtsdogmatischen und rechtspolitischen Gesichtspunkten* (Doctoral dissertation). Friedrich-Alexander-Universitaet Erlangen-Nuernberg.

Huesing, D. (1983). *Die Rechtswirklichkeit der Nebenklage-eine rechtstatsaechliche Untersuchung an 569 nebenklagefaehigen Strafverfahren* (Doctral dissertation). Georg-August-Universität Göttingen.

Jahn, M., & Bung, J. (2012). Die Grenzen der Nebenklagebefugnis. *Strafverteidiger, 12*(754), 761.

Joachimski, J. (1999). *Criminal Procedure in Germany—Lecture held in Vilnius*, Lithuania. Retrieved from http://www.joachimski.de/StPO/Rechtsvergleich/rechtsvergleich.html.

Kaiser, M. (1991). The Status of the Victim in the Criminal Justice System According to the Victim Protection Act. In G. Kaiser, H. Kury, & H.-J. Albrecht (Eds.), *Victims and Criminal Justice: Legal Protection, Restitution, and Support* (pp. 543–577). Freiburg im Breisgau: Max-Planck Institut fuer Auslaendisches und Internationals Strafrecht.

Kessler, A. (2004). Our Inquisitorial Tradition: Equity Procedure, Due Process, and the Search for an Alternative to the Adversarial. *Cornell Law Review, 90*, 1181–1276.

Kilchling, M. (1992). *Die Stellung des Verletzten im Strafverfahren: Implementation und Evaluation des Opferschutzgesetzes*. Freiburg im Breisgau: Max-Planck Institut fuer Auslaendisches und Internationales Strafrecht.

Kirchengast, T. (2008). Sentencing Law and the 'Emotional Catharsis' of Victims' Rights in NSW Homicide Cases. *Sydney Law Review, 30*, 615–637.

Kury, H., & Kilchling, M. (2011). Accessory Prosecution in Germany: Legislation and Implementation. In E. Erez, M. Kilchling, & J.-A. Wemmers (Eds.), *Therapeutic Jurisprudence and Victim Participation in Justice* (pp. 43–62). Durham: Carolina Academic Press.

Mastrocinque, J. M. (2014). Victim Personal Statements: An Analysis of Notification and Utilization. *Criminology and Criminal Justice, 14*(2), 216–234.

Mouthaan, S. (2013). Victim Participation at the ICC for Victims of Gender-Based Crimes: A Conflict of Interests. *Cardozo Journal of International and Comparative Law, 21*, 619–652.
Oxford Pro Bono Publico. (2015, April). *Victim Participation in Criminal Procedures: A Report to Assist Redress*. University of Oxford. Appendix: Country Report Denmark. Retrieved from http://ohrh.law.ox.ac.uk/opbp-makes-submissions-to-redress-on-victim-participation-in-criminal-procedures/.
Philips, J. H. (2003). Victims of Crime, Not Forgotten but Sufficiently Remembered? *Revue Internationale de Droit Comparé, 55*(1), 47–55.
Pizzi, W., & Perron, W. (1996). Crime Victims in German Courtrooms: A Comparative Perspective on American Problems. *Stanford Journal of International Law, 32*, 37–64.
Riess, P. (2007). Zur Beteiligung des Verletzten im Strafverfahren. In G. Britz, H. Koriath, K-L. Kunz, C. Momsen, E. Mueller, H. Mueller-Dietz, & H. Radtke (Eds.), *Festschrift fuer Heike Jung zum 65. Geburtstag am 23. April 2007* (pp. 751–760). Baden-Baden: Nomos.
Roberts, J. V., & Manikis, M. (2013). Victim Personal Statements in England and Wales: Latest (and Last) Trends from the Witness and Victim Experience Survey. *Criminology & Criminal Justice, 13*(3), 245–261.
Schmahl, H. L. (1980). *Das Adhaesionsverfahren im Daenischen Recht*. Itzehoe: E.A George OHG.
Schmidt, G. (1979). Die Stellung des Verletzten im schwedischen Strafprozess. In A. Kaufmann, G. Bemmann, D. Krauss, & K. Volk (Eds.), *Festchrift fuer Paul Boeckelmann zum 70. Geburtstag am 7. Dezember 1987* (pp. 847–859). Munich: Beck.
Siegismund, E. (2000). Ancillary (Adhesion) Proceedings in Germany as Shaped by the First Victim Protection Law: An Attempt to Take Stock. In H. Itsuka & R. Findlay-Debeck (Eds.), *Resource Material Series No 56* (pp. 102–113). Tokyo: United Nations Asia and Far East Institute for the Prevention of Crime and Treatment of Offenders.
South Australia Justice Strategy Unit. (1999). *Victims of Crime Review: Report One*. Adelaide: Justice Strategy Unit, Attorney General's Department.
Spiess, K. (2008). *Das Adhaesionsverfahren in der Rechtswirklichkeit*. Berlin: LIT Verlag.
Staten Offentliga Utredningar. (2013). *Brottmålsprocessen, Committee Report, 'The Criminal Trial Procedure' Sweden SOU 2013:17*. Stockholm: Staten Offentliga Utredningar.

Stoffers, K. F., & Moeckel, J. (2013). Beteiligtenrechte im Strafprozessualen Adhaesionsverfahren. *Neue Juristische Wochenschrift, 12,* 830–832.

Terrill, R. J. (2015). *World Criminal Justice Systems: A Comparative Survey* (9th ed.). New York: Routledge.

Tham, H., Roenneling, A., & Rytterbro, L.-L. (2011). The Emergence of the Crime Victim: Sweden in a Scandinavian Context. *Crime and Justice, 40*(1), 555–611.

Tumanishvili, G. (2008). *Erweiterung der strafprozessualen Rechtsstellung des Verletzten?*. Hamburg: Verlag Dr. Kovac.

Victim Support Agency. (2009). *A Victim's Voice: Victim Impact Statements in Victoria—Findings of an Evaluation into the Effectiveness of Victim Impact Statements in Victoria*. Department of Justice: Melbourne.

Victoria. (1994). Victorian Parliamentary Debates (Hansard): Legislative Assembly, 31 March 1994, 778 (Mrs Jan Wade).

Weigend, T. (1984). Viktimologische und Kriminalpolitische Ueberlegungen zur Stellung des Verletzten im Strafverfahren. *Zeitschrift fuer die Gesamte Strafrechtswissenschaft, 96*(3), 761, 793.

Weigend, T. (2011). Germany. In K. Heller & M. Dubber (Eds.), *The Handbook of Comparative Criminal Law* (pp. 252–287). Stanford, CA: Stanford University Press.

Weiner, B. (2018). Paragraph 395. In J. P. Graf (Ed.), *Strafprozessordnung-Beck'scher Online-Kommentar Strafprozessordnung* (29th ed.). Munich: C.H. Beck.

Wemmers, J.-A. (2005). Victim Policy Transfer: Learning from Each Other. *European Journal on Criminal Policy and Research, 11*(1), 121–133.

Wemmers, J.-A. (2017). *Victimology: A Canadian Perspective*. New York: University of Toronto Press.

Wilson, L. C. (2005). Independent Legal Representation for Victims of Sexual Assault: A Model for Delivery of Legal Services. *Windsor Yearbook of Access to Justice, 23*(2), 249–312.

Wolhuter, L. (2010). German and Swedish Procedures as Models for the Empowerment of Racial Minority Women in Rape Trials. *International Journal of Law, Crime and Justice, 38,* 1–16.

Wolhuter, L., Olley, N., & Denham, D. (2009). *Victimology and Victims' Rights*. London: Routledge.

Zander, S. (2011). *Das Adhaesiosnverfahren im neuen Gewand*. Berlin: Duncker & Humblot.

Cases

Bundesgerichtshof, 09 May 2012-5 StR 523/11 (Germany).
In re Bustos No. 10-2752 (7th Cir. July 26, 2010) (US) (Unpublished).
Kenna v. United States District Court, 435 F.3d 1011 (9th Cir. 2006) (US).
Levy v. Victoria (1997) HCA 31; 189 CLR 579 (Australia).
R v. Singh (2006) QCA 71 (Qld).
R v. Previtera (1997) 94 A Crim R 76 (NSW).
US v. Degenhardt, 405 F. Supp.2d 1341 (D. Utah 2005) (US).

6

Victim Participation Post Trial: Appeals and Early Release

1 Introduction

While Chapters 4 and 5 considered possibilities for victim participation before and during the trial and sentencing stage, the focus of this chapter is on the post-trial phase. It examines possibilities for victims to initiate or participate in appeals. This includes interlocutory appeals, meaning appeals in which certain pre-trial or trial decisions affecting the victim can be challenged, as well as appeals against the actual verdict or sentence the offender has received. Furthermore, it contemplates whether and how victims can be heard in the course of early-release proceedings in which relevant agencies decide on parole and its respective conditions for convicted offenders with custodial sentences. The victims' interests may be significantly affected in both contexts. Where victims' rights are violated during proceedings victims may require judicial avenues to officially complain in the form of appeal rights. They may also be dissatisfied with the outcome of proceedings or the sentence the offender has received or disagree with factual and legal aspects of the trial. Appeals could provide them with an avenue to express their dissatisfaction. Furthermore, where convicted offenders are afforded

K. Braun, *Victim Participation Rights*, Palgrave Studies in Victims and Victimology, https://doi.org/10.1007/978-3-030-04546-3_6

the possibility to serve the remainder of their custodial sentence in the community, victims' safety interests may be significantly infringed upon. Offenders released into the community can approach victims or their families more easily raising security concerns. Victims may therefore wish to have an input in the release decision or the conditions imposed on the release.

In light of the above considerations, this chapter provides a systematic and detailed analysis of available post-trial rights in all jurisdictions selected for analysis in this volume. In the context of each individual jurisdiction, it first considers the victims' right to appeal or be involved in appeals prior to assessing possibilities for victim involvement in offenders' early-release proceedings.

2 Post-trial Participation

2.1 Germany

German law differentiates between interlocutory appeals and appeals against the verdict and sentence. Where victims feel that they have been denied certain rights available to them during the pre-trial and trial stage they are able to initiate an interlocutory appeal (*Beschwerde* and *Sofortige Beschwerde*). This differs from appeals against the verdict or sentence (*Berufung* and *Revision*) the individual perpetrator has received. The latter form of appeal is limited in scope and generally only available to victims with a specific procedural role. The below first analyses the details of the appeal process prior to considering what role victims play, if any, in early-release proceedings.

2.1.1 Interlocutory Appeal

Under German criminal procedure law victims, even victims without a special procedural role such as that of Private Accessory Prosecutor (*Nebenklaeger*, *PAP*),[1] are able to complain against certain procedural decisions and orders made before or during the trial which directly affect them, so-called *Beschwerde*. Section 304(1) German Code of Criminal Procedure (*Strafprozessordnung*, StPO (Germany))[2] states that a

> complaint shall be admissible against all orders made by the courts at first instance or in appellate proceedings on fact and law and against directions given by the presiding judge, the judge in preliminary proceedings, and by a commissioned or a requested judge, unless such orders are expressly exempted from appellate remedy by law.

The section specifically refers to witnesses in Subsection 2 highlighting that 'witnesses, experts, and other persons may also lodge a complaint against orders and directions by which they are affected'. It is commonly understood that a person is directly affected by a court decision where their freedom, finance or other protected rights are infringed upon. As a consequence, a victim witness, for example, whose request to testify via video technology or in closed court is denied by court order, may submit a complaint as per the above section. The complaint is put on record at the relevant court to allow the trial judge to review their own decision first and to decide on the matter immediately. If the judge agrees with the complaint they can directly reverse their earlier decision and, for example, remove the accused while the victim testifies or exclude the public in this context. If they do not agree with the complaint, it must be passed on to the court responsible for handling such complaints within three days (StPO (Germany) s 306). As the complaint does not automatically suspend proceedings, meaning that the victim witness may have to testify in the interim with the accused or public present, the complaint becomes meaningless by the time it reaches the complaint court and will therefore be dismissed (Ullrich 1998, 175). While the trial court can suspend proceedings until a decision has been reached by the complaint court (StPO (Germany) s 307(2)), it remains in the trial court's discretion to do so.

Furthermore, in the context of complaints, a so-called immediate complaint is possible for a PAP against the court decision not to commence the main trial (StPO (Germany) ss 210, 400(2)) or the discretionary disposal of proceedings (StPO (Germany) s 153). This, however, must occur within one week of the decision becoming available (*sofortige Beschwerde*) (StPO (Germany) ss 400, 311). In these cases, the complaint is decided by a superior court which can either affirm the decision of the trial court not to commence proceedings or, where the court agrees with the complainant, order proceedings to commence.

Since law reform in 2004, victims who pursue their civil claims during criminal trials as applicants to the adhesion procedure (*Adhäsionsverfahren*) are also able to formally complain against certain court decisions which affect them (StPO (Germany) s 406a). However, in general, the standpoint of the legislature in this context appears to be that the right to complain is afforded sparingly to prevent criminal courts from having to deal with ever more civil matters (Zander 2011, 195). The applicant can complain against the court's decision to reject their adhesion application to join the criminal trial within one week of it becoming available (StPO (Germany) s 406a). Prior to 2004, it was generally assumed that a negative decision concerning the adhesion application did not legally affect applicants as they could commence civil proceedings and pursue their claim this way. For this reason, at the time, no legal right to complain was available where an application was denied. However, this issue is now viewed in a different light and the necessary legal impact on the applicant of the adhesion procedure is seen in the circumstance that they are prevented from realising their claim more speedily during the criminal trial (Zander 2011, 195).

While victims can formally complain in the above instances via an interlocutory appeal, it needs to be noted that under German law none of the above decisions give victims the right to appeal the verdict based on an error of law due to denial of their rights (Tolmein 2012, 243). For example, a victim whose request to testify using video technology has been denied cannot appeal the subsequent verdict on the basis that they should have been allowed to do so and that the denial constitutes a misapplication of the law resulting in an erroneous verdict. As a consequence of this limitation, it has been suggested that courts in practice see a low (appeal) risk of their verdicts in rejecting victims' applications for testifying via video technology or for the temporary exclusion of the defendant during the main trial. Yet, they see a higher appeal risk in granting said victims' applications. This is so because the defendant, on the other hand, has the right to appeal the verdict on the basis that the court should have rejected the victim's application (Tolmein 2012, 243). It can be imagined that in practice a lower appeal risk has the potential to sway court decisions against the victim.

In 2007, the German Federal Constitutional Court (*Bundesverfassungsgerichtshof, BVerfG*), Germany's most superior court, was called upon to comment on the availability of the victim's right to appeal the verdict in a case where authorities had disregarded the victim's procedural rights (BVerfG 2007). In the case at hand, the victim complaint to the Court that their constitutional right to be heard at trial had been violated as they had not been informed about their right to join criminal proceedings as a PAP in a specific case. The victim only found out about the trial and their right to participate months after the trial had ended and the defendant had been acquitted. While the Court ultimately rejected the victim's complaint for reasons specific to constitutional law, it did comment in passing on the consequences of victims' rights violations in relation to ordering a retrial. The Court outlined that the legislature had failed to grant victims the right to appeal the verdict where victims' rights were breached. Yet, the Court went as far as saying that this legislative decision was 'politically regrettable'.[3] Some commentators interpret this remark as the Court's call upon the legislature to carry out further law reform in this area in order to expand victims' appeal rights (Wenske 2008, 435). So far, however, the right of the victim to appeal on this basis and the possibility to achieve the opening of a retrial in which the victim can then participate as a PAP has not been introduced in German criminal procedure.

The above shows that interlocutory appeals are available to any victim who can establish that their procedural rights have been violated pre or during trial. Yet, the right to appeal the actual verdict or sentence is limited in scope and, if at all, only available to specific victims with a procedural role as the below outlines.

2.1.2 Appeal Against Verdict or Sentence

As pointed out above, victims' rights to appeal the verdict against an offender in itself are generally non-existent in Germany. The situation differs for PAPs who have been afforded more far-reaching appeal rights than other victims. In this context, a victim acting as PAP has the right to appeal completely independently from the public prosecution (StPO (Germany) s 401(1) sent. 1). Once an appeal has been initiated the prosecution has no right to terminate the PAP's appeal. Yet, the victim's right to appeal is limited in comparison with that of the public prosecution. PAPs can only appeal the verdict to a degree (StPO (Germany) ss 395(4) sent. 2, 400, 401(1) sent. 1), and not the sentence the individual offender has received. In order to appeal successfully, a PAP must demonstrate *inter alia* that they have suffered a grievance through the verdict. This is the case, where the PAP can demonstrate that the criminal offence which gave rise to their participation, for example, a sexual offence, has been assessed incorrectly during proceedings thus creating an unfair advantage for the defendant (Schroth 2012, 153). The scope of the appeal is therefore limited to those offences which allow for private accessory prosecution. The court's incorrect assessment of other offences during proceedings, for example, sexual offences against a third person, cannot justify an appeal by the PAP. An appeal is only possible against the verdict and does not cover the specific sentence imposed (e.g. the type of sentence or sentence length) (StPO (Germany) s 400(1) 1st alt). This has been the case in Germany since law reform in 1986 limited the broad appeal rights PAPs had been afforded until then. The explanatory memorandum to the bill stated that broad appeal rights for the PAP are no longer required as the PAP's role is only that of an 'extra' participant in state based criminal proceedings. A PAP, so it was described, only has a legitimate interest in whether the defendant has correctly been convicted of offences that enabled them (the PAP) to participate but not in sentences imposed or their lengths. This, according to the explanations, justified the limitation of the PAP's appeal right to verdicts alone (Bundesregierung 1986, 15). In practice, this means that PAPs can appeal an acquittal with the aim of obtaining a conviction for an offence which allows for private accessory prosecution. Furthermore, they can appeal a conviction with the aim of obtaining a further conviction for an offence which gives rise to private accessory prosecution and forms a series with the offence the defendant has already been convicted of. In cases where the public prosecution or the defendant has initiated an appeal, the PAP has the right to participate in the appeal proceedings but only in the context of PAP offences (Schroth 2012, 162).

Victims who act as applicants to the adhesion procedure do not have the right to appeal the criminal verdict or sentence (StPO (Germany) s 406a (1) sent. 2). The justification behind this is that German law only grants individuals the right to appeal where they are directly affected by a procedural decision. However, it is frequently argued that the criminal side of the verdict does not affect the applicant of the adhesion procedure as they only have a direct procedural interest in the civil side of proceedings. Furthermore, the applicant is free to pursue their claim to the extent that the criminal court has denied it in the civil courts (StPO (Germany) s 406(3) sent. 3) as additional civil law proceedings are not precluded by an adhesion verdict in Germany.

The above shows that German law affords victims some appeal remedies against certain procedural decisions directly affecting them. The right to appeal the actual verdict or sentence, on the other hand, is very limited in scope and mostly reserved for victims with a special procedural role. While victims play only a marginal role in appeal proceedings, their involvement in early-release proceedings is non-existent in Germany as the below outlines.

2.1.3 Early-Release Decisions

Early release, often referred to as parole or conditional release, includes the return of an incarcerated prisoner to the community in order to serve the remainder of their sentence in accordance with specifically imposed conditions. The German parole and probation system originally developed post-1945 with the beginnings of the Federal Republic of Germany. Prior, especially during the Nazi regime, the state took little interest in issues relating to the reintegration of offenders in society (Mutz 2008, 383). The system was greatly expanded with law reform in 1969, when the possibilities for suspended sentences and conditional release were widened. Significant reforms of the parole system followed in the 1980s.

In Germany, there are a number of ways in which an imposed custodial sentence does not have to be served or does not have to be served in full in prison. For example, the sentence can be suspended by the sentencing court under certain conditions with the consequence that the offender does not have to serve the sentence in prison unless the specific imposed conditions are violated. Furthermore, eligible convicted offenders serving a custodial sentence can be allowed semi-liberty, which means that they may leave the prison for a day or a holiday or for working and training outside of prison. Finally, the remainder of a custodial sentence can be suspended so that the offender can serve the rest in the community (Mutz 2008, 401). These decisions are usually based on reports assessing the offender and the offender's potential risk factors. Investigations are carried out into the personality of the offender, their social ties and their behaviour. The reports also often include a psycho-social diagnosis and a situation analysis and may contain recommendations for the decision to be taken (Mutz 2008, 401). A personal investigation report may also be conducted on the victim, especially on how the crime has affected them (Mutz 2008, 385).

When deciding on parole, the relevant authority can give consideration to the likely effects of parole on victims. Yet, under German law, no victim, including victims with special procedural status, has the right to make direct representations in relation to or appeal any of the above decisions. Courts have held that even PAPs have no right to submit a complaint in relation to release decisions as their procedural interests are not directly affected (Oberlandesgericht Frankfurt 1995). Even though the PAP is an additional participant in proceedings next to the prosecutor, their main procedural interests are seen to revolve around being able to participate during the trial and do not extend to the enforcement of the verdict. In line with this stance, no avenue exists for victims to complain against early-release decisions they disagree with.

Sweden, the only other jurisdiction analysed in this volume which provides victims with the possibility to receive a party-like status by supporting the prosecution, affords victims greater appeal possibilities than Germany. Yet, the involvement of victims in early-release proceedings is equally as limited in Sweden as it is in Germany.

2.2 Sweden

2.2.1 Appeals

Under Swedish law, the general rule concerning appeals is that a party who has been unsuccessful with their case may appeal to the court of appeal (Code of Judicial Procedure, *Rättegångsbalken, RB* (Sweden) Ch 49). That means that victims, who have been afforded party status, namely those supporting the prosecution and applicants to the adhesion procedure, have the right to appeal if they are not satisfied with a district court decision (European Justice 2012, 1). The supporting victim, for example, has the right to appeal acquittals which the prosecution is not pursuing to a superior court (RB (Sweden) Ch 20, s 8(2)). The applicant to the adhesion procedure may not only appeal the verdict in relation to their compensation claim but also the sentence the convicted offender has received (Carlsson 2010, 18; Brienen and Hoegen 2000, 907–908). Where the victim appeals, they must present their position to the extent necessary to consider their appeal during the main appeal hearing (RB (Sweden) Ch 51, s 18). It needs to be noted that, after the sentence enters into force, victims no longer have the right to be legally represented at the expense of the state. Where they wish to have legal representation post sentence, they must do so at their own expense (European Justice 2012).

As a consequence, victims with special procedural roles have wider appeal rights in Sweden than in Germany. They can appeal verdict and sentence and also appeal in case of an unsuccessful adhesion procedure. Yet, their involvement in early-release decisions appears equally as limited as in Germany.

2.2.2 Early-Release Decision

To better understand victim involvement in early-release proceedings some context to the Swedish conditional and early-release system is required. One of the first Swedish laws relating to the conditional release of the offender into the community was the 1918 *Conditional*

Sentence Act (Sweden) according to which a prison sentence of up to one year could be suspended (Lindholm and Bishop 2008, 1027). Since then, the Swedish Prison and Probation Service (SPPS) has been established within the Ministry of Justice which unites probation and parole in one service (Bassett 2016, 6). In this context, parole means the release of a prisoner back into the community after a certain sentence length has been served, while probation describes an alternative to incarceration and the possibility for the convicted offender to remain in the community under supervision while undergoing certain treatment or voluntary activities (Holmberg et al. 2012). The SPPS is a government agency (Lindholm and Bishop 2008, 1029), whose tasks have been described as 'performing pre-sentence investigations, executing non-custodial sanctions, supervising conditionally released parolees, and executing shorter prison sentences through electronic monitoring' (Boijsen and Tallving 2017, 4).

A report from the Swedish National Council for Crime Prevention (2007, 18) on early release of offenders with electronic monitoring in Sweden, identified *inter alia* that some of the interviewed victims felt dissatisfied with the early-release decisions made and the imposed release conditions. Nevertheless, while the SPPS is under an obligation to take the views of victims into account when making decisions (Boijsen and Tallving 2017, 9), the service does not work together with victims directly and victims do not have the right to participate in decision-making processes. That means that where a conditional or provisional release decision concerning the offender is made, the victim has no right to intervene (European Justice 2012, 1). As such victims, even if they are dissatisfied with the early-release decision, are unable to express their views in relation to the decision itself and the respective imposed conditions.

While Germany and Sweden afford victims wide participation rights at trial when they act as PAPs or in support of the prosecution these avenues of participation do not exist in France and Denmark. There, victims can generally only act as civil claimants or in the role of witnesses. What impact this has on appeal rights and participation in early-release decision in these jurisdictions is discussed below.

2.3 France

In France, victims who have not applied to join proceedings as a civil claimant have no right to appeal the judgement of the court (European Justice 2018, 1). Yet, victims who act as *partie civile* can appeal any ruling which entirely or partially rejects their civil claim within ten days (*faisant grief a ses interest civils*) (Code of Criminal Procedure, *Code de Procédure Pénale, CCP* (France) s 186-2).[4] As a consequence, the civil claimant is able to formally complain if they have been denied their active participation rights at trial. Generally, civil claimants cannot appeal the guilty or not-guilty verdict or the sentence imposed *per se* but they can challenge the specific parts of the judgement to the extent that they affect their claim (CCP (France) 380-2, 4; 497, 3, 500, 546; 567). For example, the acquittal of a defendant may directly impact the civil claim in so far as the claim is consequently rejected. In this case, the civil claimant may also appeal the criminal part of the verdict in so far as it relates to their civil claim. An appeal, however, cannot be based on the desire to achieve greater punishment. This means that victim involvement in appeals in France is limited to those victims considered parties to the proceedings, namely the victim in the role of a civil claimant. This is in line with the understanding that appeals are generally limited to the parties of a dispute and that being a victim as such does not provide an individual with a party role (European Justice 2018, 1). While victims' possibilities to participate in appeals are generally very limited in scope in France, their involvement in early-release proceedings can be described as even more minimal.

To put victims' involvement in conditional and early-release decisions into context, a brief overview of probation and parole in France is required. Probation was first formally introduced in France in 1958 by allowing judges to suspend sentences (Pelissier and Perrier 2008, 351). It has since undergone substantive law reform. The probation system is overseen by the Rehabilitation and Probation Prison Service. Upon court instruction, the service is also responsible for carrying out investigations into the social and family background of the offender in order to assist in the preparation of court decisions (CCP (France) s 574). Early-release decisions are made by specific judges responsible for the execution of sentences, so-called executing judge (*juge de l'application de peines*) where sentences are under 10 years. Where sentences are greater than 10 years, the decision is taken by the post-sentencing council (Reuflet 2013, 179). Early-release measures in France include day release and work release as well as parole in case of longer sentences. Under French law, authorities responsible for executing sentences should take the victim's interests into account during decision making (Pelissier and Perrier 2008, 359). The Rehabilitation and Probation Prison Service may be asked by the courts to gather information about the victim or to carry out in-depth interviews with the victim prior to the court decision on amending a sentence to provide them with additional information from the victim's perspective (Pelissier and Perrier 2008, 359).

French criminal procedure law now sets out that where a convicted person is likely to come into contact with a victim or civil party upon temporary or permanent release from prison and the contact is considered undesirable, the court responsible for executing sentences should prohibit such contact (CCP (France) s 712-16-2). The court is under an obligation to prohibit the contact in case of certain violent offences including sexual offences, unless otherwise explicitly justified. Only civil claimants but not victims without party role are able to appear in early-release proceedings and to make submissions upon request through their lawyer. Their appearance, however, is limited to cases where the offender has been sentenced to imprisonment for five years or more (European Justice 2018, 2). In all other cases, the CCP in s 712-16-1[5] states that

> Prior [to] any decision involving the temporary or permanent cessation of the imprisonment of a person sentenced to a custodial sentence before the due date of said sentence, the sentence enforcement courts shall take into consideration the interests of the victim or civil party in relation to the consequences of this decision.

If the court sees fit, it may allow the victim or civil party to make a written submission within 15 days (CCP (France) s 712-16-1). The statement can be submitted to the court in whatever form desired (European Justice 2018, 1). It is important to note, however, that this is a discretionary court decision and does not afford victims participation rights as such. In addition, no appeal is possible against early-release decisions in France (Dervieux 2002, 271; European Justice 2018, 2). However, where offenders are released under certain conditions and it comes to the attention of the victim that the offender is in non-compliance with said conditions, they can report them to the judge monitoring the release.

The above shows that in France only civil claimants have the right to make submissions to the early-release authority through their legal representative where the sentence term is greater than five years. Yet, in case of shorter sentences or where victims do not act as civil claimants their involvement in early-release proceedings is entirely at the discretion of the respective court.

2.4 Denmark

In Denmark, the public prosecutor can appeal an acquittal as well as the sentence (Bacik et al. 1998, 201). However, in keeping with the fact that victims are not considered parties in Danish criminal trials they generally do not have the right to appeal verdict or sentence (European Justice 2013, 1; Oxford Pro Bono Publico 2015). The right to appeal is available only for victims who have initiated proceedings through private prosecution (Oxford Pro Bono Publico 2015, 14) or in the context of the adhesion procedure. Applicants to the adhesion procedure can only appeal the aspects of the court decision relating to their civil claim. Importantly, however, this type of appeal is not dealt with as a criminal appeal but, given the nature of the claim, has to be lodged in accordance with the rules of civil procedure (European Justice 2013, 1).

After verdict and sentence enter into force the victims' role in Denmark generally comes to an end. As a consequence, their involvement in conditional or early-release proceedings is extremely limited. Since 1973, the Danish Department of Prisons and Probation, part of the Ministry of Justice, is responsible for all matters concerning the enforcement of sanctions including probation and parole (Heine 2008, 233). The Department enforces custodial sentences as well as community sanctions. Its tasks include the preparation of offender-related reports including pre-trial reports. In Denmark, prisoners may be released early from prison after they have served two-thirds of their sentence and meet certain conditions. Where a sentence is more than eight years the Department makes the decision on whether to release the convicted offender early. Prisoners who have demonstrated particular measures towards improving their situation, for example, through education or treatment initiatives, may be released early after serving 50% of their sentence (Heine 2008, 245). In accordance with the Administration of Justice Act (Denmark) (*Retsplejeloven, AJA*) s 741(g), Danish police have an obligation to notify certain victims, mostly victims of more serious criminal offences including sexual offences and violent offences against the person, in cases where an offender is released early temporarily or permanently and the victim has requested to receive such a notice. In case of other offences, the police can provide such information if there are safety concerns for the individual victim. Despite these information obligations on part of the police, victims do not have the right to participate in early-release proceedings, and probation services are not tasked with supporting victims as such (Storgaard and Skov 2017, 10). As a consequence, under Danish law, victims do not have the right to make a submission to the respective authority considering the early release of an offender as well as release conditions. Furthermore, no right exists to subsequently complain against these decisions (Oxford Pro Bono Publico 2015).

While the above focused on victim involvement in non-adversarial and mixed criminal justice systems the below considers whether and to what extent victims can participate in the context of appeals and early-release decisions in the selected adversarial systems.

2.5 Australia

2.5.1 Interlocutory Appeal

In Australia, victims are generally unable to appeal decisions made before or during the trial even where they may violate their rights. This is the case because Australian victims' legislation or charters typically do not grant victims enforcement mechanisms where their rights are not complied with. A complaint against violations is possible to specific bodies established to deal with victims' complaints if they exist in the respective jurisdiction. Yet, their investigative powers have been described as limited (Ross 2015, 223). One exception to this general stance can be found under New South Wales law. There, the *Criminal Appeal Act 1912* (NSW) allows the victim of a sexual assault, as a non-party, to appeal the pre-trial ruling of a judge allowing access to or use of documents covered by the sexual assault communication privilege (*Criminal Appeal Act 1912* (NSW) s 5F(3AA)–(3AB)). The section titled 'Appeal Against Interlocutory Judgment or Order' states the following:

> (3AA) A person who is not a party to proceedings to which this section applies may appeal to the Court of Criminal Appeal against a decision in those proceedings to grant leave under Division 2 of Part 5 of Chapter 6 of the Criminal Procedure Act 1986 or a determination in those proceedings that a document or evidence does not contain a protected confidence within the meaning of that Division, if the person is: (a) a person who, because of the leave, is required to produce a document or adduce evidence that contains a protected confidence, or (b) a protected confider in relation to a protected confidence that may be produced or adduced because of the leave, or (c) a person who claims the document or evidence does, despite the determination, contain a protected confidence in relation to which the person is a protected confider. (3AB) An appeal under subsection (3AA) may be made whether or not an appeal has been made by a party to the proceedings, but only if: (a) the Court of Criminal Appeal gives leave to appeal, or (b) the judge or magistrate of the court of trial certifies that the decision is a proper one for determination on appeal.

2.5.2 Appeal Against the Verdict or Sentence

Under common law, the right to appeal a verdict is often limited in scope to convictions and does not extend to acquittals. As a consequence, prosecutors in many jurisdictions are unable to appeal the acquittal of an offender.

They are, however, able to appeal convictions under certain circumstances as well as sentences imposed. These rights are also available to the convicted person. In no Australian jurisdiction have victims been afforded a right to appeal a conviction, acquittal or sentence. Giving victims some opportunity to be heard, one Australian jurisdiction, South Australia, has introduced the right for the victim to request that the public prosecutor consider lodging an appeal against any court determination (*Victims of Crime Act 2001* (SA) s 10A). The section states:

> Section 10A Victim may request consideration of appeal (1) A victim who is dissatisfied with a determination made in relation to the relevant criminal proceedings (being a determination against which the prosecution is entitled to appeal) may request the prosecution to consider an appeal against the determination. (2) A request under this section must be made within 10 days after the making of the determination. (3) The prosecution must give due consideration to a request made under this section.

In regard to this right Kirchengast (2016, 176) notes that this

> is not a consultative right, but the right to request consideration to appeal an outcome that the prosecutor would ordinarily be able to appeal. Although consultation is not provided for under the section, the victim's request must be given 'due consideration'. What this specifically entails has not yet been the subject of litigation, but this would arguably involve more than being informed of reasons why the prosecution is not proceeding with an appeal, or an appeal on limited issues.

In addition, on the whole, no obligations exist in prosecutor's guidelines or policy documents that require the public prosecutor to take victims' views into consideration when commencing an appeal.[6]

2.5.3 Involvement in Early-Release Decisions

So-called victim registers have been established in all Australian jurisdictions providing information about the convicted offender to certain victims, mostly victims of violent offences. Victims must apply to be on the register to receive relevant information. Upon registration, the respective state department of correctional services notifies victims of certain future events including the possibility to make submissions in the context of early-release proceedings. Generally, this type of victim submission is a 'statement, written or oral, that expresses a victim's view concerning the offence or the offender' (Black 2003, 1). Some Australian states have enshrined a direct entitlement in their victims' rights legislation for (certain) victims to make submissions to the parole board when contemplating the early release of an offender. This is the case, for example, in New South Wales and Victoria.[7] In New South Wales Section 6.16 of the Charter of Victims Rights enshrined in the *Victims' Rights and Support Act* (NSW) 2013 states the following:

> 6.16 Submissions on parole and eligibility for absence from custody of serious offenders. A victim will, on request, be provided with the opportunity to make submissions concerning the granting of parole to a serious offender or any change in security classification that would result in a serious offender being eligible for unescorted absence from custody.

It needs to be noted, however, that the operation of the charter is heavily qualified in that charter obligations need only be complied with 'as far as practicable and appropriate' (*Victims' Rights and Support Act* (NSW) 2013 s 7(1)). In addition, criminal justice officials must only have regard to the charter 'to the extent that it is relevant and practicable to do so' (*Victims' Rights and Support Act* (NSW) 2013 s 7(2)). Apart from victims' rights acts, also other pieces of legislation in Australian jurisdictions contain the right for victims to make a direct submission during parole proceedings via the victim register.[8] In general, although legislation varies between jurisdictions, the right is reserved for victims of serious violent offences and typically limited in scope to written submissions. What the statement can entail also differs between states. While some allow only for the submission of the effects of the crime on the victim others also permit comments on whether the convicted offender should receive parole and under what conditions. Comparable to the situation at sentencing, uncertainty remains as to what value the parole authority should assign to these statements in the early-release process.

Victims' rights in the post-trial context in England and Wales, as well as similarities and differences to the Australian approach, are discussed in the following part.

2.6 England and Wales

Similar to the situation in Australia, and, due to the general role of victims within the parameters of adversarial criminal justice, in England and Wales, victims are generally unable to appeal criminal verdicts or sentences the accused has received. While one Australian jurisdiction, South Australia, gives victims the right to request that the DPP consider whether to lodge an appeal, no comparable right has been introduced in England and Wales. Furthermore, victims in England and Wales have not received specific rights to appeal against interlocutory matters. This flows logically, as most obligations placed on justice authorities in relation to victims at the pre-trial and trial stage are not legally binding and thus non-enforceable. As a result, victims have no formal participation rights in the context of appeals in England and Wales.

In comparison, victims have been afforded some voice in conditional and early-release proceedings in the UK. After the introduction of the first Victims' Charter in 1990 and the second in 1996, conditional-release services were required to have contact with certain victims, especially those of more violent and sexual crimes. This obligation was subsequently enshrined in s 69 of the *Criminal Justice and Court Services Act* 2000 (see McCarva 2008, 263). Victim-related obligations for the parole board are set out in the Code of Practice for Victims of Crime (UK) 2013 (*Code for Victims*) in Section 6-part (vii) entitled 'The Parole Board and Victim Personal Statements'. Releasing authorities are under the obligation to contact victims of serious violent or sexual offences in cases where the offender has received a prison sentence greater than one year. This is organised through the Probation Service Victim Contact Scheme (Code for Victims (UK) s 6.7–6.12; see also Hall and Canton 2008, 10). The contact is meant to be facilitated through a specially trained victim contact officer asking victims whether they wish to make any representations including statements about certain victim-related conditions that can be attached to the offender's release licence (Code for Victims (UK) s 6.7; McCarva 2008, 263). The board may allow certain victims to read out their statement during parole board hearings (Code for Victims (UK) ss 6.26, 6.32; see also European Justice 2017). The above makes clear that victims cannot be heard on the question of whether the convicted offender should receive parole but only in relation to the relevant licence conditions in so far as they relate to the victim. As previously pointed out, the rights enshrined in the Code for Victims are neither legally binding nor enforceable through specific appeal processes.

That the obligation to communicate with victims and to allow them to make representations may not always be met in practice became a topic of discussion in the 2018 parole board proceedings relating to John Worboys. Worboys was convicted in 2009 of sexually assaulting 12 victims in London and was eligible for parole in 2018. Several victims alleged that the parole board did not consult them in relation to the terms of the offender's release licence (see Booth 2018). As victims in the UK have no specific right to appeal or complain against parole board decisions, the only legal remedy available to victims in the Worboys case was judicial review of the parole board decision. As pointed out in Chapter 4, the process of judicial review in England and Wales can be burdensome on victims as they must meet a high threshold. In the case of parole decisions, this means that the applicant must establish that the parole board acted illegally or that the decision was so irrational that no one else would reach the same outcome. After two victims requested judicial review, the High Court, in March 2018, ordered the parole board to carry out a new determination in the case. This was *inter alia* based on their finding that the full extent of the offending had not been taken into account in the board's decision-making process (see Bowcott 2018).

The same limitations as above concerning the victim's general role in appeals based on the adversarial nature of the criminal justice system can also be found in the US. There, however, on the federal level, the introduction of the federal Crime Victims' Rights Act has afforded victims certain enforcement remedies which go beyond those available to victims in Australia and England and Wales.

2.7 USA

Traditionally in the US, appellate proceedings have been limited to the parties of a judgement. In criminal proceedings, the parties are prosecution and defence. Consequently, the Crime Victims' Rights Act 2004 (US) (CVRA) does not afford victims, as non-parties, the right to directly appeal the verdict against a perpetrator even where the victim alleges that the court has denied their rights, potentially constituting an error of law.[9] Rather, the Act contains a different enforcement remedy. As per the provisions of the CVRA, victims who believe their rights have been denied by the district courts, as well as prosecutors on their behalf, have the right to petition the court of appeals for a writ of mandamus on the basis of the erroneous court decision; an application which must be decided within 72 hours (CVRA (US) s 3771(d)(3)). In case of a successful application, the court of appeal can instruct the district court to comply with the specific victims' rights in question by quashing a specific decision and ordering that the decision be made in accordance with the law. This can also include granting petitioners the right to pursue a motion in the trial court to reopen sentencing proceedings in cases where victims have not been properly heard during the initial trial (see, e.g., *Kenna v. United States District Court* 2006). In the first ten years after the introduction of this right, over 70 mandamus petitions had been filed, most of which, around 85%, remained unsuccessful (Tobolowsky 2015, 145). Petitions frequently related to an alleged breach of the following victims' rights contained in the CVRA: the right to confer with the prosecutor, the right to receive notice of proceedings, the right not to be excluded from proceedings, as well as the right to be heard in proceedings (Tobolowsky 2015, 151). It has been explained that the different appellate courts had developed greatly varying and partially conflicting review standards for mandamus petitions possibly contributing to disharmonious petition outcomes (Tobolowsky 2015, 132–142). In an attempt to streamline review standards, law reform in 2015 amended the CVRA by inserting that courts shall apply 'ordinary standards' of appellate review in relation to mandamus provisions.

Where appeals are already under way, courts may allow victims to intervene under specific, possibly limited, circumstances. For example, the victim was allowed to intervene in order to defend their restitution order in *United States v. Laraneta* (2012) after the defendant had initiated the appeal. At the same time, the court (*United States v. Laraneta* 2012, 986) noted that

> [t]he case for intervention is most compelling when a person has a direct financial stake in a case and cannot be certain that any party has an interest in defending that stake. The government has no financial stake in restitution to victims of crime. And judicial power to allow intervention at the appellate level can be exercised in a case such as this without causing the problems that intervention in the district court would cause—indeed without causing any problems at all that we can see.

Through the introduction of the right to file a writ of mandamus, the CVRA has significantly expanded victims' enforcement rights in the US on the federal level, especially when compared to the situation for victims in England and Wales.

The Act also sets out victims' rights in relation to early-release proceedings. Under the CVRA, victims have been afforded the right to be heard in relation to parole decisions in case of federal offences (CRVA (US) s 3771(a)(4)). Similar provisions exist on the state level in most of the US. The effects of these statements, be it on parole outcomes or on individual victims, are largely under-researched and the small amount of research available has drawn diverging conclusions (for recent research see, e.g., Young 2016). Similar to the situation in England and Wales and Australia, and comparable to the use of Victim Impact Statements at the sentencing stage, it remains unclear what evidential value is meant to be attributed to these statements by parole decision-making bodies in the US.

3 Discussion

Appeal rights in the form of interlocutory appeals or appeals against verdict and sentence have been afforded sparingly to victims in many jurisdictions. In line with the understanding of the adversarial criminal justice systems that only parties to proceedings should be able to appeal, victims, as non-parties, have not received a specific right to appeal the verdict in any of the analysed common law jurisdictions. Relief regarding possible victims' rights denials at the pre-trial and trial stage is available in the US under the CVRA in the form of mandamus petitions. No similar enforcement mechanisms have been introduced in Australia and England and Wales. The situation concerning appeals of verdict and sentence differs for some victims in non-adversarial and mixed criminal justice systems which have taken up a specific legal status, including applicants to the adhesion procedure and PAP participants. While these victims have received the right to appeal, it is noteworthy that their right, in most of the analysed jurisdictions except for Sweden, is more limited than that of the public prosecutor. For example, the right to appeal for applicants to the adhesion procedure, where available, is frequently limited to the civil aspects of the criminal verdict. PAPs in Germany can only appeal the verdict but not the sentencing decision. In addition, the verdict is only subject to appeal in so far as it concerns an offence which gave rise to the victim's PAP participation.

Participation possibilities for victims in early-release decisions are even less frequent. None of the non-adversarial systems analysed had enacted legislation giving victims the right to directly participate in early-release proceedings. This is perhaps unsurprising given that the 2012 EU Directive on Minimum Standards on the Rights, Support and Protection of Victims of Crime (*EU Directive*) does not require Member States to implement such a right. The situation differs in adversarial jurisdictions, which allow (some) victims to submit statements to early-release authorities to varying degrees. It appears, however, that violations of this right are only subject to an enforcement mechanism in the US, namely the CVRA mandamus review scheme, but not in Australia and England and Wales.

4 Concluding Remarks

Chapter 4 assessed victim's participatory rights at the pre-trial stage and found that existing rights were fragmented and that no holistic concept to victim participation between jurisdictions, and sometimes within jurisdictions, could be detected. However, many victims in Europe have been afforded the right to request a review, be it internal, judicial or both, of the non-prosecution decision. As such, at least in the analysed European jurisdictions, victims may be able to participate in relation to this particular decision at the pre-trial stage through requesting a review. In relation to the trial stage, Chapter 5 found that victims have the fewest possibilities to participate during trial and sentencing in adversarial jurisdictions. Their involvement is mostly limited to making a submission to the court at the sentencing stage explaining how the crime has affected them. The evidential value of these submissions is unclear in most jurisdictions. Victims have more far-reaching opportunities to participate during the trial in Germany, although this is limited to certain victims deemed particularly worthy of participation, and in Sweden, where they are able to act as a second prosecutor. Victims with financial losses are able to participate in relation to their civil claim in proceedings in Germany, Sweden, Denmark and France. Lastly, victim witnesses are able to participate to a limited degree through their legal representative in relation to matters concerning testifying and protection in Germany, Sweden, Denmark and the US.

While victims' rights at the pre-trial and trial phase already appear limited in scope this chapter has shown that participatory rights after the conclusion of the trial are even less frequently available for the majority of victims. Nevertheless, victims' interests continue to be affected even after the trial proper concludes. The significant decrease of participatory rights for victims between the first two stages and the last stage of proceedings may perhaps be related to the fact that victims are generally required as witnesses during the pre-trial and trial phase and are therefore afforded some rights to entice their cooperation (see also discussion in van der Aa 2015, 240). However, their testimony and assistance are no longer needed at the enforcement stage potentially affecting the availability of participatory rights.

Chapters 4–6 have drawn a systematic picture of victims' participatory rights in different jurisdictions at the pre-trial, trial and post-trial stage. Based on these findings, Chapter 7, undertakes a case study of Germany, a mostly inquisitorial country and Australia, a largely adversarial system, to identify the general position of the victim in criminal trials within these two structures. The point of the exercise is to understand how the victim's role is comprehended in each country in order to subsequently ponder what consequences this understanding may have on future law reform in the context of victims' participation rights.

Notes

1. Referred to as Private Accessory Prosecutor in the English translation of the German Code of Criminal Procedure. Also translated as 'additional private prosecutor' or 'auxiliary private prosecutor' in comparative legal literature.
2. An English translation of the German StPO is available on the German Ministry of Justice website: https://www.gesetze-im-internet.de/englisch_stpo/.
3. The original German wording used was *rechtspolitisch bedauerlich*.
4. An unofficial 2006 English translation of the French Code of Criminal Procedure is available online: http://www.legislationline.org/documents/section/criminal-codes/country/30.
5. Translation of the French section into English available in Gogorza (2017, 51).
6. As per the Director of Public Prosecutions Guidelines (NSW) Guideline 31 'Retrial', the victims' views must be sought in relation to a retrial but not regarding an appeal.
7. See, for example, *Victims' Rights and Support Act* (NSW) 2013 s 6.16; *Victims Charter Act 2006* (Vic) s 17(3)(a); *Corrections Act 1986* (Vic) s 74A.
8. See, for example, *Crime (Sentence Administration) Act 2005* (ACT) s 215; *Corrective Services Act 2006* (Qld) s 320; *Corrections Act* 1997 (Tas) s 87A.
9. On the possibility for victims to appeal an interlocutory court decision concerning the admissibility of past sexual behaviour evidence, see *Doe v. United States* (1981).

Legislation and Related Sources

Administration of Justice Act (Denmark), Retsplejeloven
Code de Procédure Pénale (France), Code of Criminal Procedure
Code of Practice for Victims of Crime (UK) 2013
Conditional Sentence Act (Sweden)

Corrections Act 1997 (Tas)
Corrections Act 1986 (Vic)
Corrective Services Act 2006 (Qld)
Crime (Sentence Administration) Act 2005 (ACT)
Criminal Appeal Act 1912 (NSW)
Criminal Justice and Court Services Act 2000 (UK)
Crime Victims' Rights Act 2004 (US)
Director of Public Prosecution Guidelines (NSW) (version of 1 June 2007)
Rättegångsbalken (Sweden), Code of Judicial Procedure
Strafprozessordnung (Germany), Code of Criminal Procedure
Victims Charter Act 2006 (Vic)
Victims of Crime Act 2001 (SA)
Victims' Rights and Support Act (NSW) 2013.

References

Bacik, I., Maunsell, C., & Gogan, S. (1998). *The Legal Process and Victims of Rape*. Dublin: Dublin Rape Crisis Centre.

Bassett, R. (2016). *Parole in Sweden and Canada: A Cross-Cultural Review of Risk and Electronic Monitoring Parole Practices*. Thesis in Criminology, Malmoe University, Sweden. Retrieved from https://muep.mau.se/bitstream/handle/2043/21598/Parole%20in%20Sweden%20and%20Canada%2C%20Bassett%202016.pdf?sequence=2&isAllowed=y.

Black, M. (2003). *Victim Submission to Parole Boards: The Agenda for Research*. Australian Institute of Criminology. Trends & Issues in Crime and Criminal Justice 251. Canberra: Australian Institute of Criminology.

Boijsen, G., & Tallving, G. (2017). Probation in Europe-Sweden. In A. M. van Kalmthout & I. Durnescu (Eds.), *Probation in Europe*. Nijmegen: Wolf Legal Publishers. 2008; Updated Chapter (pp. 1–30). Utrecht: Confederation of European Probation.

Booth, R. (2018, January 10). Victims of John Worboys Not Consulted Over Terms of His Release. *The Guardian* (online). Retrieved from https://www.theguardian.com/uk-news/2018/jan/10/victims-of-john-worboys-not-consulted-over-terms-of-his-release.

Bowcott, O. (2018, March 29). High Court Overturns Decision to Release John Worboys. *The Guardian* (online). Retrieved from https://www.theguardian.com/uk-news/2018/mar/28/parole-board-must-reconsider-decision-to-release-john-worboys.

Brienen, M. E. I., & Hoegen, E. H. (2000). *Victims of Crime in 22 European Criminal Justice Systems: The Implementation of Recommendation (85) 11 of the Council of Europe on the Position of the Victim in the Framework of Criminal Law and Procedure*. Nijmegen: Wolf Legal Publishers.
Bundesregierung der Bundesrepublik Deutschland. (1986, April 10). Gesetzentwurf der Bundesregierung Entwurf eines Ersten Gesetzes zur Verbesserung der Stellung des Verletzten im Strafverfahren, Bundestag, BT Drucksache 10/5305.
Carlsson, J. (2010). *Right to Counsel for the Injured Party—A Comparative Study of Sexual Assault Victims' Rights in Sweden, Arizona & Massachusetts* (Master thesis). Lund University Libraries, Faculty of Law. Retrieved from http://lup.lub.lu.se/luur/download?func=downloadFile&recordOId=1628195&fileOId=16281.
Dervieux, V. (2002). The French System. In M. Delmas-Marty & J. Spencer (Eds.), *European Criminal Procedures* (pp. 218–292). Cambridge: Cambridge University Press.
European Justice. (2012, May 2). *Sweden—My Rights After the First Trial*. Retrieved from https://e-justice.europa.eu/content_rights_of_victims_of_crime_in_criminal_proceedings-171-SE-maximizeMS-en.do?clang=en&idSubpage=3&member=1.
European Justice. (2013, September 10). *Denmark—My Rights After the (First) Trial*. Retrieved from https://e-justice.europa.eu/content_rights_of_victims_of_crime_in_criminal_proceedings-171-dk-en.do?member=1.
European Justice. (2017, September 21). *England and Wales—My Rights After Trial*. Retrieved from https://e-justice.europa.eu/content_rights_of_victims_of_crime_in_criminal_proceedings-171-EW-maximizeMS-en.do?clang=en&idSubpage=7&member=1.
European Justice. (2018, July 4). *France—My Rights After Trial*. Retrieved from https://e-justice.europa.eu/content_rights_of_victims_of_crime_in_criminal_proceedings-171-FR-maximizeMS-en.do?clang=en&idSubpage=7&member=1.
Gogorza, A. (2017). Life Imprisonment and Terrorism: The Consolidation of a Repressive Subsystem. *Montesquieu Law Review, 5*, 46–61.
Hall, S., & Canton, R. (2015). England and Wales. In A. M. van Kalmthout & I. Durnescu (Eds.), *Probation in Europe*. Nijmegen: Wolf Legal Publishers. 2008; Updated Chapter (pp. 1–48). Utrecht: Confederation of European Probation.
Heine, L. (2008). Denmark. In A. M. van Kalmthout & I. Durnescu (Eds.), *Probation in Europe* (pp. 231–254). Nijmegen: Wolf Legal Publishers.

Holmberg, S., Kindgren, J., & Bogestam, N. (2012). *Non-custodial Care in Sweden: A Summary of Three Evaluations*. Stockholm: Swedish National Council for Crime Prevention.

Kirchengast, T. (2016). *Victimology and Victim Rights: International Comparative Perspectives*. Oxon, UK: Routledge.

Lindholm, M. & Bishop, N. (2008). Sweden. In A. M. van Kalmthout & I. Durnescu (Eds.), *Probation in Europe* (pp. 1025–1044). Nijmegen: Wolf Legal Publishers.

McCarva, R. (2008). England and Wales. In A. M. van Kalmthout & I. Durnescu (Eds.), *Probation in Europe* (pp. 255–288). Nijmegen: Wolf Legal Publishers.

Mutz, J. (2008). Germany. In A. M. van Kalmthout & I. Durnescu (Eds.), *Probation in Europe* (pp. 281–416). Nijmegen: Wolf Legal Publishers.

Oxford Pro Bono Publico. (2015). *Victim Participation in Criminal Procedures: A Report to Assist Redress*. University of Oxford, April 2015. Appendix: Country Report Denmark. Retrieved from http://ohrh.law.ox.ac.uk/opbp-makes-submissions-to-redress-on-victim-participation-in-criminal-procedures/.

Pelissier, B., & Perrier, Y. (2008) France. In A. M. van Kalmthout & I. Durnescu (Eds.), *Probation in Europe* (pp. 349–380). Nijmegen: Wolf Legal Publishers.

Reuflet, K. (2013). France. In N. Padfield, D. Van Zyl Smit, & F. Dünkel (Eds.), *Release from Prison: European Policy and Practice* (pp. 169–184). London: Routledge.

Ross, S. (2015). Victims in Australian Criminal Justice Systems: Principles, Policy and (Distr)action. In D. Wilson & S. Ross (Eds.), *Crime, Victims, and Policy International Contexts, Local Experiences* (pp. 214–239). Basingstoke: Palgrave Macmillan.

Schroth, K. (2012). *Die Rechte des Opfers im Straprozess* (2nd ed.). Munich: C.F. Mueller.

Storgaard, A., & Skov, L. (2017). Denmark. In A. M. van Kalmthout & I. Durnescu (Eds.), *Probation in Europe*. Nijmegen: Wolf Legal Publishers. 2008; Updated Chapter (pp. 1–33). Utrecht: Confederation of European Probation.

Swedish National Council for Crime Prevention. (2007). *Extended Use of Electronic Tagging in Sweden: The Offenders' and the Victims' View, Report 2007: 3*. Stockholm: Brå. Retrieved from https://www.bra.se/download/18.cba82f7130f475a2f1800024290/1371914733858/20.

Tobolowsky, P. M. (2015). Mandamus Muddle: The Mandamus Review Standard for the Federal Crime Victims' Rights Act. *University of Denver Criminal Law Review, 5*, 108–171.

Tolmein, O. (2012). Nebenklage-Eine Erweiterung, keine Demontage des liberalen Strafverfahrens. In S. Barton & R. Koebel (Eds.), *Ambivalenzen der Opferzuwendung des Strafrechts: Zwischenbilanz nach einem Vierteljahrhundert opferorientierter Strafrechtspolitik in Deutschland* (pp. 233–251). Baden-Baden: Nomos.

Ullrich, C. (1998). *Schutz des verletzten Zeugen durch Entfernung des Angeklagten gemäß § 247 StPO im Bereich der Sexualdelinquenz*. Hamburg: LIT Verlag.

van der Aa, S. (2015). Post-trial Victims' Rights in the EU: Do Law Enforcement Motives Still Reign Supreme? *European Law Journal, 21*(2), 239–256.

Wenske, M. (2008). Weiterer Ausbau der Verletztenrechte? Über zweifelhafte verfassungsgerichtliche Begehrlichkeiten. *Neue Zeitschrift fuer Strafrecht, 28*(8), 434–437.

Young, K. M. (2016). Parole Hearings and Victims' Rights: Implementation, Ambiguity, and Reform. *Connecticut Law Review, 49*(2), 431–498.

Zander, S. (2011). *Das Adhaesiosnverfahren im neuen Gewand*. Berlin: Duncker & Humblot.

Cases

Bundesverfassungsgericht, BverfG 9 October 2007 – 2 BvR 1671/07.

Doe v. United States, 666 F. 2d. 43 (4th Cir. 1981) (US).

Kenna v. United States District Court, 435 F.3d 1011 (9th Cir. 2006) (US).

Oberlandesgericht Frankfurt, OLG Frankfurt, 25 July 1995 – 1 Ws 120, StV 1995, 594.

United States v. Laraneta, 700 F.3d 983 (7th Cir. 2012).

7

Limits of Victim Participation in Adversarial and Non-adversarial Systems—A Case Study of Germany and Australia

1 Introduction

This chapter builds on Chapters 4–6 by providing a detailed case study on the general position of victims in criminal trials in Germany, an inquisitorial system, and Australia, a mostly adversarial system. In doing so, it also takes into account the traditional understanding of criminal justice focused on retribution, deterrence and prevention outlined in Chapter 3, which generally does not include individual victims. Groenhuijsen (2004, 64) uses the term 'contradictio in terminis', meaning words which are *per se* in conflict with one another, when describing the introduction of victims' rights in a retributive system, a system not originally designed to accommodate victims. This chapter questions whether the two jurisdictions, Germany and Australia, have moved away from the traditional aims of criminal law and procedure, thus creating a changed understanding of criminal justice and the role of the victim within. In light of the analysis, the chapter subsequently ponders whether future law reforms in the area of procedural rights for victims are likely to be successful. Possible consequences of these findings are examined further in Chapter 8.

K. Braun, *Victim Participation Rights*, Palgrave Studies in Victims and Victimology, https://doi.org/10.1007/978-3-030-04546-3_7

2 The Perception of Victim Participation in Germany

In comparative literature, Germany, a mostly inquisitorial system, is frequently used as an example of a European country which affords victims a great participatory role in criminal proceedings. Because of the status quo of victims' rights, especially at the trial stage, Germany may appear like a jurisdiction which has built up its criminal justice process to 'a participatory model of justice' (Kirchengast 2016, 34)[1] in which victims play an important procedural role. This may seem especially so in light of the numerous law reforms undertaken over a relatively short period of time regarding the participation of Private Accessory Prosecutors (*Nebenklaeger, PAP*).[2] The reforms eventually resulted in an increased number of victims eligible to participate at trial and a respective expansion of their participatory rights. At first glance, it could be suggested that perhaps the inquisitorial nature of proceedings makes German criminal justice more willing to afford victims active participation rights at trial. Against this backdrop, this chapter analyses whether modern criminal procedure in Germany aims to reintegrate victims into proceedings by providing them with a general right to participation. It thus ponders whether a departure from the traditional understanding of criminal justice as a state-based conflict in which the victim plays no role has occurred in the German context over the past decades.

2.1 Traditional Understanding of Criminal Justice in Germany

Chapter 3 analysed the role of victims in criminal theories including the classical schools of retributivism and utilitarianism. In the German context, it appears doubtful that retributivism in the traditional sense, namely as punishment exclusively for the sake of punishment itself, has any remaining supporters (Hoernle 2011, 28). Rather, German criminal justice appears heavily dominated by the collectivistic interests of society. The activity of the state in the criminal sphere is based on, and justified in accordance with, the interests of the general community

(Hoernle 2006, 951; Kilchling 2002, 58).[3] The underlying aims of German criminal procedure are described as punishing a breach of society's norms, on the one hand, and as granting the defendant a fair trial on the other (see Walther 1999, 129–130; Stoffers and Moeckel 2013, 830). It is said that German criminal law does not deal with interpersonal matters, but with acts and omissions which can endanger the current social and economic order (Weigend 2010, 42).[4]

State-based criminal procedure was originally introduced to replace the system of private prosecutions often associated with individual vengeance, which was seen as endangering the peace and order of society (see Weigend 2010, 43). As a consequence, a criminal justice system largely independent from victims' wishes evolved. In this system, the state is responsible for reacting to violations of society's norms (Weigend 2010, 43; Reemtsma 2005, 86–87; Meier 2009, 34). German criminal law and procedure therefore developed through the 'cutting' of the 'injuring thread' (Hassemer and Matussek 1996, 10) between victim and offender by the state. This led to the 'neutralisation' of the victim and to a 'de-emotionalisation' of criminal procedure (Hassemer 1990, 70; Hoernle 2006, 953). According to this traditional view of criminal justice, the individual violation of a victim's right is consumed by the respective violation of societal norms (see Kilchling 2002, 58). Thus, the limited participatory status for victims in general in Germany is 'no accident in the history of criminal procedure' (Weigend 2010, 43; see also Christie 1977) but the logical consequence of the de-privatisation of conflicts. Some conclude that under these circumstances there is no basis 'for regarding the victim as a "natural" party in the criminal process' (Horovitz and Weigend 2011, 298). The individual victim's interest to participate during the trial does not seem especially relevant in German criminal procedure (see Kilchling 1992, 70) because the criminal process is regarded 'a matter between the suspect and the state and therefore does not accord the victim an independent active role' (Horovitz and Weigend 2011, 297).

On this basis, some authors have commented that restoring victims, including allowing them to actively participate, should be the aim of civil proceedings which deal with individual conflicts between victims and offenders (torts), but not criminal trials (Frehsee 2000, 125;

see also Walther 1999, 131).[5] This view has been supported by the argument that criminal courts are not responsible for providing closure for victims but only for judging a matter brought to their attention by the prosecution. Assuming that a criminal court could be obligated to undertake a 'therapy session' (Volckart 2005, 183) for victims, is seen as problematic and foreign to German criminal proceedings. Noting the difficulties with accommodating victims' rights in the traditional criminal justice arena others have suggested the introduction of separate proceedings, so-called parallel justice proceedings (see Deutscher Anwaltsverein 2014, 9). Parallel justice in the German context has been described as a process outside of the criminal justice system focusing on the victim with the aim of providing compensation as well as offering support (von Galen 2012).

Dearing (2017, 6) describes the rationale of traditional German criminal justice in the following words:

> However, in the traditional perspective, the rationale of criminal justice is to effectively assert a state's substantive criminal law, which is depicted as protecting— not the rights of individuals, but— public interests or common goods or some similar collective asset. The relevant German term is '*Rechtsgut*', which denotes virtually any interest protected by a criminal law provision. If an interest is protected by criminal law, it is thereby acknowledged as a public interest. By threatening criminal sanctions, the law demonstrates its authority and upholds public trust in its rule and its ability to protect and defend public or common interests (or *Rechtsgüter*).

Thus Dearing (2017, 7) concludes that

> the victim is not a main figure, if a figure at all. The offence is not perceived as a violation of an individual's rights but as an infringement of a state's laws. Strictly speaking, the state, is the real victim and therefore entitled to the punishment of the offender. In German legal language the state's right to the punishment of the offender is called '*staatlicher Strafanspruch*' and denotes precisely what, in this system, criminal proceedings are mainly about. The offender has violated the laws of the state; hence the state is entitled to the punishment of the offender....

The above suggests that due to the de-privatisation of conflict victim participation cannot be considered an underlying value or aim of traditional criminal justice in Germany. To the contrary, criminal procedure appears to be shaped by the intentional 'neutralisation' of the victim. Nevertheless, victim-related law reform, also in relation to participatory rights, has occurred frequently in Germany, especially over the last decades. This gives rise to the question of whether the ongoing law reforms in the victims' rights arena can be seen as a victim-centred reorientation of criminal procedure and the birth of a victim-focused process model in Germany.[6] The below addresses these questions by considering possible motives behind the introduction of victims' rights legislation as well as by pondering the reactions of the legal profession, political bodies and academic scholars to the enacted reforms.

2.2 Victim Participation—A Reconceptualisation of Criminal Justice?

2.2.1 Legislature's Motives

When expanding the eligibility criteria for PAP participation to more victims in 2004, members of the German Parliament and the German Government explicitly clarified that the right to act as a PAP was never intended to serve as a 'general right to victim participation'. The right was expanded only to protect certain victims who had suffered the physical consequences of an aggressive crime and thus, in the government's view, were in need of specific protection in order to avoid further trauma and shock (Bundesregierung der Bundesrepublik Deutschland (*Bundesregierung*) 2003, 13; 2009, 30–31; see also Hermann 2010, 241). The argument was presented that a general right for victims to participate is foreign to German criminal procedure and would result in a redistribution of the roles of participants in German criminal trials, which was not desired (Bundesregierung 2003, 13). Yet, in 2009, only five years after explaining that a general participation right was foreign to German criminal procedure, legislation was passed allowing courts to grant victims of all offences the right to participate as a PAP if they considered the participation particularly necessary. However, according to the explanatory memorandum to the bill, parliament seemed to have reserved this right mainly for 'victims of personal offences' who had suffered physical or psychological damages to a significant extent. It was explained that the right was not introduced to allow general participation for all victims in Germany but to support victims who seemed particularly worthy of protection (Bundesregierung 2009, 31). These annotations speak against the assumption that victim participation in general has become an aim of German criminal procedure. Rather, the explanations offered for the introduction of the legislation indicate that victim participation rights in Germany are still deliberately afforded mostly to victims who want to claim financial losses and victims of sexual and other more violent offences. A general right for victims to be heard at trial continues to be perceived as 'inconsistent' with criminal procedure in Germany (see Anders 2012, 392). This is further supported by parliamentary explanations in the context of the Third Victims' Rights Reform Act of 2015. In the explanatory memorandum to the bill, the government, once again, explicitly pointed out that victims will not receive a general right to be heard during criminal proceedings under German law. As a justification for this decision, it remarked that victims already had the opportunity to be heard in all criminal proceedings, at least in writing (Bundesregierung 2015, 16). It should be noted that this *opportunity* to be heard, however, is neither a specific procedural right nor is it available exclusively to victims. Rather, every individual capable of writing and finding out the address of the public prosecutor, so it has been explained, can comment on criminal proceedings in writing by mailing a letter containing their views (Weigend 2017, 785). That does not mean, however, that criminal justice authorities are under any obligation to consider these views and even less to address them in the decision-making process. Consequently, the Third Victims' Rights Reform Act does not offer additional active procedural participation rights to victims. Rather, its focus is greater victim protection by introducing the right for vulnerable victims to have access to a psycho-social support person before, during and after the main trial (German Code of Criminal

Procedure (*Strafprozessordnung*, StPO (Germany)) s 406g; see also Ferber 2016, 281).[7] The support person has no legal training but a background in social work, pedagogy or psychology. Their primary task is to look after the well-being of the victim during proceedings in order to reduce potential secondary victimisation and to enhance the quality of victim witness testimony. The introduction of the psycho-social support person has been labelled by some as a 'milestone' of victim protection in Germany (Ferber 2016, 282).

Lastly, it needs to be taken into account that parliament has stopped short of granting victims proper appeal rights against the verdict in cases where their rights have been violated before and during proceedings. For example, as explained in Chapter 6, where criminal justice authorities fail to inform victims about their right to PAP participation and victims therefore miss their opportunity to partake they are unable to appeal the subsequent verdict with the aim of obtaining a retrial. This suggests that even the role of PAPs is not intended to be that of an equal participant in criminal proceedings in Germany.

2.2.2 Reactions Within the Legal Profession, Political Institutions and Scholarship

That victim participation has not become an aim of German criminal procedure is reinforced by the opposition to expanding victims' participatory rights to more or all victims within the legal profession, political institutions and academic scholarship. Although not by all,[8] the continuous enhancement of victims' participatory rights in Germany has been met with great criticism.

The Federal Bar Association, an organisation representing the interests of the German legal profession, has heavily criticised the expansion of the right to act as a PAP. According to the Association, the expansion of victim categories eligible to participate as PAPs is likely to 're-introduce' vengeance in criminal procedure. This, it argues, impedes rational, non-subjective conflict processing which is an aim of German criminal trials (Bundesrechtsanwaltskammer 2009, 6–7). Likewise, the German Judge Association, the largest professional association of judges and prosecutors in Germany, warned that further extension of victims' participatory rights could lead to an equality in victims' and defendants' rights, which could endanger the basic structure of German criminal procedure as a 'de-privatised' conflict. It concluded that the victim's need to be heard at trial is generally not worthy of protection, except in cases where private accessory prosecution is already possible and thus rejected a 'general right to be heard' at trial for victims of crime (Deutscher Richterbund 2010, 141–142). In 2009, the *Bundesrat* (German Federal Council, similar to a second chamber of parliament) also strongly criticised the ongoing expansion of the listed criminal offences enabling private accessory prosecution and asserted that the right to participation in Germany should not be afforded to all victims (Bundesrat 2009, 9–10).[9]

Some submit that the ongoing victims' rights reforms will make victims *de facto* parties to the proceedings, an outcome foreign to the German criminal justice system (Bundesregierung 1986, 14–15; Schroth 2009, 2919). Expanding victims' rights and thus *de facto* turning criminal proceedings into a 'party process', so it has been argued, holds the risk of impacting the objective function of criminal procedure and of introducing retribution and vengeance into the justice process (Schroth 2009, 2919). For this reason, a number of commentators have referred to the expansion of victims' participatory rights as a 'historic step back' because victims would once again be tasked with crime control (Bung 2009, 434; Schroth 2009, 2919; Schuenemann 2002, 32).[10] Opponents to enhancing victims' participatory rights during the trial stage have gone as far as asserting that expanding victims' rights to participate in Germany could cause the 'decline of the constitutional and democratic state' (Schroth 2009, 2918). Scholars have cautioned that enhancing victim participation in criminal procedure could have a significant impact on a criminal justice system which is not equipped for this kind of participation and could lead to a 'privatisation' of criminal conflicts (see Riess 2009, 477). Others conclude that ultimately victims' interests in criminal procedure must remain subordinate to the public interests of truth finding at trial (Hassemer and Matussek 1996, 23). While some see a need to afford victims a minimum set of rights including information rights, more extensive rights, including general participation rights, have been labelled 'incompatible with state criminal proceedings as a primarily formalised conflict between the state and the accused' (Duenkel 2001, 190). With regard to the above, Duenkel (2001, 190) comments that victims' 'active rights to codetermination as they exist in Germany only in connection with private or joint prosecution can therefore hardly be generalised'. Further criticism relates to the fact that the 'new' role PAPs received with the introduction of extensive procedural rights in the 1980s was simply tagged onto existing criminal procedure without consideration of the potentially far-reaching procedural consequences, especially for defendants (Barton and Flotho 2010, 28).

The resistance to the expansion of victims' participatory rights in Germany raises significant doubts as to whether a truly victim-focused process model has emerged. The noticeable opposition evident in both academic scholarship and legal-political discourse suggests that this is not currently the case. In this respect, Horovitz and Weigend (2011, 293) caution that 'the thesis that the inquisitorial German system is abundantly victim friendly is not really supported by the evidence' and that it is unlikely that the German inquisitorial system will recognise the victim as a full party (Horovitz and Weigend 2011, 294). Against this background, the question arises what motives have contributed to the expansion of victims' participatory rights in Germany.

2.3 Possible Explanations for the Expansion of Procedural Rights

When contemplating reasons for the frequent enhancement of victims' participatory rights in Germany, electoral politics or 'political opportunism' cannot be ignored (Schuenemann 2009, 492). It can be beneficial to a political party to promote the better treatment of victims (Weigend 1987; Kilchling 2010, 39), since the general public, as potential voters, considers protecting victims an important political goal (Barton 2012, 22).[11] Victims receive much sympathy from the general public while defendants usually do not (Kilchling 2010, 41). For this reason, no politician wants to get their 'fingers burned' on this topic (Pollaehne 2012, 11), turning victim protection into the 'favourite-child' of German politics surrounding criminal law and procedure (Anders 2012, 382). In light of this development, some suggest that the term 'victim' has taken on a 'magical' meaning in German political jargon (Pollaehne 2016, 671). Furthermore, the political activism in regard to victim participation is seen as an attempt to satisfy the ongoing lobbying for participatory rights by influential victim support organisations and pressure groups (Schuenemann 2009, 492; see also Kilchling 2010, 48). This explanation is in line with the fact that victims' rights law reforms in Germany are introduced with increasing frequency but without much or any empirical assessment of the effectiveness of already existing schemes. As a result, reforms continue to occur in this area without empirical insight into what is actually working for victims in practice and relatedly what aspects are in need of reform. The Deutsche Anwaltverein, the German Association of Lawyers, calls this approach to law reform 'regrettable' (Deutscher Anwaltsverein 2014, 7).

The above discussion indicates that victim participation has not become a genuine aim or underlying principle of 'modern' German criminal procedure which appears largely dominated by the traditional understanding of criminal justice as the 'de-privatisation' of conflict. Dearing notes that if 'a crime is essentially a violation of public interests vindicated by state authorities, it is indeed not clear why the victim should be involved in proceedings' (Dearing 2017, 9). Ultimately, in Germany there is a noticeable discrepancy between the traditional and continuing theoretical understanding of criminal justice and what criminal procedure is factually morphing into through the increasing number of law reforms concerning victim involvement (Schiemann 2012, 162). Based on this discrepancy, some scholars have emphasised the need to re-evaluate the traditional understanding of criminal justice in the German context (Meier 2009, 35).

2.4 Possible Implications

The debate on what role victims should have in German criminal procedure is ongoing with no consensus in reach (Doelling 2007, 85). It is true that expanding victims' participatory rights to more or all victims would change the character of the German criminal justice system to some extent as victims would obtain a more prominent and influential role in proceedings (see Altenhain 2001, 792 commenting on

PAP participation). Such an expansion of victims' rights in the German context requires discussion and consensus on whether there should be a general right for victims to be heard during proceedings (Anders 2012, 392), and relatedly, whether it is still justified to mainly base the participation of victims on the type of crime that has been committed against them. Debate on changes to victims' participatory rights could potentially trigger a 'landslide' of other fundamental and individual questions about crime and punishment in Germany for which no solution is currently at hand. Some have therefore cautioned that law reform in this area is an altogether risky undertaking (Walther 1999, 123). Even though in Germany criminal law reform has occurred over the past decades in general (Riess 2009, 467), and in particular in regard to victims' rights,[12] it does not appear that the question of the victims' role in proceedings will be sufficiently answered or even addressed in the near future. On this basis, some scholars have concluded that due to the current lack of societal consensus on the basic values of a new process model in Germany, it may be preferable that an overall reform of German criminal procedure is not attempted at the moment (see Riess 2009, 481). This appears in line with victim-related law reform efforts in other European jurisdictions where the motivation seems to be to improve the situation for victims as long as this does not drastically change the existing criminal justice structures (Shapland 2010, 368).

The traditional understanding of criminal justice in the Australian adversarial system and whether victim participation has become an aim or principle of modern Australian criminal procedure is subsequently discussed.

3 The Perception of Victim Participation in Australia

3.1 Traditional Understanding of Criminal Justice in Australia

Much as in Germany, crime is considered an offence against the norms of society and not against the individual victim in Australia (Victim Support Agency 2009, 4; for general discussion on the issue see also Erez and Bienkowska 1993, 48). Criminal justice was specifically designed to allow the state to take over proceedings from the victim (Douglas and Laster 1994; Karmen 2012, 26), so as to end blood feuds between kinship groups and to put a stop to private vengeance which characterised the time of early private prosecution (Sankoff and Wansbrough 2006, 6). For this reason, the determination of the existence of a criminal offence has been placed in the sphere of the state (van Caenegem 1999, 70; Findlay et al. 2009, 372). The state therefore plays a double role, that of the prosecutor and of the adjudicator (Shapland and Hall 2010, 163). The decision-making power the victim held before the development of the current criminal justice system has generally been taken over by the public prosecution service on behalf of society (Garkawe 2003, 35; Victim Support Agency 2009, 18). The aims of criminal procedure in Australia have been described as threefold: protecting defendants by having open trials with procedural safeguards,[13] punishing offenders and protecting the general community (Lanham et al. 2006, 1–15). Restoring victims has not been described as an aim of Australian criminal justice. Similar to Germany, crime is seen as a wrong against society and the demands of 'individual' victims in adversarial systems are traditionally not significant (Bednarova 2011, 10; Sankoff 2007, 461). This is further evidenced by the fact that no common law principles exist which safeguard the possibility for victims to be heard at trial (Victim Support Agency 2009, 4). Hence, the exclusion of the victim from criminal proceedings cannot be seen as a coincidental occurrence in the history of criminal procedure but an intentional decision in order to avoid emotionality and subjectivity in criminal trials (Sankoff and Wansbrough 2006, 2; Garkawe 1994, 600). In light of the above, the victim's role in adversarial criminal procedure currently lies primarily in being a witness for the prosecution (Kirchengast 2006, 172; Sankoff 2007, 461) with the consequence that victims are not parties to proceedings in common law jurisdictions (Rock 2014, 24). Doak (2005, 300) describes the role of victims in adversarial systems as follows:

> Although many victims may feel as though they are 'owed' a right to exercise a voice in decision-making processes, such as prosecution, reparation

and sentencing, the criminal justice system places such rights or interests in a firmly subservient position to the collective interests of society in prosecuting the crime and imposing a denunciatory punishment.

As in Germany, some commentators in adversarial systems see the task of restoring victims, which may also include restoring victims emotionally by allowing them to participate, as an aim of civil proceedings and not of criminal trials (see discussion in Doak 2005, 299).[14] It has been argued that civil law processes allow victims to make demands and provide them with veto powers. According to this argument, civil trials are better equipped for victim participation when compared to the criminal justice system. This is because burdens of proof can be more lenient in civil trials and defendants may not have the same protections they are afforded under criminal law. An example of this is that defendants in civil trials are often under the positive duty to incriminate themselves in the course of discovery and the interrogation process. This does not apply to criminal trials (see explanations in Douglas and Lester 1994, 3–4). Others explain that a changed perception of crime and criminal justice that emphasises the importance of victim participation cannot be found in traditional criminal justice systems but only outside of this setting in restorative justice movements. These movements consider crime as harm to the individual victim, the state and the community (Daigle 2012, 127)[15] and processes are designed to allow victim participation (Miller and Hefner 2015, 162).[16]

Therefore, conceptually, victims have a limited role in criminal procedure in adversarial systems (Doak 2005, 299).[17] Commentators have argued that victims' participatory rights *de facto* challenge the general conception of crime as a violation of the state's interest rather than that of the individual victim (Elizabeth 2008). For this reason, the (re-) introduction of victims as participants is seen as 'reinterpreting centuries of practice' in criminal procedure (see Goodey 2005 cited in Bednarova 2011, 12). This conceptualisation of common law criminal justice has the consequence that '[v]ictims are not to be trusted as full participants in the criminal justice system ... They may not have a voice in the decision to charge, in sentencing and parole. What claims they may have are not enforceable' (Rock 2014, 26).

In light of the above, victim participation appears generally inconsistent with Australian criminal procedure and its underlying principles.

3.2 Victim Participation—A Reconceptualisation of Criminal Justice?

Despite the apparent consensus that crime is an offence against the norms of society and not against the individual, victim participation, for example, in the form of Victim Impact Statement (VIS) schemes, has been introduced for eligible victims in all Australian jurisdictions. Why this cannot be seen as a paradigm shift in Australian criminal justice and a reorientation towards a more victim-focused trial system, however, is discussed below.

In a first attempt to introduce VIS schemes in New South Wales in 1987, Premier at the time Unsworth declared that the introduction of VIS schemes was a 'historic step for a common law jurisdiction like New South Wales where the criminal trial has been exclusively a relationship between the state and the offender' (New South Wales Legislative Assembly 1987, 915 cited in Baptie 2004, 76). However, the perception of these schemes in scholarship and by actors in the criminal justice system makes the assumption that victim participation can be considered one of the principles of Australian criminal procedure questionable. A small number of Australian cases have considered the aims of criminal justice and the role of crime victims in a procedural context. For example, in the Victorian case of *DPP v. Dupas* (2007, [16]), Cummins J. found that generally there needs to be more balance between victims' and defendants' rights. In the case, the defendant could not be sentenced beyond the term of imprisonment he was already serving. In this instance, the judge explained that the trial was conducted exclusively for the vindication of the individual victim and for the vindication for all victims of crime in general. Such views, however, remain the exception.

VISs have been described as ill-fitting in common law systems where victims generally have no standing. Since the introduction of VIS schemes, Australian courts have mostly applied caution when considering the content of VISs in order to remain objective and to sentence in a detached fashion (Baptie 2004, 88). Due to the values underlying criminal justice and sentencing, all Australian jurisdictions have struggled to some extent with the question of what influence VISs should have on the sentencing decision (Kirchengast 2010, 199). State authorities have also generally expressed concerns in regard to victim participation in sentencing contending that the exercise of victim power is incompatible with the state's power to punish (Kirchengast 2006, 187). The participatory inclusion of victims via the right to make a VIS remains an 'ambivalent and contested space' even some 30 years after their first introduction in Australia, particularly from the viewpoint of the legal profession (Booth and Carrington 2018, 304). Garland (2001, 4) notes that among other reforms the introduction of VISs has created an 'unfamiliar territory where the ideological lines are far from clear and where the old assumptions are an unreliable guide'.

Furthermore, the concept of victim involvement during proceedings at large has remained unchanged in Australia over the past century (Garkawe 2003, 35). There has been no reconceptualisation of the actual understanding of the victim's role: victims are still regarded largely as witnesses, despite the introduction of the right to make a VIS (Wolhuter et al. 2009, 181 referring to the UK situation). Dearing (2017, 20) notes that essentially 'by delivering such a statement, the victim provides evidence of certain aspects of the offence, which fits the victim's role as a witness'. On the possibility of changing or expanding the victim's role in criminal procedure to that of an active participant, the Victorian Law Reform Commission (2016, 133) comments that they do not recommend giving victims a role similar to that of the prosecution as this would 'fundamentally alter Victoria's criminal justice system'; a result considered undesirable. That victim participation has not become an aim of criminal procedure in Australia is further evidenced by the extremely limited role victims play during all stages of proceedings. For example, formal rights allowing victims to request a review of prosecutorial or police decisions at the pre-trial stage, including the non-investigation and non-prosecution decision, do not exist as such. The victim's involvement is also limited post trial, as victims have little or no direct input in appeals and only certain victims may submit a statement in the context of parole decisions in some Australian jurisdictions.

On the role of victims in Australian jurisdictions today, the Victorian Law Reform Commission (2016, 14) comments that regarding 'the criminal trial process, victims' needs and interests are better acknowledged and accommodated although, in practice, gaps and inconsistencies remain'. This conclusion is perhaps based on the introduction of victim-centred information and support obligations in Australian jurisdictions rather than on the introduction of substantive procedural rights affording victims active participation possibilities, as these remain extremely limited. Similarly, Rock (2014, 18) suggests in the adversarial context that 'with a few apparent exceptions, almost all victims' rights fall at the aspirational pole as they take the form of affirmations of principle and statements about standards of good practice, rather than of justiciable entitlements'.

Scholars remark on victims' rights in the common law context that 'the notion of rights has in practice met with substantial resistance from lawyers, practitioners and politicians' (Rock 2014, 20). This is also true in Australia, where there is noticeable opposition to expanding victims' participatory rights within the legal profession, the judiciary and legal-political institutions due to fears that this may upset the balance of the adversarial trial.[18] One major underlying reason for the opposition to victim participation may be the traditional understanding of crime as a state-based conflict and, relatedly the 'reluctance to cede real power to victims as participants in justice processes' (Ross 2015, 214).

The introduction of the right to make a VIS therefore neither suggests that victim participation has become an established value of Australian criminal procedure *per se*, nor that the traditional understanding of the role of the victim, namely that of a witness for the prosecution, has changed.

3.3 Possible Explanations for the Expansion of Procedural Rights

The question then arises why victims' participatory rights, for example, in the form of VISs, were introduced in Australia at all, when adversarial criminal procedure 'rests on the cogent philosophical foundation'

(Sankoff 2007, 467) that the views and wishes of the individual victim are overridden by the general good of society. Some commentators have suggested, in the US context, that the primary reason for the introduction of VIS schemes was largely politically motivated: politicians wanted to show that 'something was being done' for victims (Williams 2005, 103). This has also been suggested for the UK, where it has been proposed that such statements were introduced to show that victims were not forgotten in the criminal justice process. Alas, the actual Victim Personal Statement (VPS) scheme enacted in the UK has been criticised as 'unclear in its aims and justifications, with the victim left inexorably an ambiguous participant' (Newlove 2015, 8). The eagerness for the adoption of VIS schemes in other jurisdictions, such as Australia, might be explained by the same political enthusiasm (Williams 2005, 102–103). In practice, supporting victims has become a 'catchphrase' for most Australian political parties (Booth and Carrington 2007, 383). Australian politicians, similar to their German counterparts, have found it politically beneficial to introduce regulations that attempt to protect victims and punish offenders (Booth and Carrington 2007, 383). Victims' rights campaigns are considered 'risk-free political pandering for professional politicians' (Stevens 2000, [10]). It has been proposed in the Australian context that the introduction of VISs may in fact have been mere 'window dressing' to demonstrate that the situation for victims is being actively improved (Cook et al. 1999, 62; Grant et al. 2002, 291). Similar to Germany, the expansion of victims' participatory rights in adversarial systems, such as Australia, has also been linked to the lobbying efforts of influential victim support groups (Goodey 2000, 13, 23; Kirchengast 2013, 569).

3.4 Possible Implications

Overall, the introduction of VIS schemes cannot be seen as a changed perception of victims or their participatory role at trial. To the contrary, these schemes seem to have been introduced to uphold the 'time-honoured tradition of excluding victims from criminal justice with a thin veneer of being part of it' (Erez and Roeger 1999, 234–235). As such, law reforms relating to victims' participatory rights may perhaps be more 'attributed to the lucrative political appeal of the crime victim … rather than any desire to grapple with such problems in a principled and systemic manner' (Doak 2015, 140). Principled and systematic reform may also likely require the amendment of adversarial trial structures in order to allow further victim participation without violating defendants' rights. Due to the bipartisan nature of adversarial proceedings, victim participation without an infringement of defendants' rights is only possible during the trial stage to a limited extent. Based on their structure, inquisitorial systems are, in theory, capable of accommodating victims to a greater extent (see Sanders and Jones 2012). Reforms 'within' the adversarial system intended to allow victims to present views and concerns have therefore been described as solely playing around with existing structures instead of challenging the actual problem, namely the concept of the adversarial system as a bipartisan contest (Ericson and Baranek 1982, 225 cited in Doak 2004, 342).[19] On this basis, it may be that 'the adversarial paradigm remains, at its core, fundamentally ill-equipped to provide a platform for the meaningful participation of victims' (Doak 2004, 342). To allow for further victim participation in the Australian adversarial system, without endangering the rights of the defendant, some adversarial features might have to be replaced with inquisitorial ones (for the UK context see Doak 2004, 380–383). Yet, many supporters of the adversarial system believe that it is this bipartisan structure which is best equipped to provide procedural fairness for the defendant (Plater and Line 2012, 69; Corrado 2010, 289). So far, no attempt has been made, or even been investigated, to amend the actual structures of the Australian criminal justice system to enhance victim participation. On this basis, it seems unlikely that Australian criminal procedure will embrace more holistic participatory rights for victims in the near future.

4 Concluding Remarks

At heart, the desire to afford victims' greater participation rights and to reintegrate them into proceedings is incompatible with the traditional understanding of criminal justice as a conflict between state and offender from which the victim has been intentionally excluded. In other words, victim participation in proceedings does not fit well in those criminal justice systems, inquisitorial and adversarial alike, whose concepts are heavily influenced by traditional criminal theories. It would appear that where crime and criminal justice continue to be understood in the traditional sense, there is no room or rationale for systematic reform of the role of victims at the pre-trial, trial and post-trial stage. Horovitz and Weigend (2011, 298) comment in their research on victims' rights in the German and Israeli context that the critical issue for victim participation

> is whether the criminal process against the suspect/offender is (also) the victim's process. If that is the case, the victim may have a right not only to address the court and to present his views, but to also co-determine the outcome. If, on the other hand, the criminal process is primarily a matter between the state and the accused, the victim has not claim to allocution rights or to an even more active role. In such a case, the victim is, structurally, a mere by-stander ... However great the individual victim' s interest in the conviction and sentencing of "his" offender may be, it remains true that the criminal process, regardless of its adversarial or inquisitorial structure, is about the defendant' s responsibility toward the state. It is the state that imposes, through its courts, criminal sanctions, and it is the state that enforces them [footnote omitted].

This may shed some light on why, in most jurisdictions, the introduction of victims' participatory rights has occurred sparingly and in an unsystematic and piecemeal fashion. Dearing (2017, 3) notes that

> [v]ictims' rights have scarcely been incorporated into the theory of punishment and criminal justice and therefore—even where they gradually make their way into procedural law—they find themselves in a delicate and exposed position because of the complexities and inconsistencies within the theory and practice of criminal justice.

Indeed, a traditional understanding of criminal justice may be the reason why holistic reintegration of the victim into criminal procedure so far is 'unattained and perhaps unattainable' (Hall 2017, 151). It appears that in order for real progress to occur in relation to the implementation of victims' participatory rights in a procedural context the traditional understanding of criminal justice needs to be replaced with a new and more inclusive one (see also discussion in Groenhijusen 2004, 65–66). As such, what may be required to truly change the role of victims in criminal procedure is a fundamental shift, referred to by some as a paradigm shift, in national criminal justice (see, e.g. Fattah 2004, 16–17). As long as the criminal act is considered an offence against the state, the victim's role in criminal procedure is likely to remain that of an alien. Especially in the Australian context, it has been reiterated that change of the victim's role depends 'on overcoming vested criminal justice interests that, among other thing, continue to relegate the victims' status to no more than a witness for the state, as investigator and prosecutor' (O'Connell 2015, 262).[20] However, given the identified resistance by many to such change and, relatedly, the deep-rooted prevailing traditional understanding of criminal justice, scepticism remains as to whether this is likely to occur in the near future.

Pemberton and Aarten (2017, 316) suggest that perhaps the time has come to reflect on the possibility that 'victimisation is fundamentally at odds with features of criminal justice systems' and that the traditional criminal justice system may be unable to deliver the benefits envisioned for victims. What consequences this may have in practice is analysed in Chapter 8.

Notes

1. Kirchengast is referring to European criminal justice systems in general and not to Germany in particular.
2. Referred to as Private Accessory Prosecutor in the English translation of the German Code of Criminal Procedure. Also translated as 'additional private prosecutor' or 'auxiliary private prosecutor' in comparative legal literature.
3. Recent German academic scholarship has started to explore how victims' interests can fit with existing criminal theories. For further discussion see Anders (2012, 394–408).

4. In that regard, Walther (1999, 131) promotes a holistic view of crime which goes beyond seeing crime as an exclusive violation of society's norms.
5. Walther (2008, 406) argues that the constitutional guaranteed right to human dignity prohibits treating victims as witnesses without their own rights in German criminal procedure.
6. For further consideration of the question of a paradigm shift and victims' rights on a German but also international level, see Safferling (2011).
7. An English translation of the German StPO is available on the German Ministry of Justice website: https://www.gesetze-im-internet.de/englisch_stpo/.
8. In 2007, Riess (2007, 760) pointed out that German reforms to the victims' role were generally limited due to the tension with defendants' rights and the interest of truth finding at trial. He argued that victim related law reform in Germany up until that point in time, however, still fit within these parameters.
9. Groenhuijsen (2014, 42) explains that the opposition to victims' rights appears to have increased in judicial circles and in academic scholarship. He relates these developments to the introduction of victims' rights that are 'over the top'.
10. Barton (2012, 41) highlights that German criminal procedure is not turning into a party process as such because searching for the truth and investigating through the power of the court's office (*ex-officio*) remains the obligation of the court.
11. Among others, the changed public perception of crime victims in different jurisdictions has been attributed to extended (partially unobjective) media focus and coverage on victim-related matters. See Karmen (2007, 31) and Kilchling (2010, 41).
12. After the Victim Protection Act was enacted in 1986, it took 12 years until an act on witness protection was passed in 1998. Subsequently, it took only 8 years until the First Victims' Rights Reform Act was passed in 2004 which, five years later, was followed by the Second Victims' Rights Reform Act in 2009. Subsequently, it took only 2 years until in 2011 legislation to strengthen the rights of sexual assault victims was passed and lastly an additional 4 years until the Third Victims' Rights Reform Act was passed in 2015.
13. The due-process model based on considerations of what best protects defendants' rights has dominated the 'normative paradigm of common lawyers' (Kirchengast 2013, 573).

14. It is possible in Australian jurisdictions to receive a compensation order from the court in criminal trials for the harm suffered, which breaks the traditional criminal law/civil law divide. Yet, victim participation is traditionally still suggested in the context of civil trials or in restorative justice programmes (Karmen 2012, 26).
15. In regard to the failure of adversarial systems to recognise victims as parties, see Sanders and Jones (2012, 284).
16. For an overview of restorative justice in Australia, see O'Connell (2015, 256–257).
17. Commenting on adversarial systems in general.
18. See, for example, the submissions partially viewing expansion of victim participation rights critically in the context of the consultation of the Victorian Law Reform Commission: Submission 10a (Victoria Legal Aid), Submission 23 (DPP), Submission 25 (Law Institute of Victoria), Submission 27 (Supreme Court of Victoria), Submission 29 (Victorian Bar and Criminal Bar Association), Submission 43 (Liberty Victoria); All of these submissions can be retrieved from http://www.lawreform.vic.gov.au/projects/victims-crime-criminal-trial-process/submissions/victims-crime-criminal-trial-process.
19. In Doak's (2004, 342) opinion reforming the different elements of the adversarial system in order to accommodate victims to a greater extent cannot change the underlying 'ethos' of the system as a bipartite contest between the State and the defendant.
20. Discussing findings of the national Victims of Crime Workgroup.

Legislation and Related Source

Strafprozessordnung (Germany), Code of Criminal Procedure.

References

Altenhain, K. (2001). Angreifende und verteidigende Nebenklage. *Juristen Zeitung, 2001*(15), 791–801.

Anders, R. P. (2012). Straftheoretische Anmerkungen zur Verletztenorientierung im Strafverfahren. *Zeitschrift fuer die gesamte Strafrechtswissenschaft, 124*(2), 374–410.

Baptie, J. (2004). The Effect of the Provision of Victim Impact Statements on Sentencing in the Local Courts of New South Wales. *The Judicial Review, 7*(1), 73–88.

Barton, S. (2012). Opferanwaelte im Strafverfahren: Auf dem Weg zu einem neuen Prozessmodell? In H. Pollaehne & I. Rode (Eds.), *Opfer im Blickpunkt-Angeklagte im Abseits: Probleme und Chancen zunehmender Orientierung auf die Verletzten in Prozess, Therapie und Vollzug* (pp. 21–42). Hamburg: LIT Verlag.

Barton, S., & Flotho, C. (2010). *Ofperanwaelte im Strafverfahren*. Baden-Baden: Nomos.

Bednarova, J. (2011). The Heart of the Criminal Justice System: A Critical Analysis of the Position of the Victim. *Internet Journal of Criminology*, 1–46. Retrieved from www.internetjournalofcriminology.com/Bednarova_The_Heart_of_the_Criminal_Justice_System.pdf.

Booth, T. (2007). Penalty, Harm and the Community: What Role Now for Victim Impact Statements in Sentencing Homicide Offenders in NSW. *University of New South Wales Law Review, 30*(3), 664–685.

Booth, T., & Carrington, K. (2007). A Comparative Analysis of the Victim Policies Across the Anglo-Speaking World. In S. Walklate (Ed.), *Handbook of Victims and Victimology* (1st ed., pp. 380–416). Devon: Willan Publishing.

Booth, T., & Carrington, K. (2018). Victims Support in Policy and Legal Process in Australia-Still an Ambivalent and Contested Space. In S. Walklate (Ed.), *Handbook of Victims and Victimology* (2nd ed., pp. 293–307). London: Taylor and Francis.

Bundesrat der Bundesrepublik Deutschland. (2009, April 3). Gesetzesentwurf der Bundesregierung: Entwurf eines Gesetzes zur Staerkung der Rechte von Verletzten und Zeugen im Strafverfahren (2. Opferrechtsreformgesetz), BR-Drucks 178/09.

Bundesrechtsanwaltskammer. (2009). *Stellungnahme der Bundesrechtsanwaltskammer, zum Gesetzesentwurf der Bundesregierung zur Staerkung der Rechte von Verletzten und Zeugen im Strafverfahren (2. Opferrechtsreformgesetz-BT-Drucks 16-12098) BRAK-Stellungsnahme-Nr. 2009/9*. Retrieved from https://www.brak.de/zur-rechtspolitik/stellungnahmen-pdf/stellungnahmen-deutschland/2009/maerz/stellungnahme-der-brak-2009-09.pdf.

Bundesregierung der Bundesrepublik Deutschland. (1986, April 10). Entwurf eines Gesetzes zur Verbesserung der Stellung des Verletzten im Strafverfahren, BT-Drucks 10/5305.

Bundesregierung der Bundesrepublik Deutschland. (2003, November 11). Entwurf eines Gesetzes zur Verbesserung der Rechte von Verletzten im Strafverfahren (Opferrechtsrefromgesetz-OpferRG) text identitical with Entwurf eines Gesetzes zur Verbesserung der Rechte von Verletzten im Strafverfahren (Opferrechtsreformgesetz-OpferRG) der Fraktionen der SPD und B90/GR, BT-Drucks 15/1976.

Bundesregierung der Bundesrepublik Deutschland. (2009, March 3). Entwurf eines Gesetzes zur Staerkung der Rechte von Verletzten und Zeugen im Strafverfahren (2. Opferrechtsreformgesetz) identical with Gesetzesentwurf der Fraktionen der CDU/CSU und SPD Entwurf eines Gesetzes zur Staerkung der Rechte von Verletzten und Zeugen im Strafverfahren (2. Opferrechtsreformgesetz), BT-Drucks 16/12098.

Bundesregierung der Bundesrepublik Deutschland. (2015, April 15). Entwurf eines Gesetzes zur Stärkung der Opferrechte im Strafverfahren (3. Opferrechtsreformgesetz), BT-Drucks 18/4621.

Bung, J. (2009). Zweites Opferrechtsreformgesetz: Vom Opferschutz zur Opferermaechtigung. *Strafverteidiger, 2002*, 430–434.

Christie, N. (1977). Conflicts as Property. *British Journal of Criminology, Delinquency and Deviant Social Behaviour, 17*(1), 1–15.

Cook, B., David, F., & Grant, A. (1999). *Victims' Needs, Victims' Rights: Policies and Programs for Victims of Crime in Australia* (Research and Public Policy: Series No. 19). Canberra: Australian Institute of Criminology.

Corrado, M. L. (2010). The Future of Adversarial Systems: An Introduction to the Papers from the First Conference. *North Carolina Journal of International Law & Commercial Regulation, 35*(2), 285–296.

Daigle, L. (2012). *Victimology: The Essentials*. Thousand Oaks, CA: Sage.

Dearing, A. (2017). *Justice for Victims of Crime: Human Dignity as the Foundation of Criminal Justice in Europe*. Cham, Switzerland: Springer.

Deutscher Anwaltsverein. (2014). *Stellungnahme des Deutschen Anwaltvereins durch die Task Force "Anwalt für Opferrechte" unter Beteiligung des DAV-Ausschusses Strafrecht zum Referentenentwurf des Bundesministeriums der Justiz und für Verbraucherschutz Entwurf eines Gesetzes zur Stärkung der Opferrechte im Strafverfahren (3. Opferrechtsreformgesetz) Stellungnahme Nr.: 66/2014, Dezember 2014*. Retrieved from https://www.bmjv.de/SharedDocs/Gesetzgebungsverfahren/Stellungnahmen/2014/Downloads/12162014_Stellungnahme_DAV_RefE_Staerkung_Opferrechte_Strafverfahren.pdf?__blob=publicationFile&v=1.

Deutscher Richterbund. (2010). *Gutachten der Großen Strafrechtskommission, Staerkung der Rechte des Opfers auf Gehoer im Strafverfahren*. Germany: Deutscher Richterbund.

Doak, J. (2004). *Victims' Rights and the Adversarial Trial: The Impact of Shifting Parameters* (Doctoral dissertation). Queen's University Belfast.

Doak, J. (2005). Victims' Rights in Criminal Trials: Prospects for Participation. *Journal of Law and Society, 32*(2), 294–316.

Doak, J. (2015). Enriching Trial Justice for Crime Victims in Common Law Systems: Lessons from Transitional Environments. *International Review of Victimology, 21*(2), 139–160.

Doelling, D. (2007). Zur Stellung des Verletzten im Strafverfahren. In G. Britz, et al. (Eds.), *Festschrift fuer Heike Jung zum 65. Geburtstag am 23. April 2007* (pp. 77–86). Baden-Baden: Nomos.

Douglas, R., & Laster, K. (1994). *Victim Information and the Criminal Justice System: Adversarial or Technocratic*. Bundoora, VIC: Criminology Research Council.

Duenkel, F. (2001). The Victim in Criminal Law—On the Way from Offender-Related to Victim Related Criminal Justice. In E. A. Fattah, S. Parmentier, & T. Peters (Eds.), *Victim Policies and Criminal Justice on the Road to Restorative Justice: A Collection of Essays in Honour of Tony Peters* (pp. 167–211). Leuven: Leuven University Press.

Edwards, I. (2002). The Place of Victims' Preferences in the Sentencing of "Their" Offenders. *Criminal Law Review, 2002*, 689–702.

Elizabeth, S. (2008). The Newest Spectator Sport: Why Extending Victims' Rights to the Spectators' Gallery Erodes the Presumption of Innocence. *Duke Law Journal, 58*(2), 275–309.

Erez, E., & Bienkowska, E. (1993). Victim Participation in Proceedings and Satisfaction with Justice in the Continental Systems: The Case of Poland. *Journal of Criminal Justice, 21*(1), 47–60.

Erez, E., & Roeger, L. (1999). Victim Impact Statements and Sentencing: Outcomes and Process. *British Journal of Criminology, 39*(2), 216–239.

Ericson, R., & Baranek, P. (1982). *The Ordering of Justice: A Study of Accused Persons as Dependants in the Criminal Justice Process*. Toronto: University of Toronto Press. Cited in Doak, J. (2004). *Victims' Rights and the Adversarial Trial: The Impact of Shifting Parameters* (p. 342) (Doctoral dissertation). Queen's University Belfast.

Fattah, E. (2004). Gearing Justice Action to Victim Satisfaction Contrasting Two Justice Philosophies: Retribution and Redress. In H. Kaptein & M.

Malsch (Eds.), *Crime, Victims and Justice: Essays on Principles and Practice* (pp. 16–30). Aldershot: Ashgate.

Ferber, S. (2016). Stärkung der Opferrechte im Strafverfahren – Das 3. Opferrechtsreformgesetz. *Neue Juristische Wochenschrift, 2016*(69), 279–283.

Findlay, M., Odgers, S., & Yeo, S. (2009). *Australian Criminal Justice* (4th ed.). Melbourne, VIC: Oxford University Press.

Frehsee, D. (2000). Wiedergutmachung und Taeter-Opfer Ausgleich im deutschen Strafrecht- Entwicklung, Moeglichkeiten und Probleme. In B. Schuenemann & M. D. Dubber (Eds.), *Die Stellung des Opfers im Strafrechtssystem: Neue Entwicklungen in Deutschland und in den USA* (pp. 117–137). Koeln: Carl Heymanns.

Garkawe, S. (1994). The Role of the Victim During Criminal Court Proceedings. *The University of New South Wales Law Journal, 17*(2), 595–616.

Garkawe, S. (2003). The History of the Legal Rights of Victims of Crime in the Australian Criminal Justice System. In Victims of Crime Bureau, NSW Attorney-General's Department (Ed.), *Raising the Standards: Charting Government Agencies' Responsibilities to Implement Victims' Rights* (pp. 35–42). Sydney: Victims of Crime Bureau.

Garland, D. (2001). *The Culture of Control: Crime and Social Order in Contemporary Society*. Oxford: Oxford University Press.

Goodey, J. (2000). An Overview of Key Themes. In A. Crawford & J. Goodey (Eds.), *Integrating a Victim Perspective Within Criminal Justice: International Debates* (pp. 13–34). Aldershot: Ashgate.

Goodey, J. (2005). *Victims and Victimology: Research, Policy and Practice*. Harlow, UK: Person Longman. Quoted in Bednarova, J. (2011). The Heart of the Criminal Justice System: A Critical Analysis of the Position of the Victim. *Internet Journal of Criminology*, 1–46. Retrieved from www.internetjournalofcriminology.com/Bednarova_The_Heart_of_the_Criminal_Justice_System.pdf.

Grant, A., David, F., & Cook, B. (2002). Victims of Crime. In A. Graycar & P. Grabosky (Eds.), *The Cambridge Handbook of Australian Criminology* (pp. 281–293). Cambridge: Cambridge University Press.

Groenhuijsen, M. S. (2004). Victims' Rights and Restorative Justice: Piecemeal Reform of the Criminal Justice System or a Change of Paradigm? In H. Kaptein & M. Malsch (Eds.), *Crime, Victims and Justice: Essays on Principles and Practice* (pp. 63–79). Aldershot, Hampshire: Ashgate.

Groenhuijsen, M. (2014). The Development of International Policy in Relation to Victims of Crime. *International Review of Victimology, 20*(1), 31–48.

Hall, M. (2017). *Victims of Crime, Construction, Governance and Policy*. Cham, Switzerland: Palgrave Macmillan.

Hassemer, W. (1990). *Einfuehrung in die Grundlagen des Strafrechts*. Munich: C.H. Beck.

Hassemer, W., & Matussek, K. (1996). *Das Opfer als Verfolger*. Franfurt am Main: Peter Lang.

Herrmann, J. (2010). Die Entwicklung des Opferschutzes im deutschen Strafrecht und Strafprozessrecht-Eine unendliche Geschichte. *Zeitschrift fuer Internationale Strafrechtsdogmatik, 3*, 236–245.

Hoernle, T. (2006). Die Rolle des Opfers in der Straftheorie und im materiellen Strafrecht. *Justisten Zeitung, 19*, 950–958.

Hoernle, T. (2011). Gegenwärtige Strafbegründungstheorien. Die herkömmliche deutsche Diskussion. In A. von Hirsch, U. Neumann, & K. Seelmann (Eds.), *Strafe – Warum? Gegenwärtige Strafbegründungen im Lichte von Hegels Straftheorie* (pp. 11–30). Baden-Baden: Nomos.

Horovitz, A., & Weigend, T. (2011). Human Dignity and Victims' Rights in the German and Israeli Criminal Process. *Israeli Law Review, 44*, 263–300.

Karmen, A. (2007). *Crime Victims: An Introduction to Victimology* (6th ed.). Belmont, CA and Wadsworth: Cengage Learning.

Karmen, A. (2012). *Crime Victims: An Introduction to Victimology* (8th ed.). Belmont, CA and Wadsworth: Cengage Learning.

Kilchling, M. (1992). *Die Stellung des Verletzten im Strafverfahren: Implementation und Evaluation des Opferschutzgesetzes*. Freiburg im Breisgau: Max-Planck Institut fuer Auslaendisches und Internationales Strafrecht.

Kilchling, M. (2002). Opferschutz und der Strafanspruch des Staates- ein Wiederspruch. *Neue Zeitschrift fuer Strafrecht, 22*, 57–66.

Kilchling, M. (2010). Veraenderte Perspektiven auf die Rolle des Opfers im gesellschaftlichen, sozialwissenschaftlichen und rechtspolitischen Diskurs. In J. Hartmann (Ed.), *Perspektiven professioneller Opferhilfe* (pp. 39–50). Wiesbaden: VS Verlag.

Kirchengast, T. (2006). *The Victim in Criminal Law and Justice*. New York: Palgrave Macmillan.

Kirchengast, T. (2010). Proportionality in Sentencing and the Restorative Justice Paradigm: 'Just Deserts' for Victims and Defendants Alike? *Criminal Law and Philosophy, 4*, 197–213.

Kirchengast, T. (2013). Victim Lawyer's, Victim Advocates, and the Adversarial Criminal Trial. *New Criminal Law Review, 16*, 568–594.

Kirchengast, T. (2016). *Victims and the Criminal Trial*. London, UK: Palgrave Macmillan.

Lanham, D., Bartal, B., Evans, R., & Wood, D. (2006). *Criminal Laws in Australia*. Annandale, NSW: The Federation Press.

Meier, B.-D. (2009). *Strafrechtliche Sanktionen* (3rd ed.). Berlin: Springer.

Miller, S. L., & Hefner, M. K. (2015). Procedural Justice for Victims and Offenders? Exploring Restorative Justice Processes in Australia and the US. *Justice Quarterly, 32*(1), 142–167.

Newlove, B. H. (2015). *The Silenced Victim: A Review of the Victim Personal Statement*. London: Office of the Commissioner for Victims and Witnesses.

New South Wales Legislative Assembly. (1987). *Second Reading Speech, Crimes (Sentencing Speech, Crimes (Sentencing) Amendment Bill*. New South Wales Parliamentary Debates, November 12, 1987, 915 (Barrie John Unsworth, MP) cited in Baptie, J. (2004). The Effect of the Provision of Victim Impact Statements on Sentencing in the Local Courts of New South Wales. *The Judicial Review, 7*(1), 73–88.

O'Connell, M. (2015). The Evolution of Victims' Rights and Services in Australia. In D. Wilson & S. Ross (Eds.), *Crime, Victims, and Policy International Contexts, Local Experiences* (pp. 240–278). Basingstoke: Palgrave Macmillan.

Pemberton, A., & Aarten, P. G. M. (2017). A Radical in Disguise: Judith Shklar's Victimology and Restorative Justice. In I. Aertsen & B. Pali (Eds.), *Critical Restorative Justice* (pp. 315–330). Oxford: Hart Publishing.

Plater, D., & Line, L. (2012). Has the 'Silver Thread' of the Criminal Law Lost Its Lustre? The Modern Prosecutor as a Minister of Justice. *The University of Tasmania Law Review, 31*(2), 55–95.

Pollaehne, H. (2012). Opfer im Blickpunkt- Taeter im Toten Winkel. In H. Pollaehne & I. Rode (Eds.), *Opfer im Blickpunkt-Angeklagte im Abseits. Probleme und Chancen zunehmender Orientierung auf die Verletzten in Prozess, Therapie und Vollzug* (pp. 5–20). Hamburg: LIT Verlag.

Pollaehne, H. (2016). Zu viel geopfert!? Eine Kritik der Viktimisierung von Kriminalpolitik und Strafjustiz. *Strafverteidiger, 10*, 671–678.

Reemtsma, J. P. (2005). Was sind eigentlich Opferinteressen. *Rechtsmedizin, 15*, 86–91.

Riess, P. (2007). Zur Beteiligung des Verletzten im Strafverfahren. In G. Britz, et al. (Eds.), *Festschrift fuer Heike Jung zum 65. Geburtstag am 23. April 2007* (pp. 751–760). Baden-Baden: Nomos.

Riess, P. (2009). Entwicklungstendenzen in der deutschen Strafprozessgestaltung seit 1950. *Zeitschrift fuer Internationale Strafrechtsdogmatik, 10*, 466–483.

Rock, P. (2014). Victims' Rights. In I. Vanfraechem, A. Pemberton, & F. M. Ndahinda (Eds.), *Justice for Victims, Perspectives on Rights, Transition and Reconciliation* (pp. 11–31). London: Routledge.

Ross, S. (2015). Victims in Australian Criminal Justice Systems: Principles, Policy an (Distr)action. In D. Wilson & S. Ross (Eds.), *Crime, Victims, and Policy International Contexts, Local Experiences* (pp. 214–239). Basingstoke: Palgrave Macmillan.

Safferling, C. (2011). The Role of the Victim in the Criminal Process—A Paradigm Shift in National German and International Law. *International Criminal Law Review, 11*(2), 183–215.

Sanders, A., & Jones, I. (2012). The Victim in Court. In S. Walklate (Ed.), *Handbook of Victims and Victimology* (pp. 282–308). London: Taylor and Francis.

Sankoff, P. (2007). Is Three Really a Crowd? Evaluating the Use of Victim Impact Statements Under New Zealand's Revamped Sentencing Regime. *New Zealand Law Review, 3,* 459–498.

Sankoff, P., & Wansbrough, L. (2006). *Is Three Really a Crowd? Thoughts About Victim Impact Statements and New Zealand's Revamped Sentencing Regime.* Paper Presented at the 20th International Conference of the International Society for the Reform of Criminal Law Brisbane, July 2–July 6, 2006.

Schiemann, A. (2012). Macht des Opfers – Ohnmacht des Beschuldigten: – Vom Ungleichgewicht der Rechte und Pflichten im deutschen Strafverfahren. *Kritische Vierteljahresschrift für Gesetzgebung und Rechtswissenschaft, 95*(2), 161–173.

Schroth, K. (2009). 2. Opferrechtsreformgestz- Das Strafverfahren auf dem Weg zum Parteienprozess? *Neue Juristische Wochenschrift, 62*, 2916–2919.

Schuenemann, B. (2002). Wohin treibt der Deutsche Strafprozess? *Zeitschrift fuer die Gesamte Strafrechtswissenschaft, 114*(1), 1–62.

Schuenemann, B. (2009). Risse im Fundament, Flammen im Gebaelk: Die Strafprozessordnung nach 130 Jahren. *Zeitschrift fuer Internationale Strafrechtsdogmatik, 10,* 484–494.

Shapland, J. (2010). Victims and Criminal Justice in Europe. In S. G. Shoham, P. Knepper, & M. Kett (Eds.), *International Handbook of Criminology* (pp. 347–372). Boca Raton, FL: CRC Press.

Shapland, J., & Hall, M. (2010). Victims at Court: Necessary Accessories or Principal Players at Centre Stage. In A. Bottoms & J. Roberts (Eds.), *Hearing the Victim, Adversarial Justice, Crime Victims and the State* (pp. 163–199). Cullompton: Willian Publishing.

Stevens, M. (2000). Victim Impact Statements Considered in Sentencing. *Berkeley Journal of Criminal Law, 2*(1), 1–13.

Stoffers, K. F., & Moeckel, J. (2013). Beteiligtenrechte im Strafprozessualen Adhaesionsverfahren. *Neue Juristische Wochenschrift, 12,* 830–832.
van Caenegem, W. (1999). Advantages and Disadvantages of the Adversarial System in Criminal Proceedings. Law Faculty Publications, Paper 224. Bond University E-publications, pp. 69–102.
Victim Support Agency. (2009). A Victim's Voice: Victim Impact Statements in Victoria—Findings of an Evaluation into the Effectiveness of Victim Impact Statements in Victoria. Melbourne, Department of Justice.
Victorian Law Reform Commission. (2016). *The Role of Victims of Crime in the Criminal Trial Process—Final Report.* Melbourne: Victorian Law Reform Commission.
von Galen, M. G. (2012). *'Parallel Justice' für Opfer von Straftaten, Ein Verfahren mit, Opfervermutung' außerhalb des Strafrechts, Beitrag zum 36. Strafverteidigertag,* Hannover 2012 (pp. 69–89). Retrieved from http://www.strafverteidigervereinigungen.org/Material/Themen/Opferrechte/36_Galen_opfer.pdf.
Volckart, B. (2005). Opfer in der Strafrechtspflege. *Juristische Rundschau, 5,* 181–187.
Walther, S. (1999). Was soll "Strafe". *Zeitschrift fuer die Gesamte Strafrechtswissenschaft, 111,* 123–143.
Walther, S. (2008). Interessen und Rechtsstellung des Verletzten im Strafverfahren. *Juristische Rundschau, 2008,* 405–410.
Weigend, T. (1987). Das Opferschutzgesetz-kleine Schritte zu welchem Ziel? *Neue Juristische Wochenschrift, 40,* 1170–1177.
Weigend, T. (2010). „Die Strafe fuer das Opfer"? Zur Rennaisance des Genugtuungsgedankens im Straf- und Strafverfahrensrecht. *Zeitschrift fuer Rechtswissenschaftliche Forschung, 1,* 39–57.
Weigend, T. (2017). Alle sind sich einig-und das Opfer? In C. Safferling, G. Kett-Straub, C. Jaeger, H. Kudlich, & F. Streng (Eds.), *Festschrift fuer Franz Streng zum 70. Geburtstag* (pp. 781–798). Heidelberg: D.F. Mueller.
Williams, B. (2005). *Victims of Crime and Community Justice.* London: Jessica Kingsley Publishers.
Wolhuter, L., Olley, N., & Denham, D. (2009). *Victimology and Victims' Rights.* London: Routledge.

Case

DPP v. Dupas [2007] VSC 305 (Victoria).

8

Victim Participation: An Enhanced Focus on Legal Representation for Victims

1 Introduction

The emergence of victims' rights has led some scholars to remark that the 'twenty-first century criminal trial is increasingly modified to benefit the needs of crime victims' (Kirchengast 2016, 1). This may well be the case for some victims in some instances. For example, it appears that the obligations placed on criminal justice authorities to provide information to victims about the trial process or the individual case at hand and to offer support in this context have increased over the past 30 or so years. In addition, as Chapter 4 has shown, victims in some jurisdictions have received participation rights in relation to specific decisions, for example, the decision not to prosecute. Moreover, the analysis in Chapters 4–6 highlights that in some jurisdictions certain victims, frequently victims of sexual violence or other serious offences, have been afforded ample participation rights during specific stages of the proceedings. While all analysed adversarial and non-adversarial systems allow victims some form of participation at some stage of the proceedings, the

K. Braun, *Victim Participation Rights*, Palgrave Studies in Victims and Victimology, https://doi.org/10.1007/978-3-030-04546-3_8

overall picture emerged in this volume that victims, on the whole, have not been afforded holistic and systematically implemented participation rights at the pre-trial, trial and post-trial stage.

The noticeable limitations to victim participation may be due to concerns for the rights of the accused and a fair trial as well as be based on the underlying traditional understanding that victim participation is foreign to state-run, de-privatised criminal conflicts. As shown in Chapter 2, victims were once the main actors in criminal justice. Yet, their role decreased significantly in adversarial and non-adversarial system alike with the introduction of a public police and prosecution service and the related deprivatisation of the criminal conflict. Indeed, over a relatively short period of time, the role of victims became so marginalised that the increased scholarly and political attention victims received in the 1970s and 1980s was termed the 'rediscovery' of the victim in criminal procedure.

That victims were not considered key players in the criminal justice system during most of the nineteenth and twentieth century is also evidenced by their absence from traditional criminal theories analysed in Chapter 3. Victims and their needs do not feature in non-consequentialist criminal justice theories and are only marginally relevant for consequentialist theories and only in so far as victims form part of the wider community. While some more recent theoretical approaches have specifically focused on victims and their needs, for example, restorative justice approaches, these remain fairly new ways of conceptualising victims and their role and mostly concern victims' involvement outside of the traditional criminal justice arena.

Even in Germany, which is frequently used as an example of a country which offers victims broad participation rights due to the possibility to become a Private Accessory Prosecutor (*Nebenklaeger, PAP*),[1] a strong resistance to furthering victims' participatory rights can be detected. Chapter 7 highlighted that politicians, the judiciary and scholars alike have pointed out that a general right to victim participation is foreign to German criminal procedure and cannot be brought into conformity with the aims of German criminal justice. Nevertheless, the right to PAP participation has continuously been expanded to more victim categories, especially over the past 15 years. Yet, explanations offered by members of parliament and government when introducing said law reforms seem to suggest that the expansion was never intended to provide a general right to victim participation but only to protect those victims deemed particularly worthy of protection in the state's view. Allowing victims to participate to a greater extent, so it is feared by many in Germany, will allow vengeance and retribution back into proceedings; a result considered undesirable. While some participatory rights have been introduced or expanded this may be more related to political opportunism than the desire to holistically reposition the victim in the criminal justice system. In other words, it does not appear that the introduction of further participatory rights for victims has gone hand in hand with a radical departure from the values, principles and objectives which traditionally underlie criminal justice. Crime continues to be classically perceived as an offence against the state—a perception which appears to exclude victims from becoming key players in criminal conflicts.

A traditional understanding of criminal justice and its related consequences for victims in a procedural setting is not an exclusively German phenomenon. In the context of European jurisdictions, Dearing (2017, 10) notes that

> in the settings of criminal courts in Europe, individual victims have for a long time been—and in some countries still are—denied a significant role in criminal proceedings and often only appear in court when called upon as witnesses to fulfil their duties in supporting law enforcement, i.e. the conviction and, in appropriate cases, also punishment of offenders to which the state—on behalf of 'society'—is entitled.
>
> The traditional paradigm reduces the victim to the function of delivering evidence in favour of a state's efforts to investigate and prosecute an offender and negates that the victim has suffered wrong, a violation, that is, of her rights. In traditional criminal justice systems, the position of the victim was and very often still is that of a witness obliged to support public interests by delivering their statement to the police and evidence in court. Reducing the role of the victim to the obligation to support the administration of criminal justice as a witness is the clearest expression of the traditional, state-centred understanding of criminal justice and shows disrespect of the victim as a rights-holder.

2 An Enhanced Focus on Legal Representation

In light of the generally limited and disjointed participatory rights for victims and the continuous and noticeable resistance to their expansion, even in jurisdictions which have introduced ample rights for some victims, it is doubtful that an underlying consensus for affording victims holistic and structured participation possibilities exists at this point in time. Such a general restructure would, so it has been suggested by some, require a paradigm shift concerning the victims' role in criminal procedure (see discussion in Groenhuijsen 2004, 65–67). Some propose that effective change for victims can also be accomplished by continuous piecemeal reforms of the 'current paradigm' rather than angling for a radical departure from the traditionally held views on crime and punishment (Groenhuijsen 2004, 75–76). Scholars have cautioned that pursuing victims' rights reforms which are not broadly supported in society can lead to opposition and resistance, possibly negatively impacting other law reform efforts concerning less contested victims' rights (Groenhuijsen 2014, 42). Aiming to introduce or expand what some consider excessive victims' rights may therefore become counterproductive (Groenhuijsen 1999, 26). Thus, the question arises whether—at this stage—there may be greater benefit in focusing on better protecting victim witnesses during proceedings and strengthening the enforcement of existing rights to improve their position rather than continuing to pursue greater participation rights *per se*. It is true that this approach may not touch on or change the basic position of victims in traditional criminal justice. Yet, this may also be the advantage of this less interventional focus especially in light of the identified reluctance to fundamentally change the victims' role in criminal procedure in many criminal justice systems.

This chapter explores this proposition by considering the merits of legal representation schemes for victims at different stages of proceedings. In this context, it is important to note that the victim in criminal proceedings mainly acts alone and may frequently not be aware of the rights already available to them, including, for example, the right to be informed about certain aspects of the proceedings or to receive specific support. As a consequence, although victims' rights may exist on paper in a particular jurisdiction, many victims may not or only sparingly exercise them in practice. Germany is an example of a jurisdiction with numerous victims' rights, including service and information rights, which are not easily accessible to victims in practice. There, the fifth section of the StPO, called the fifth book, ((*Strafprozessordnung, StPO*) (Germany) ss 374–406h)[2] is entitled 'Participation of the Injured Person in Proceedings'. Although this may suggest that all victims' procedural rights are exclusively contained in this section providing transparency on the issue, this is not actually the case. Despite the section title, victims' rights can be found all through the German StPO. As a consequence, victims' rights are neither confined to a single section nor are they placed close together in the Code. This makes it extremely difficult for a lay person to identify what their rights are and how to exercise them. While criminal justice authorities have been placed under the duty to inform victims of their rights to enhance transparency and accessibility this does not always occur in practice. For example, a 2017 German study on the impact of pre-trial proceedings on victims found that victims were confused about the particulars of procedure and highlighted a lack of information available to them. While broad information obligations on the part of criminal justice authorities have been included in German criminal procedure law, victims did not feel that they received the necessary information in practice. The study confirmed that the victims' perceptions of being under-informed by authorities were at least partially accurate. The review of relevant court files in the respective cases showed that some criminal justice authorities had indeed failed to adequately discharge their information obligations towards the individual victims in the particular cases at hand (Weisser Ring 2017, 183).

These problems could be overcome, or at least reduced, where a legal representative provides victims with the necessary information and exercises respective rights on their behalf. Overall, this could contribute to a strengthened position of victims in practice without necessarily affording them greater procedural participation rights as such. Analysis of legal representation schemes for victims and victim witnesses including their current availability in the selected criminal justice systems and the merits of their introduction is provided below.

2.1 Status Quo of Legal Representation Schemes for Victims in Selected Jurisdictions

Whether legal representation for victims is available in a particular state as well as what role a victim's legal representative holds is at the discretion of the respective jurisdiction. The particulars of the legal representation are often heavily dependent on what role the individual victim has been afforded in the distinct criminal justice system. For example, where the role of a victim is mainly or exclusively that of a witness without additional legal status, victims' legal representatives are frequently exclusively tasked with ensuring that existing victims' rights, such as, the right to be informed and treated respectfully, are complied with. Victims' legal representatives are not necessarily afforded additional rights and their role may therefore be perceived as generally less controversial. The availability and particulars of victim legal representation schemes in the jurisdictions selected for analysis in this volume vary to a significant extent. The below therefore first outlines the modalities of legal representation for victims, or the lack thereof, in the analysed adversarial and non-adversarial-jurisdictions. It then considers the merits of introducing legal representation schemes in jurisdictions in which these arrangements are currently unavailable before pondering identified practical problems with existing schemes in Germany, Sweden and the US. The point of the exercise is to assess whether potential problems can likely be overcome to enhance the overall experience of represented victims in criminal procedure.

Some of the analysed adversarial jurisdictions, namely England and Wales and some Australian states, do not allow for any form of legal representation for victims during proceedings. Others, even though their criminal trial is (at least partially) based on the adversarial model, such as the US, Sweden and Denmark, have afforded victims legal representation during proceedings to various degrees. Legal representation for (some) victims is also available in the mostly inquisitorial criminal justice systems of Germany and France. The below provides detailed analysis on the particulars of the relevant legal representation arrangements in each jurisdiction contained in this volume.

2.1.1 Germany

As demonstrated in Chapters 4–6, victims in the German criminal justice system can have several roles and rights ranging from active PAP participation to merely being a witness in proceedings. In line with this differentiation, the rights a legal representative can exercise vary depending on whether they represent a PAP or a victim witness. That means that the role of a legal representative is closely entwined with the procedural status of their individual client.

Legal Representation of PAPs

Victims who are eligible to participate as PAPs, whether they elect to participate in proceedings or not, have the right to be legally represented even before the main trial commences (StPO (Germany) s 397a). In many cases, especially where sexual offences, homicide offences or severe assaults have occurred, the representative, once requested, is state funded (StPO (Germany) s 397a(1)). That means the lawyer is paid for by the state no matter what the financial situation of the individual victim is. In other cases, victims eligible for PAP participation can apply for legal aid to cover the costs of their lawyer if they meet the standard eligibility criteria (StPO (Germany) s 397a(2)), including insufficient personal financial means. In this case, the victim has to provide the court with information about their personal and financial situation. Furthermore, to receive legal aid the victim must demonstrate that they are unable to protect their own interests during proceedings. This is assumed to be the case, for example, where the matter is legally or factually challenging. The funding available to PAPs emphasises their privileged role in comparison with victims without this special procedural status whose funding opportunities are more limited.

The legal representative of a PAP can exercise all rights available to the victim on their behalf. Legal representatives for PAPs also have the right to review court and prosecutorial files without having to establish a justified interest in reviewing these documents (StPO (Germany), s 406e (1) sent. 1). In comparison, lawyers acting on behalf of victims without PAP status who wish to inspect court files have to demonstrate to the court that they have a vested interest in reviewing the requested file. During the main trial, the legal representative of a PAP has the right to be present and to exercise all procedural rights available to the victim. Research by Barton and Flotho (2010, 248) on legal representation for PAPs showed that in practice, in 94% of all cases analysed in the study, PAPs were legally represented by a state-funded lawyer. The study also examined what trial strategies legal representatives for PAPs mainly used during the trial proper. It found that the work of victims' lawyers at trial almost exclusively focused on asking questions and giving statements during proceedings, including a closing statement, while other procedural rights, including formal applications and objections, were exercised rather sparingly (Barton and Flotho 2010, 236–237).

Legal Representation of Victim Witnesses

Victim witnesses, who are not eligible to participate as a PAP, nevertheless have the right to legal representation (*Zeugenbeistand/Verletztenbeistand*) in their role as a victim witness (StPO (Germany), ss 68b, 406f). The legal representative is neither witness nor party to the proceedings but derives their rights exclusively from the rights available to the victim witness (Daimagueler 2016, 54). The role of the legal representative of a victim witness in the German context is seen as supporting their client in properly exercising their existing rights. This includes explaining available rights as well as offering advice on whether and how to best make use of them during proceedings (Daimagueler 2016, 55).

The representation is not limited to the trial stage but can commence earlier. For example, at the pre-trial stage, a victim witness has the right to be legally represented, and the legal representative has the right to be present during questioning by the police, the public prosecutor and the courts (StPO (Germany) s 68b(1)). Yet, German law does not require criminal justice agencies to inform the legal representative of any scheduled interviews (Wessing and Ahlbrecht 2013, 13). It therefore falls upon the individual witness to ensure that their lawyer has knowledge of, and is present at, the time of questioning. Where a witness is not legally represented during an interview and it is believed that their interests cannot be protected holistically without representation, the courts are under a duty to order a legal representative for them for the duration of the interview at public expense (StPO (Germany) s 68b(2)). The victim can also apply to the court to make such an order (Daimagueler 2016, 63). Before the interview commences, the legal representative must be informed about the main content of the interview and must have the opportunity to discuss this, as well as possible rights and strategies, with their client. Rare circumstances allow for the exclusion of the representative from the interview, for example, if the representative is suspected of being a party to the offence in question (StPO (Germany), s 68b (1) sent. 4).

The legal representative's role in these instances concentrates on the examination of witnesses (both in interviews as well as in case of physical examination), reviewing judicial files and providing general advice to their client. To illustrate this point further, the StPO allows for the physical examination of witnesses even against their will under certain circumstances, such as, securing evidence on the victim's body (StPO (Germany) s 81c). Generally, a judicial order will be necessary for the examination. However, the prosecution or police can make such orders if loss of evidence is expected by the time a judicial order can be obtained. Examinations can include mucous and vaginal smears depending on the offence in question. While the witness does not have to actively partake in the examination, they have to attend said examinations, undress where required, and take certain poses necessary for respective procedures. In this context, the legal representative can generally object to unreasonable examinations on behalf of the victim witness (StPO (Germany) s 81c(4)). Whether the legal representative has a right to be present in person during these examinations, however, is not explicitly regulated under German law (Wessing and Ahlbrecht 2013, 19).

One controversially debated right the legal representative of a victim witness has in the German context is the right to apply to the public prosecutor or the court to review judicial files and to inspect evidence. To do so, and in comparison with the legal representative of the PAP, who is exempt from this requirement, the legal representative must explicitly demonstrate that they have a justified interest in the file and the review does not endanger or significantly lengthen proceedings (StPO (Germany) s 406e). The existence of a justified interest has been denied in cases where the application was solely intended to discover what evidence existed against the defendant (Wessing and Ahlbrecht 2013, 27). A justified interest has been frequently acknowledged, however, where the aim of the inspection is to prepare a civil claim for compensation and damages against the defendant (Daimagueler 2016, 56).

The legal representative of a victim witness is furthermore tasked with providing general advice to their client in relation to the upcoming questioning at trial and the general operation of the criminal process. In that regard, the representative advises the victim witness on potential rights available to them during the main trial. One of these is the right not to testify, for example, in case of spousal privilege or where the right against self-incrimination applies (StPO (Germany) ss 52, 53, 55). Another is the availability of protective measures during proceedings, such as testifying via video technology. The legal representative must also ensure that their client is aware that they have an obligation to testify truthfully at trial while pointing out the legal consequences which apply in case of providing false testimony.

During the actual trial, the legal representative can generally only exercise the rights available to the victim witness they are representing. The representative has the right to be present when the victim is questioned as a witness at trial and, according to the majority opinion in legal scholarship and jurisprudence, has the right to attend the entire trial even before and after the questioning of their client (StPO (Germany) s 406f; Wessing and Ahlbrecht 2013, 19). As pointed out above, prior to questioning, the lawyer can make applications to the court on behalf of the victim including the exclusion of the public during examination of the witness (Court Organisation Act, *Gerichtsverfassungsgestz, GVG* s 171b), exclusion of the defendant during examination of the witness (StPO (Germany) s 247(1)), and allowing victims to testify using video technology (StPO (Germany) s 247a). The task of the legal representative during examination is to object to abusive, compromising, disrespectful and inadmissible questions thereby ensuring that the existing witness protection legislation is complied with (StPO (Germany) ss 55, 58, 68a, 241(2)). Apart from explaining why they object to certain questions, the legal representative does not have the right to speak independently at trial and to make statements (StPO (Germany) s 406f; Wessing and Ahbrecht 2013, 33). Where a court believes this to be necessary, however, they can allow questions from the legal representative on a case by case basis (Wessing and Ahlbrecht 2013, 34).

As a general rule, the costs for the lawyer of a victim witness fall onto the individual victim. This is based on the understanding that a witness who has been properly instructed should be able to exercise their own rights independently. The exception to this general rule is the above discussed Section 68b StPO (Germany), which allows or requires the ordering of a state-funded lawyer for a specific interview if it is believed that the victim is unable to exercise their own rights.

The above shows that the role of the legal representative in Germany is closely entwined with the status of the individual victim. This is also the case in France, where the availability of legal representation differs for victims who act as a civil party and thus uphold a specific legal status, and those victims who do not.

2.1.2 France

As pointed out in Chapter 5, victims in France who act as civil claimants are afforded party status and therefore have the right to be legally represented. The legal representation can already commence during the pre-trial stage (*Code de Procédure Pénale, CCP* (France) s 115).[3] The representative needs to be notified at least five days prior to a scheduled interview with their client and has the right to be present during this interview (CCP (France) s 114). As a consequence, the civil party cannot be interviewed in their absence unless the civil party has explicitly waived their right to legal representation (CCP (France) s 114). The lawyer has the right to obtain access to the dossier of evidence including results of forensic tests, expert witness reports and written opinions of the judge (Bacik et al. 1998, 214). The civil claimant also has the right to be legally represented during the main proceedings (CCP (France) ss 346, 418, 424, 536). Once a legal representative has been engaged the victim can no longer be questioned during the main trial without their lawyer present. If the victim wishes not to attend proceedings, the legal representative can exercise the victim's rights on their behalf (CCP (France) s 424). The costs for the legal representation generally fall onto the victim with legal aid being available for eligible victims who do not have the required financial means (*aide judiciaire*) (Stehle 2007, 177). Victims who are ineligible for legal aid may recoup their costs from the defendant if a conviction occurs (CCP (France) ss 475, 543). Victims who do not act as civil claimants in criminal proceedings, for example, because they elect to pursue their claims in the civil courts or for other motives, generally do not have the right to be legally represented during proceedings (Stehle 2007, 175).

Comparable to Germany and France, in Scandinavian criminal justice systems, the role and rights a victims' lawyer can exercise are also heavily entwined with the specific role the individual victim is afforded. For this reason, victim lawyers have different rights in Sweden than they have in Denmark.

2.1.3 Scandinavia

In both Denmark and Sweden, victims of certain offences have had the right to legal representation by private counsel since the 1980s (Temkin 2002, 281).

In Denmark, legal representation developed in the early 1980s to accommodate victims of certain sexual offences including rape (Temkin 2002, 287). The Danish legal representation scheme originally developed from a single case in which a female lawyer sought court approval to represent a female crime victim during proceedings. Although no such right existed at the time, the court allowed the representation in so far as it also related to a civil damage claim the victim intended to pursue (Caringella 2009, 276–277). On this basis, the lawyer was subsequently able to represent a number of female crime victims in different cases. This ultimately resulted in law reform in the area and the introduction of an official legal representation scheme for rape victims in 1987 (Amnesty International 2010, 38). Due to the positive results of its operation, the legal representation scheme has since been expanded to include victims of other sexual and violent crimes including robbery (Temkin 2002, 288; Bacik et al. 1998, 199).

A memo accompanying the introduction of the original legislation highlights that the lawyer's role in Denmark is not meant to be that of a second prosecutor (Bacik et al. 1998, 199). Rather, lawyers provide victims with legal advice before the trial, explain how the trial will proceed, provide moral support and advise on possible compensation and restoration claims. Victims have the right to be legally represented early on in proceedings, including when reporting an offence to the police and during initial questioning. Moreover, police officers must inform qualifying victims of their right to legal representation if they are unrepresented. Whether victims wish to have a lawyer is up to them. If they select to be legally represented questioning cannot commence before the lawyer is present. Victims furthermore have the right to be legally represented during the main trial and their lawyer has the right to be present when they testify in court. The legal representative will generally not interrupt the questioning unless improper questions, for example, those relating to the victim's past sexual conduct, are asked. The lawyer's role is not to advise the victim on how to respond to questions but simply to ensure their respectful treatment during the interview process in order to reduce feelings of anxiety in a possibly unfamiliar interview situation (on all of the above see Temkin 2002, 289). The lawyer may apply to court to allow the victim to testify in the absence of the defendant or using video technology (Temkin 2002, 290). As identified in Chapter 5, the role of victims in Denmark during the trial is limited to that of a witness and they are generally not considered parties to the proceedings. It is for this reason that their lawyer 'cannot make statements . . . , put questions to the accused or in any other way take part in the proceedings. The lawyer can request the prosecutor to present additional evidence, but the prosecutor alone decides which evidence is to be presented to the court' (Amnesty International 2010, 38). An exception to the general rule that legal representatives cannot call evidence applies where the victim acts as an applicant to the adhesion procedure and the evidence is necessary to support their civil claim during the criminal trial (Bacik et al. 1998, 200).

Legal representation for victims is also widely used in Sweden and is state funded for certain victims, mostly those of serious violent and sexual offences. Legal representation is regulated by the Counsel for the Injured Party Act *(Lag om Målsägandebiträde)* (1988:609) which was originally introduced in 1988. Its introduction was based on victimology research highlighting the risks of secondary victimisation of an already victimised individual through the criminal justice process. The law was therefore part of a strategy aimed at improving the situation for crime victims in the criminal justice system (Lindgren et al. 2012, 168). The law sets out that the counsel for the injured party shall provide support and assistance for the victim. Specific tasks of Swedish victim lawyers include 'participating in police interrogations, explaining legal matters, keeping her [the victim] informed, giving her [the victim] support through the whole legal process, and also putting forward claims for damages on her [the victim's] behalf' (Lindgren et al. 2012, 168; see also Staten Offentliga Utredningar 2007, 30–36). The overall aim of legal representation in Sweden has been described as 'mitigating stress in connection with the investigation' (Staten Offentliga Utredningar 2007, 35). As the role of victims who support the prosecution in Sweden is more active than the role of other victims, their legal representative can also be more actively involved in proceedings. For example, as discussed in Chapter 5, the legal representative of a victim who supports the prosecution in Sweden can examine witnesses and request the introduction of certain evidence. Concerning the practical use of victims' lawyers, Tham et al. (2011, 580) explain that:

> [i]n 2007–8 almost 14,000 complainants, two-thirds of them women, were assigned injured-party counsel. The costs associated with injured-party counsel increased by 1 million euros each year during the decade to 2007. On average, the costs of an injured-party counsel amount to three-quarters of the costs of the defense lawyer in the same case.

While inquisitorial and mixed criminal justice systems look back on a longer tradition of affording victims legal representation during proceedings, adversarial systems, with some exceptions, have not introduced such schemes at all or only to a marginal extent as highlighted below.

2.1.4 United Kingdom and the Republic of Ireland

The availability of legal representation for victims is generally very limited in the United Kingdom and the Republic of Ireland. Since 2001, Ireland allows minimal legal representation for victims of sexual offences during hearings in front of a judge deciding on the defendant's application to introduce evidence about the victim's past sexual history (inserted as per the *Sex Offenders Act 2001* (Ireland) s 34). This does not mean, however, that victims have the right to be legally represented during the trial proper (Rape Crisis Network Ireland 2012, 3).

In Scotland, in 2013 an amendment to the *Victims and Witnesses Bill* (Scotland) was tabled which suggested the right to legal representation in cases where information about health or other sensitive information about a sexual offence victim was sought (Chalmers 2014, 186). This amendment was rejected through vote by the Scottish Parliament in 2013. However, in 2016, a rape victim applied to the Scottish Government for state-funded legal representation in order to object to the defendant's application to access all her medical, psychiatric and psychological files. While no legislation existed in Scotland to obtain legal aid to oppose such applications, Scottish ministers can grant legal aid in circumstances not covered by the legislation (*Legal Aid (Scotland) Act 1986* s 4(2)(c)). The ministers denied the request. On judicial review, this denial was seen as a violation of the victim's human rights although no express provisions in Scotland afforded the victim standing and legal representation in relation to this type of application at the time (*WF, Petitioner* 2016; see also No Author 2016).

In 2005, the Labour Government indicated that it would introduce legal representation for certain victims, including family victims of homicide as well as victims of rape and domestic violence (Reeves and Dunn 2010, 60). It was envisioned that the scheme would allow barristers to provide legal advice to victims and their families and to object to certain inadmissible questions posed by defence lawyers (No Author 2005). At the time, the Lord Chancellor, Lord Falconer of Thoroton QC, was quoted saying that 'Labour is on the side of victims of crime - and for the first time Labour will make sure that victims and their families will have the right to be represented in court' (No Author 2005).

In addition to the representation, the government announcement proposed the introduction of the right for victims to make a statement after the conviction of an offender and before sentencing. After a pilot of the advocacy scheme from April 2006 (Reeves and Dunn 2010, 61), a decision was made against rolling out legal representation for victims (Hoyano 2015, 116). In 2014, the United Kingdom Ministry of Justice (2014, n. 30) in its 'Report on Review of Ways to Reduce Distress of Victims in Trials of Sexual Violence' suggested it should be examined further 'whether steps could be taken to address the seeming inequality of arms for victims (whose interests are not represented by the prosecution and they are not parties to the proceedings)' with reference to legal representation. Thus far, however, legal representation for victims has not been implemented in legislation.

2.1.5 United States

Sexual assault victims in the US military justice system have the right to have legal counsel in the form of a Special Victim Counsel (SVC) aimed at establishing a client-attorney relationship (10 US Code s 1044e).[4] SVCs provide their clients with information about the military justice system and represent their interests during all stages of the proceedings. Their tasks include attending client interviews with defence counsel and law enforcement agencies, asserting their clients' privacy rights during discovery, providing advice on immunity and assistance with Freedom of Information Act requests (see Garvin and Beloof 2015, 74). A US Air Force study surveying sexual assault victims showed that 92% of legally represented victims were 'extremely satisfied' with the advice and support of their SVC during their hearing and 98% would recommend that other victims use legal representation in the form of SVCs (see discussion of the study in Garvin and Beloof 2015, 74).

The US non-military criminal justice system, on the other hand, offers no comparable agency for victims of sexual or other offences. Due to enacted crime victims' rights legislation in most US states and on the federal level, many victims have received the right to be represented by their own attorney. On the federal level, legal representatives may file motions in relation to victim's rights including, for example, applications to prevent the victim's personal information from being made public. In addition, they may address the court at the sentencing stage (Federal Bureau of Investigation, no date). Yet, legal representation schemes are usually not state funded and only a negligible number of pro bono victim lawyers or legal clinics exist (Garvin and Beloof 2015, 80). As a consequence, mostly only affluent victims can afford to be legally represented. Garvin and Beloof (2015, 82) conclude that although victims' rights exist on the books in the US they continue to be disregarded where no legal representation is available for victims at trial to enforce said rights and guarantees.[5]

2.1.6 Australia

Legal representation for victims is available only to a very limited degree in few Australian jurisdictions. Since 2011, New South Wales has introduced a state-funded legal representation scheme for sexual assault victims when addressing the court in relation to the prevention or restriction of disclosure of protected sexual assault counselling notes (*Criminal Procedure Act 1986* (NSW) s 299A). The section states that:

> A protected confider who is not a party may appear in criminal proceedings or preliminary criminal proceedings if a document is sought to be produced or evidence is sought to be adduced that may disclose a protected confidence made by, to or about the protected confider.

The scheme is publically funded through legal aid. These arrangements, however, do not extend to the trial proper.

In South Australia, victims have the right to apply to the Victims of Crime Commissioner to be legally represented in cases that involve 'consultation with prosecution, in criminal and civil proceedings and coronial inquests, as well as initiated legal matters that affect victims in general' (O'Connell, n.d., 7). This includes sexual assault cases in which an application is made to disclose details of the victim's protected communication, for example, in the therapeutic context (*Evidence Act 1929* (SA) s 67F(7)).

2.2 Merits of Introducing/Enhancing Legal Representation Schemes

The above shows that not all of the analysed jurisdictions have enacted legal representation schemes for victim witnesses or that the actual legal representation under some schemes is minimal. Especially, the common law jurisdictions England and Wales and Australia offer very limited, if any, opportunities for victims to be legally represented during proceedings. In contrast, most European jurisdictions and the US on the federal level allow for legal representation of (certain) victims. While legal representation appears to be a more recent development in the US, lawyers for victims have been available in some European jurisdictions including Denmark and Sweden for decades. The below first considers the merits of introducing legal representation schemes for victim witnesses in jurisdictions in which this right is currently not available. It particularly contemplates their compatibility with adversarial parameters, a criticism often relied upon to rebut their introduction in common law systems. It subsequently ponders difficulties associated with existing schemes in the US, Germany and Sweden in an attempt to identify whether and how implemented arrangements could be enhanced.

2.2.1 The Introduction of Legal Representation Schemes

Currently, legal representation for victim witnesses is not available at all in England and Wales. Furthermore, its availability is very limited in Australia. The question therefore arises what benefits could be gained from introducing such arrangements and what the associated risks are.

Protection Gaps

One of the underlying objectives of legal representation schemes for victims is the better protection of victims' interests during criminal proceedings. Legal representatives could be tasked with providing information to victims and ensuring their protection and support. Some may argue that the introduction of such a role is superfluous because existing actors in the criminal justice system already sufficiently support victims in this context. This overlooks the fact, however, that it is not the primary function of the courts or the public prosecution service to act as the protectors of victims' rights and that both also have to consider the public interest and the interests of the accused to a fair trial (Smythe 2002, 2; 2005, 180–181; see also Raitt 2013, 734–739). Courts and public prosecution have to consider different interests and the interests of the victim cannot be given and are not given due attention at all times. For example, although courts are often under a statutory duty to prevent unnecessary, misleading, unduly annoying, belittling and stereotypical questions in the examination of witnesses, they have been found to be reluctant to intervene to protect witnesses in criminal trials (Australian Law Reform Commission 2010, 1335–1336). In light of the situation in practice, the introduction of a separate victims' legal representative, who has the right to make applications for protective measures to the courts, could make the needs of victims overall more visible and increase the sensitivity surrounding these matters. The victims' lawyer could thus perform the role that is not, or only inconsistently, performed by the courts.

Moreover, the task of safeguarding and representing victims' interests can not always be carried out efficiently by the public prosecutor. That is because the public prosecutor is not the representative of the victim but the representative of the state and the public interest (Doak 2008, 139). Although the public prosecutor is obligated to consider the interests of the victim during the criminal trial they also have to consider the public interest and the rights of the defendant in order to guarantee a fair trial. Situations can arise where the interests of the prosecution and the interests of the victim collide. For example, a survey by Brown et al. (1992 cited in Doak 2008, 140) regarding Scottish sexual offence trials found that there are instances where prosecutors do not shield witnesses from character attacks for tactical reasons. Some practitioners believe that too many objections to the questions of the defence counsel can make the jury suspicious because it implies that counsel is hiding something and that a witness suffering at the hands of the defence could win the jury's sympathy for the prosecution (Doak 2005, 307). Similarly, in the context of rape victims, Smythe outlines that prosecutors may have an interest in courts seeing the victim tearfully defending their credibility (Smythe 2005, 181) thus perhaps limiting their objections to the defence's line of questioning. These examples illustrate the conflict between various interests having to be taken into account by the public prosecution at the same time. The role of the prosecution makes it therefore impossible to efficiently protect victims' interests during trial. Ultimately, leaving the protection of victims' rights up to the parties or the judge means allowing third parties, and not the victim, to determine the scope of victim protection in light of their own agenda. This essentially renders the victim powerless once more (Garvin and Beloof 2015, 85).

The role of protecting the victim can also not be carried out as efficiently by witness assistance services or other victim support persons whose role it is to generally inform victims and, in some cases, accompany the victim to court. The victim and their legal representative can form a close relationship during their consultations leading up to the trial allowing the victim to build up trust and be well prepared to testify. This is not always possible in the case where a victim support worker provides advice. Victim support workers employed by the government or in a non-governmental organisation can be under a much greater workload and may have many victims assigned to them to work with. In addition, depending on the jurisdiction, these services are assigned on an ad hoc basis and are often reserved for victims who appear particularly vulnerable (see Office of the Victims of Crime Commissioner (Victoria) 2015, 3). As a consequence, not all victims who require support will be able to access it. Moreover, victim support services are not always staffed with lawyers and are unable to assist victims with legal matters such as information about the content of Victim Impact Statements and other substantive rights victims have been afforded during proceedings (Doak 2015, 13). This is especially true as many obligations owed to victims are set out in different pieces of legislation and policy. Providing a holistic legal overview of available victims' rights may therefore not be possible for victim support workers with no legal background.

Furthermore, the support victim services can offer is limited especially at court due to lack of legal standing, leaving victims in a very vulnerable position when testifying at trial (Temkin 2002, 302).

The support person generally does not have the right to object to any questions during cross-examination, be heard concerning applications for the introduction of the victim's sexual history or apply for the use of protective measures when victims give evidence.

While the availability of lawyers for victims may close existing protection gaps, the schemes may also be advantageous from the point that they can enhance the flow of information and support between victim and state and contribute to an increase in the overall transparency of the criminal justice system.

Enhanced Flow of Information, Support and Transparency

Legal representation for victims may contribute to ensuring that victims are better informed about relevant stages of proceedings and the flow of the trial process. Where information is not forthcoming, for example, from the police or courts, a victim's legal representative is in a position to follow up on missing content. While keeping victims informed about certain steps in proceedings and the court process is a general obligation placed on criminal justice authorities in many jurisdictions, they often find themselves managing a substantial caseload. It may perhaps be for this reason that research in a number of jurisdictions indicates that there is a lack of communication between justice officials and victims (see Victorian Law Reform Commission 2016, 121; Kirchengast 2014, 141–142). Wilson (2008, 15) remarks in this context that:

> [t]he introduction of an independent, legally trained advocate would represent a very positive development for all concerned. A victim's lawyer could track the progress of the case, facilitate the flow of information, provide a single contact point for the victim, and significantly reduce time pressures currently imposed on police and the Crown.

This was confirmed in a study by Bacik et al. (1998, 17) which found that surveyed victims who were legally represented reported greater ease in obtaining information regarding the investigation and trial process and considered their lawyer to be the main source for the provision of information on particular aspects of the proceedings.

On the benefits of legal representation for victims at the pre-trial stage, a German study by Weisser Ring (2017, 100) found that some of the surveyed victims felt that the investigation could have been less traumatising for them had they been legally represented early on in proceedings. This was the case, so participating victims explained, because the whole process would have been more transparent to them and they would have been better prepared to encounter potentially difficult aspects. Similarly, an Irish study on legal representation for rape victims in different jurisdictions found that having access to a legal representative increased victims' satisfaction with the criminal justice process (Bacik et al. 1998, 17).

Introducing a lawyer for victims in criminal proceedings may also result in greater compliance of criminal justice authorities with existing victims' rights legislation thus serving as an additional safeguard.

Greater Compliance with Existing Victims' Rights

Legal representation for victims may contribute to keeping checks on criminal justice authorities during different stages of proceedings and may ensure that existing rights are complied with to the required extent. For instance, a legal representative will know where information or other support to which victims are entitled has not been adequately provided and will likely address this shortfall where relevant. The knowledge that the victim's lawyer is tasked with identifying and raising potential breaches, thus bringing greater awareness to potential underperformances, may be enough to encourage criminal justice authorities to take their obligations towards victims more seriously. This is less likely to be the case where victims are informed and supported by a myriad of different support workers at different stages of proceedings as consistency and continuity of support may be lacking. In 2014, O'Connell, South Australian Commissioner for Victims' Rights at the time, therefore outlined that 'if victims had legal counsel, that would better give them a sense of having genuine rights, legitimacy and identity in the justice process' (O'Connell cited in Fewster and Hyde 2014).

Legal representation schemes appear to offer victim witnesses several advantages and may allow for their better protection during proceedings. This may contribute to an overall enhanced position in criminal trials. While the existence of certain benefits cannot be denied, some have cautioned that legal representation for victims is an exclusively non-adversarial phenomenon which is ill-suited for adversarial criminal justice systems. On this basis, some commentators in the common law context firmly oppose the introduction in adversarial systems.

Compatibility with the Parameters of Different Criminal Justice Systems

It is acknowledged that broad participation rights for legal representatives of victims, such as those acting on behalf of PAPs, may be difficult, if not impossible, to incorporate into adversarial criminal justice systems with a different trial structure. Pizzi and Perron (1996, 41) argue that the German model of PAP participation is unique to the inquisitorial system and cannot be transplanted into adversarial criminal procedure due to structural issues. They opine that because trials in Germany are judge dominated and not set out like a battle between two parties it is easier to make room for the victim without offsetting the balance of the parties at trial (Pizzi and Perron 1996, 41). Concurring, Doak (2005, 298) suggests that the integration of a third party, the victim, could cause the traditional distribution of roles in the adversarial system between state and defendant to be set off balance. Others propose that, for the same reason, legal representation for victims cannot be accommodated in adversarial criminal justice systems as they differ structurally to a great extent from inquisitorial systems, where such representation is frequently possible (see discussion in Hoyano 2015, 115, 117). It needs to be appreciated, however, that legal representation does not have to be understood as legal representation for PAPs or civil claimants, meaning victims with additional legal status. Therefore, it does not have to take the same shape as some broad forms of victim participation in inquisitorial systems. Rather legal representation is also possible to exclusively safeguard the existing rights of victim witnesses and therefore can be tailored to fit within existing adversarial parameters. It is submitted that a narrowly tailored role in which the legal representative merely safeguards the victim's existing rights and provides information and support does not violate adversarial structures or defendants' due process rights in principle (see also Braun 2014, 829; Raitt 2010, 53; 2013, 742).

Another common criticism of legal representation schemes for victims is that they will increase the length of trials and thus place a greater financial and administrative burden on the criminal justice system. Why this argument falls short, however, is discussed below.

Length of Trials

Some fear that trials will become longer and more complex where another person, a victims' lawyer, is involved. While this may well be the case for legal representatives who have broad rights including the right to introduce and examine additional evidence, this is less likely to be the case under more narrowly tailored schemes. Especially in cases where a legal representative derives their rights exclusively from the victim witness, it is unclear why trials should become significantly longer. The rights a lawyer can exercise on behalf of a victim witness can be limited and many, for example, the exclusion of the public when testifying, do not appear to have the potential to lengthen proceedings considerably at all. The complexity and length of trials are therefore questions associated with the particulars of the introduced representation schemes but do not constitute an insurmountable hurdle to their operation.

While legal representation schemes for victims have been available in European countries including Germany and Sweden for some time now and more recently in the US, their operation has not been without criticism in practice. The below traces common problems and inefficiencies associated with these arrangements in order to assess whether and how their effectiveness could be improved in practice.

2.2.2 Problems with Existing Legal Representation Schemes for Victims

To date, only few studies have examined the operation of legal representation schemes for victims in practice. Available research has identified problems with lack of funding as well as with lack of information or misinformation about availability and content of these arrangements. Another contested issue revolves around lawyers' qualifications required for this type of work and the general availability (or lack) of qualified lawyers to perform this role. These issues are discussed below in turn prior to considering their implications for the future of legal representation schemes in general.

Funding

One of the main problems identified with existing legal representation schemes is that state funding is frequently not available at all or that funding is limited to certain victim categories, mostly those of serious violent or sexual offences. Especially in the US context, where legal representation schemes are generally not state funded, it has been submitted that only very limited opportunities for pro bono representation exist (Garvin and Beloof 2015, 80). While victims in some jurisdictions, for example, in Germany, may be able to recoup their legal fees from the defendant in case of conviction, the victim carries the financial risk for their legal costs and requires sufficient initial resources to outlay these fees. That is why in practice, depending on the jurisdiction, only affluent victims may be able to afford legal representation and receive legal advice. In reality, this *de facto* distorts legal representation for victims intended to safeguard their rights and interests during proceedings into a two-class system.

Information

Another problematic issue concerning victims' effective legal representation revolves around the lack of information or misinformation about legal representation schemes for victims.

A 2017 German study on victims in pre-trial proceedings revealed that during initial police questioning less than 1.5% of witnesses were legally represented despite the right to obtain such representation (see Truscheit 2017). This was partially attributed to a poor understanding of the nature of legal representation schemes for victims.

For instance, some interviewed victims thought they did not need a legal representative as they had done nothing wrong. This stance is rooted in the belief that only people who commit crimes require representation and shows a misapprehension of the general underlying aims of legal representation schemes for victims. Others stated that the mere act of finding a competent representative was too complex in their situation. Given that lawyers cannot formally specialise in victims' rights in Germany and add this to their qualifications it was difficult, according to some interviewed victims, to identify which lawyers worked in this area. Furthermore, a number of victims indicated that they struggled to understand the different financial implications of legal representation, ranging from state funded over legal aid to recuperation from the convicted offender, depending on what category of victim they classified as. Due to fears of becoming financially liable, these victims refused to engage legal advice. Others misunderstood the role of the public prosecution and initially believed they would represent their interests (on all of the above see Weisser Ring 2017, 172–173). This shows that the role a legal representative for victims plays is perhaps not adequately understood in society including by victims of crime themselves. Additional information in this context may be required to allow victims to make a more informed decision on whether they wish to be legally represented and what costs, if any, this may entail. This may also include providing them with access to a list of experienced lawyers working in this area to simplify the initial selection and appointment process.

Similar concerns have been raised in the Swedish context. The Swedish Government Official Committee Service reviewing the Counsel for the Injured Party Act and its effectiveness in 2007 found in its official report that lack of information or misinformation about legal representation for victims complicated the appointment process of the injured party counsel (Staten Offentliga Utredningar 2007, 30). In their inquiry, the Committee highlighted that in some instances information on the availability of legal representatives was not or not correctly provided to victims. In order to allow victims to be holistically represented from the preliminary investigation stage, the report emphasised the need to provide information about legal representation early on, for example, as soon as the victim reported to the police (Staten Offentliga

Utredningar 2007, 31). A study by Lindgren et al. (2012, 170–171) on the extent to which criminal justice is afforded to assaulted women in Sweden found that prosecutions were more prevalent in cases where victims were legally represented. In this context, the researchers identified a link between the willingness of counsel to cooperate with authorities and the frequency of cases going to court. On this basis, they concurred with the 2007 Swedish Government report and reiterated the importance of providing legal counsel to victims at an early stage of proceedings (Lindgren et al. 2012, 171).

While the situation in both Germany and Sweden shows that lack of information or misinformation can significantly impact the effective operation of legal representation schemes, another concern associated with their adequate operation identified in both countries is the qualification of lawyers acting in this role.

Qualification of Lawyers

Whether victims receive adequate legal representation in practice is often dependent on the availability of qualified lawyers. A 2017 German study on legal representation identified a general lack of available and qualified lawyers. A number of surveyed legal professionals raised the issue that legal representation of victim witnesses at the pre-trial stage was financially unattractive to them and prevented them from taking on this type of work. For example, where the lawyer was court appointed for a victim interview, they could charge a maximum of 136 Euro for accompanying the victim to up to three different interview sessions potentially taking up three days of work (Weisser Ring 2017, 173). As a result, many lawyers who are able to obtain higher fees by doing other work in their field may choose to do so over representing victims. Relatedly, at the moment, any lawyer in Germany can represent a victim and there is no specialisation or specific requirement for this role. That means that the expertise of victims' lawyers may vary greatly in practice. It has been found that mainly four different types of lawyers take up work as victims' legal representatives. These are: lawyers whose work generally focuses on victims, lawyers who have an interest in victims' rights issues, lawyers who occasionally do work involving victims and specialised defence lawyers (Barton and Flotho 2010, 242). While some lawyers have broad expert knowledge on victim protection and the availability of existing rights others have been found to have serious knowledge gaps in this area. The quality divide between lawyers is seen as so extensive in practice that the work of some representatives has been described as a 'de-professionalisation' of victims' lawyers (Barton and Flotho 2010, 243).

The qualification of the injured party counsel has also arisen as an issue in Sweden. There, the representation can be undertaken by non-qualified lawyers who are not part of the Swedish Bar Association (Staten Offentliga Utredningar 2007, 33). The quality of legal representation for victims, or lack thereof, was reiterated in a 2016 official Swedish report investigating sexual offences (Staten Offentliga Utredningar 2016, 54). In relation to the qualifications of lawyers, the report (Staten Offentliga Utredningar 2016, 60) states that:

> assignments as injured party counsel are often given to relatively inexperienced lawyers at law firms with or without members of the Swedish Bar Association. For the injured party counsel to be able to provide support for the injured party, and also for the counsel to have an equal standing with the prosecutor and the defence counsel, there is, in our view, reason to set stricter requirements concerning the experience and suitability of the injured party counsel in particularly sensitive cases such as in investigations of sexual offences and offences in close relationship, for instance.

This indicates that both Germany and Sweden struggle with aspects concerning the practical operation of legal representation schemes for victims.

2.3 The Future of Legal Representation Schemes for Victims

The above shows that many benefits may lie in legal representation schemes for victims during criminal proceedings. Legal representation may offer victims greater protection in the criminal justice process by providing them with a person exclusively responsible for representing their interests. This way, victims are more in control of their own protection rather than having to rely on third parties, including the prosecution and courts, to exercise rights on their behalf. The introduction of an official actor on behalf of the victim with standing in certain instances may also enhance the compliance of criminal justice authorities with existing victims' rights legislation and obligations. These schemes may furthermore allow for a greater flow of information between state and victim and lead to increased victim awareness as to what they can expect in proceedings. Ultimately, legal representation schemes can be tailored to fit adversarial trial structure and are unlikely to significantly lengthen proceedings depending on their particular modalities. As such, victims in jurisdictions in which legal representation schemes are currently unavailable may benefit from their introduction. This is the case, even though the victim's role as a witness in proceedings is not significantly altered.

Existing research in the US, Germany and Sweden, jurisdictions in which legal representation for victims has been available to varying degrees for some time, has shown that the schemes require some modifications and streamlining to enhance their effectiveness in practice. Problems identified with existing schemes revolve around lack of funding as well as lack of information or misinformation about legal representation and issues surrounding the quality of legal representatives themselves. These issues, while relevant in practice, do not appear so paramount in nature that they cannot be overcome through the development of tactical solutions. These could include a realignment of funding concepts as well as the introduction of specific training courses which allow lawyers to obtain particular qualifications in the victims' rights area to close quality gaps. As a result, even though problems remain, it is submitted that these are not so severe that they justify the categorical dismissal of legal representation schemes aimed at improving the experience of victims in criminal proceedings.

3 Concluding Remarks

The question of what role victims should play in criminal proceedings has been on the political agenda in many jurisdictions for decades. The answer, however, remains highly contested and elusive. While law reform appears to occur frequently in this area, perhaps due to electoral politics, the overall situation of victim participation rights in most jurisdictions at the pre-trial, trial and post-trial stage remains fragmented. In the analysed jurisdictions, no comprehensive approach to victim participation is detectable. Because of the remaining controversy surrounding victim participation rights, this chapter contemplated whether a focus on legal representation for victim witnesses could be more beneficial—at least for the time being—to enhance the overall position of victims in criminal justice systems.

Focusing on the increased availability of victim lawyers during proceedings may prove advantageous from multiple perspectives including increased availability of information and transparency of proceedings as well as the fostering of greater compliance with existing victims' rights norms within criminal justice agencies. While legal representation schemes may have the potential to provide victims with an improved experience in the criminal justice system, their introduction may not be without controversy, especially in adversarial systems to which this right is foreign. Yet, it is important to acknowledge that legal representation schemes, depending on their particular modalities, do not give rise to the same concerns regarding the transformation of the traditional criminal trial structure as the introduction of active procedural rights for victims during proceedings does.

Notes

1. Referred to as Private Accessory Prosecutor in the English translation of the German Code of Criminal Procedure. Also translated as 'additional private prosecutor' or 'auxiliary private prosecutor' in comparative legal literature.
2. An English translation of the German, StPO is available on the German Ministry of Justice website: https://www.gesetze-im-internet.de/englisch_stpo/.
3. An unofficial 2006 English translation of the French Code of Criminal Procedure is available online: http://www.legislationline.org/documents/section/criminal-codes/country/30.

4. Title 10 of the US Code outlines the role of the armed forces. See in particular wording of subsections (a)–(c) of 10 US Code, § 1044e: (a) Designation; Purposes—(1) The Secretary concerned shall designate legal counsel (to be known as 'Special Victims' Counsel') for the purpose of providing legal assistance to an individual described in paragraph (2) who is the victim of an alleged sex-related offense, regardless of whether the report of that offense is restricted or unrestricted... (b) Types of Legal Assistance Authorised—The types of legal assistance authorised by subsection (a) include the following: (1) Legal consultation regarding potential criminal liability of the victim stemming from or in relation to the circumstances surrounding the alleged sex-related offense and the victim's right to seek military defence services. (2) Legal consultation regarding the Victim Witness Assistance Programme, including—(A) the rights and benefits afforded the victim; (B) the role of the Victim Witness Assistance Programme liaison and what privileges do or do not exist between the victim and the liaison; and (C) the nature of communication made to the liaison in comparison to communication made to a Special Victims' Counsel or a legal assistance attorney under Section 1044 of this title. (3) Legal consultation regarding the responsibilities and support provided to the victim by the Sexual Assault Response Coordinator, a unit or installation Sexual Assault Victim Advocate, or domestic abuse advocate, to include any privileges that may exist regarding communications between those persons and the victim. (4) Legal consultation regarding the potential for civil litigation against other parties (other than the United States). (5) Legal consultation regarding the military justice system, including (but not limited to)—(A) the roles and responsibilities of the trial counsel, the defence counsel and investigators; (B) any proceedings of the military justice process in which the victim may observe; (C) the Government's authority to compel cooperation and testimony; and (D) the victim's responsibility to testify and other duties to the court. (6) Representing the victim at any proceedings in connection with the reporting, military investigation and military prosecution of the alleged sex-related offense. (7) Legal consultation regarding eligibility and requirements for services available from appropriate agencies or offices for emotional and mental health counselling and other medical services; (8) Legal consultation and assistance—(A) in personal civil legal matters in accordance with Section 1044 of this title; (B) in any proceedings of the military justice process in which

a victim can participate as a witness or other party; (C) in understanding the availability of, and obtaining any protections offered by, civilian and military protecting or restraining orders; and (D) in understanding the eligibility and requirements for, and obtaining, any available military and veteran benefits, such as transitional compensation benefits found in Section 1059 of this title and other State and Federal victims' compensation programmes. (9) Legal consultation and assistance in connection with—(A) any complaint against the Government, including an allegation under review by an inspector general and a complaint regarding equal employment opportunities; (B) any request to the Government for information, including a request under Section 552a of title 5 (commonly referred to as a 'Freedom of Information Act request'); and (C) any correspondence or other communications with Congress. (10) Such other legal assistance as the Secretary of Defence (or, in the case of the Coast Guard, the Secretary of the Department in which the Coast Guard is operating) may authorise in the regulations prescribed under subsection (h). (c) Nature of Relationship—the relationship between a Special Victims' Counsel and a victim in the provision of legal advice and assistance shall be the relationship between an attorney and client.

5. See, for example, Kenna (2006), where the victim's request to make a verbal Victim Impact Statement during sentencing was initially denied by the district court which argued that the right merely related to a written statement. This restricted interpretation was later successfully challenged by the victim via a writ of mandamus petition to the Court of Appeal.

Legislation and Related Sources

Administration of Justice Act (Denmark), Retsplejeloven
Code de Procédure Pénale (France), Code of Criminal Procedure
Criminal Procedure Act 1986 (NSW)
Evidence Act 1929 (SA)
Lag om Målsägandebiträde (Sweden), Counsel for the Inured Party Act
Legal Aid (Scotland) Act 1986 (Scotland)
Rättegångsbalken (Sweden), Code of Judicial Procedure
Sex Offenders Act 2001 (Ireland)
Strafprozessordnung (Germany), Code of Criminal Procedure.

References

Amnesty International. (2010, March 8). *Case Closed: Rape and Human Rights in the Nordic Countries*. London: Amnesty International. Retrieved from https://amnesty.dk/media/1557/case-closed.pdf.

Australian Law Reform Commission. (2010). *Family Violence: A National Legal Response*—Final Report (ALRC Report 114). Sydney, Australia.

Bacik, I., Maunsell, C., & Gogan, S. (1998). *The Legal Process and Victims of Rape*. Dublin: Dublin Rape Crisis Centre.

Barton, S., & Flotho, C. (2010). *Opferanwaelte im Strafverfahren*. Baden-Baden: Nomos.

Braun, K. (2014). Legal Representation for Sexual Assault Victims—Possibilities for Law Reform. *Current Issues in Criminal Justice, 25,* 819–837.

Brown, B., Burman, M., & Jamieson, L. (1992). *Sexual History and Sexual Character Evidence in Scottish Sexual Offence Trials*. Edinburgh: Scottish Office Central Research Unit.

Caringella, S. (2009). *Addressing Rape Reform in Law and Practice*. New York: Columbia University Press.

Chalmers, J. (2014). Independent Legal Representation for Complainers in Sexual Offence Cases. In J. Chalmers, F. Leverick, & A. Shaw (Eds.), *Post-corroboration Safeguard Review Report of the Academic Expert Group* (pp. 185–189). Edinburgh: The Scottish Government.

Daimagueler, M. G. (2016). *Der Verletzte im Strafverfahren: Handbuch fuer die Praxis*. Munich: C.H. Beck.

Dearing, A. (2017). *Justice for Victims of Crime: Human Dignity as the Foundation of Criminal Justice in Europe*. Cham, Switzerland: Springer.

Doak, J. (2005). Victims' Rights in Criminal Trials: Prospects for Participation. *Journal of Law and Society, 32*(2), 294–316.

Doak, J. (2008). *Victims' Rights, Human Rights and Criminal Justice: Reconceiving the Role of Third Parties*. Portland: Hart Publishing.

Doak, J. (2015, October 20). *Victims of Crime in the Criminal Trial Process: Submission 31 to the Victorian Law Reform Commission*. Received October 20, 2015. Retrieved from http://www.lawreform.vic.gov.au/sites/default/files/Submission_CP_31_Professor_Johnathon_Doak_20-10-15.pdf.

Federal Bureau of Investigation. (n.d.). *A Brief Description of the Federal Criminal Justice Process*. Retrieved from https://www.fbi.gov/resources/victim-services/a-brief-description-of-the-federal-criminal-justice-process.

Garvin, M., & Beloof, D. E. (2015). Crime Victim Agency: Independent Lawyers for Sexual Assault Victims. *Ohio State Journal of Criminal Law, 13*, 67–88.
Groenhuijsen, M. (1999). *Victims' Rights in the Criminal Justice System: A Call for More Comprehensive Implementation Theory*. Keynote Lecture Delivered to the Ninth International Symposium on Victimology, August 27, 1997, Amsterdam, The Netherlands. Retrieved from https://pure.uvt.nl/portal/files/673773/amsterdawsv.PDF.
Groenhuijsen, M. (2014). The Development of International Policy in Relation to Victims of Crime. *International Review of Victimology, 20*(1), 31–48.
Groenhuijsen, M. S. (2004). Victims' Rights and Restorative Justice: Piecemeal Reform of the Criminal Justice System or a Change of Paradigm? In H. Kaptein, & M. Malsch (Eds.), *Crime, Victims and Justice: Essays on Principles and Practice* (pp. 63–79). Aldershot, Hampshire: Ashgate.
Hoyano, L. (2015). Reforming the Adversarial Trial for Vulnerable Witnesses and Defendants. *Criminal Law Review, 2*, 107–129.
Kirchengast, T. (2014). *Participation of Victims of Crime in New South Wales Court Processes: A Study Commissioned by Victims Services*. NSW: Final Report—Full Report Including All Appendices, November 2014. Sydney: Victim Services. Retrieved from http://www.victimsclearinghouse.nsw.gov.au/Documents/Kirchengast_Victim%20Participation%20Study%20Final%20Report.pdf.
Kirchengast, T. (2016). *Victims and the Criminal Trial*. London, UK: Palgrave Macmillan.
Lindgren, M. S., Renck, B., & Diesen, C. (2012). Criminal Justice for Assaulted Women in Sweden—Law Versus Practice. *Review of European Studies, 4*(1), 167–178.
No Author. (2005, April 27). Victims' Advocates Plan for Murder and Rape Cases. *The Guardian* (online). Retrieved from https://www.theguardian.com/uk/2005/apr/26/ukcrime.election2005.
No Author. (2016, February 12). Anti-rape Groups Hail Legal Aid Ruling. *BBC News Scotland*. Retrieved from http://www.bbc.com/news/uk-scotland-35562009.
Office of the Victims of Crime Commissioner (Victoria). (2015, August 21). *The Role of Victims in the Criminal Trial Process, Submission 14 to the Victorian Law Reform Commission*. Received September 30, 2015. Retrieved from http://www.lawreform.vic.gov.au/sites/default/files/Submission_CP_14_Office_of_the_Victims_of_Crime_Commissioner_30-09-15.pdf.

O'Connell, M. (2014, June 3). Cited in Fewster, S., & Hyde, B. 'SA Victims' Rights Commissioner Says Victims Should Be Represented by Lawyers During Criminal Sentencing Hearing. *The Advertiser* (online). Retrieved from https://www.adelaidenow.com.au/news/south-australia/sa-victims-rights-commissioner-says-victims-should-be-represented-by-lawyers-during-criminal-sentencing-hearings/story-fni6uo1m-1226940821137.

O'Connell, M. (n.d.). *Victims' Rights: Integrating Victims in Criminal Proceedings, Commission for Victims' Rights*. Adelaide: Government of South Australia. Retrieved from http://www.voc.sa.gov.au/sites/default/files/OConnell_Integrating%20Victims.pdf.

Pizzi, W., & Perron, W. (1996). Crime Victims in German Courtrooms: A Comparative Perspective on American Problems. *Stanford Journal of International Law, 32,* 37–64.

Raitt, F. (2010). *Independent Legal Representation for Complainers in Sexual Offence Trials, Research Report for Rape Crisis Scotland*. Glasgow: Rape Crisis Scotland.

Raitt, F. (2013). Independent Legal Representation in Rape Cases: Meeting the Justice Deficit in Adversarial Proceedings. *Criminal Law Review, 9,* 729–749.

Rape Crisis Network Ireland. (2012). *Previous Sexual History Evidence and Separate Legal Representation: RCNI Position Paper*. Dublin: Rape Crisis Network Ireland.

Reeves, H. D., & Dunn, P. (2010). The Status of Crime Victims and Witnesses in the Twenty-First Century. In A. Bottoms & J. Roberts (Eds.), *Hearing the Victim, Adversarial Justice, Crime Victims and the State* (pp. 46–71). Cullompton: Willan Publishing.

Smythe, D. (2002). *Parliamentary Submissions to the South African Parliament by the University of Cape Town, Sexual Offences Submission*. Chapter 8: Legal Representation for Victims of Sexual Offences. Retrieved from www.ghjru.uct.ac.za/sexual-offence-bill/Legal-Representation-for-Victims-of-Sexual-Offences.pdf.

Smythe, D. (2005). Moving Beyond 30 Years of Anglo-American Rape Law Reforms: Legal Representation for Victims of Sexual Violence. *South African Journal of Criminal Justice, 2,* 167–186.

Staten Offentliga Utredningar. (2007). *Committee Report, Målsägandebiträdet-Ett aktivt stöd i rättsprocessen: The Injured Party Counsel: An Active Support in the Legal Process, SOU 2007:6*. Stockholm, Sweden: Swedish Government Official Reports.

Staten Offentliga Utredningar. (2016). *Committee Report, Ett starkare skydd för den sexuella integriteten: A Stronger Protection for Sexual Integrity; SOU 2016:60*. Stockholm, Sweden: Swedish Government Official Reports.
Stehle, S. (2007). *Das Strafverfahren als immaterielle Wiedergutmachung*. Hamburg: Verlag Dr Kovac.
Temkin, J. (2002). *Rape and the Legal Process* (2nd ed.). Oxford: Oxford University Press.
Tham, H., Roenneling, A., & Rytterbro, L.-L. (2011). The Emergence of the Crime Victim: Sweden in a Scandinavian Context. *Crime and Justice, 40*(1), 555–611.
Truscheit, K. (2017, July 5). „Wir brauchen Opferanwälte". *Frankfurter Allgemeine Zeitung* (online). Retrieved from http://www.faz.net/aktuell/gesellschaft/kriminalitaet/opferschutzverband-weisser-ring-fordert-anwaelte-fuer-opfer-15092629.html.
United Kingdom Ministry of Justice. (2014). *Report on Review of Ways to Reduce Distress of Victims in Trials of Sexual Violence*. Retrieved from https://www.gov.uk/government/uploads/system/uploads/attachment_data/file/299341/report-on-review-of-ways-to-reduce-distress-of-victims-in-trials-of-sexual-violence.pdf.
Victorian Law Reform Commission. (2016). *The Role of Victims of Crime in the Criminal Trial Process—Final Report*. Melbourne: Victorian Law Reform Commission.
Weisser, R. (2017). *Forschungsprojekt Belastungen von Opfern in Ermittlungsverfahren Forschungsbericht*. Mainz: Weisser Ring Stiftung. Retrieved from https://weisser-ring-stiftung.de/sites/default/files/domains/weisser_ring_stiftung/downloads/wrsforschungsberichthp_1.pdf.
Wessing, J., & Ahlbrecht, H. (2013). *Der Zeugenbeistand*. Munich: C.H. Beck.
Wilson, L. (2008). *Victims of Sexual Assault: Who Represents Them in Criminal Proceedings? (Windsor, ON)*. Unpublished Paper Delivered at the Eleventh Colloquium on the Legal Profession, University of Windsor, October 24, 2008. Retrieved from https://lawsocietyontario.azureedge.net/media/lso/media/legacy/pdf/e/eleventh_colloquium_wilson.pdf.

Cases

Kenna v. US District Court for the Central District of California 435 F.3d 1011 (9th Cir. 2006) (US).
WF, Petitioner [2016] CSOH 27 (Scotland).

9

Victim Participation: Review and Conclusions

1 Introduction

It is no longer true that victims can be considered forgotten persons in most Western justice systems, at least not in legal and political discourse and academic scholarship. While different jurisdictions have introduced varying types of victims' rights and standards, some rights remain more contested than others. This book focused on one of the most heavily debated rights: the right for victims to participate in criminal proceedings.

Chapter 1 gave a short introduction to the general developments concerning victim participation on the national and international level and provided an overview of the adversarial, inquisitorial and mixed criminal justice systems selected for analysis in this book. Chapters 2 and 3 were concerned with presenting context for subsequent analysis by tracing the historical developments regarding the victims' role in national criminal justice systems and in traditional criminal theories. This was followed by Chapters 4–6, which examined what participatory rights are available to victims at the pre-trial stage, the trial stage and the post-trial stage in each of the selected jurisdictions. Subsequently,

K. Braun, *Victim Participation Rights*, Palgrave Studies in Victims and Victimology, https://doi.org/10.1007/978-3-030-04546-3_9

Chapter 7 drew on these findings and contemplated whether the introduction of victims' participatory rights in Germany and Australia could be considered a changed understanding of criminal justice and a reconceptualisation of the existing criminal justice system. Drawing on these themes, Chapter 8 contemplated whether, at present, greater benefits could be derived from better protecting victim witnesses rather than from the pursuit of active procedural participation rights.

The below brings together all previous discussion and findings in order to provide a holistic examination of victim participation in the selected jurisdictions, its limitations and the possible implications for future law and policy reform.

2 Historical Developments Regarding the Victims' Role and Conceptualisation of Victims in Criminal Theories

Historically, all countries analysed in this volume relied heavily on victims for the prosecution of offences. This was to do with the fact that a distinction between civil law, which relates to violations of individual rights and interests, and criminal law, which is concerned with the violation of public norms, did not exist in early justice systems. As such, a victim was traditionally able to seek recovery of their losses from the offender by pursuing different forms of prosecution. Overall, there was little state involvement in these processes. Even when a changed understanding emerged in states that crime is an offence against the sovereign or the state and not against the individual victim, many criminal justice systems, especially common law systems, continued to rely heavily on victims as private prosecutors. This was often related to the fact that no public police or prosecution service existed at the time, not the least due to questions of financing such services. Yet, with the introduction of modern police and prosecution services, tasked with investigating and prosecuting offences, the role of the victim gradually decreased over the centuries and ultimately became that of a witness for the prosecution in many jurisdictions.

Increased state-control over criminal proceedings from around the nineteenth century onward also led to a new focus in academic scholarship and national law and policy on how to best protect the individual defendant against the superior powers of the state. This ultimately contributed to the development of criminal justice principles and doctrines in many states, including, the fair trial principle as well as principles surrounding equality of arms and the presumption of innocence. The emerging emphasis on defendants and their rights and needs further usurped consideration of victims and their role in criminal procedure. As a consequence, prior to the 1970s, victims and their interests were largely ignored in many Western systems. It was not until the second half of the twentieth century that scholars and policy makers 'rediscovered' victims and their plight. In many of the analysed jurisdictions, the rediscovery of victims in criminal procedure was closely related to the feminist movement of the 1960s and 1970s pointing out shortfalls regarding the treatment of rape victims in criminal trials and victims' potential secondary victimisation through the criminal process.

In accordance with the limited emphasis on victims prior to the second half of the twentieth century is the absence of victims from traditional criminal theories—theories developed to explain the underlying reasons for punishment and criminal justice. Chapter 3 considered how the two main traditional theories, non-consequentialist and consequentialist theories in the form of retributivism and utilitarianism, relate to victims of crime. Non-consequentialist theories focus on retribution and are based on the assumption that any infringement of criminal law must be punished *per se*. An underlying reason for the punishment is not required according to strictly non-consequentialist theories. In contrast, consequentialist criminal theories consider punishment only justified if it serves a specific purpose, for example, the prevention of future crime or the protection of the community. Exploring how victims fit within criminal theories is important as the theories have the potential to shape society's understanding of crime and justice and, in turn, to inform certain criminal justice responses relating to victims and their role in criminal procedure. The chapter concluded that all traditional theories have in common that they see crime as a conflict between offender and state but not between victim and offender. Consequently, in their classical sense, criminal theories do not focus on victims of crime and their individual interests. Particularly the pure non-consequentialist theories do not take into account the consequences of punishment on anyone, including the perpetrator, society or the victim. Consequentialist theories, on the other hand, focus mainly on prevention or deterrence and may therefore take the perpetrator and society but not the individual victim into account. Nothing suggests that traditional criminal theories envision a central role for victims in criminal procedure. National criminal justice systems heavily influenced by retributivism or utilitarianism may therefore be less likely to provide victims with a central role in proceedings based on the lack of theoretical and philosophical underpinning and relatedly the more limited interpretation of the victims' role.

With the refocus on victims in criminal law and policy since the 1970s, a gap between victims' rights in practice and the classic theoretical underpinnings of such rights seems to have emerged. In front of this background, more contemporary criminal justice theories have developed with a specific focus on victims and their role within and outside traditional criminal justice parameters. These include expressive theory and restorative justice, which take victims and their interests into account to a greater extent. Especially expressive theory, however, does not appear to attract the same level of support as classical criminal theories do. In addition, restorative justice in general does not focus on the role of victims within the traditional justice system. Rather, it seeks to afford victims participation possibilities outside of this traditional arena. Accordingly, the actual victims' role in traditional criminal procedure remains largely unaffected by this approach.

It appears that the understanding of crime and criminal justice, which has in turn influenced the structures of numerous national justice system, is frequently based on traditional theories with a focus on the state, the community at large or individual defendants but without reference to victims.

3 Victim Participation in National Criminal Justice Systems: Review of Key Findings

In front of this backdrop, Chapters 4–6 set out to identify what participatory rights are available to victims in criminal proceedings by undertaking a detailed analysis of said rights at the pre-trial, trial and post-trial stage in the selected adversarial, inquisitorial and mixed criminal justice systems. The point of the exercise was to identify whether a shift from the traditional understanding of criminal justice as a conflict between defendant and state towards a more victim-focussed criminal justice process through victim integration could be detected. This was followed in Chapter 7 by a comprehensive analysis of the role of victims in criminal procedure and the perception of this role in legal-political discourse and academic scholarship in a case study of Germany and Australia, as examples of largely inquisitorial and mostly adversarial criminal justice systems. Subsequently, Chapter 8 drew on the themes emerging from the previous chapters by contemplating the merits of introducing or expanding legal representation schemes for victims to improve their overall position during criminal proceedings.

3.1 Pre-trial Rights in National Criminal Justice Systems

Chapter 4 was concerned with ways in which victims can participate in different decision-making processes during the pre-trial phase which may significantly affect their interests. These include the non-investigation and non-prosecution decision, the decision to afford a defendant release from incarceration while awaiting trial and the decision of prosecution and defence to enter into an agreement in exchange for certain sentencing conditions.

The chapter found that pre-trial, many European countries afford victims the right to request a review of the decision not to prosecute, either through some form of internal review (within the office of the police or public prosecution), judicial review or through both types of review. The availability of this right across the different European jurisdictions is likely related to EU obligations placed on Member States in this regard. The situation in Germany makes it particularly clear, however, that the right to request a review of the non-prosecution decision was not primarily introduced to provide victims with a possibility to participate and be heard in proceedings. Rather, the right was originally introduced to ensure that general prosecutorial obligations, namely the obligation to prosecute where sufficient evidence exists, became subject to judicial review through the assistance of the victim. The right to review a non-prosecution decision is not available to the same degree in the non-European jurisdictions analysed: Australia and the US. There, victims have been afforded few official avenues to seek a review or to request a court determination of the legitimacy of said decisions. This may be closely linked to the broad discretion prosecutors have been afforded in these adversarial systems and the related understanding that their discretionary decisions can only be subjected to limited avenues for review.

Furthermore, the possibilities for victims to participate during the pre-trial release decision of the offender (frequently referred to as bail) vary greatly between the analysed jurisdictions. In the context of adversarial systems, it appears that only victims in the US have an enforceable right to be heard in relation to early-release proceedings. While victims in the UK and some Australian jurisdictions may be able to present a submission to the release decision-making body, such rights, where they do exist, are frequently neither statutory nor enforceable. As a result, it is less clear whether in practice victims receive the possibility to participate in this context. The possibilities for victims to participate in this situation are even more reduced in the analysed European inquisitorial and mixed criminal justice systems. That is in France, Germany, Sweden and Denmark, a right for victims to participate in relation to pre-trial release does not exist at all.

Lastly, in all of the countries analysed but for Sweden, some form of agreement in exchange for certain sentencing conditions appears to be available to defendants. Particulars of the agreements vary and depend on the respective jurisdiction. Yet, as a consequence of such agreements between defence and prosecution, many defendants will not undergo a trial or, at least, not a complete trial. Although defendants admit guilt in relation to a specific offence within these agreements, victims may not feel that the offence agreed upon adequately reflects the harm done to them. Thus although victims' interests may be particularly affected by these agreements, none of the analysed jurisdictions but for the US, and arguably only after charges have been presented, afford victims a statutory right to participate in relation to this decision. No jurisdiction has afforded victims the right to request a review of the agreement itself.

Although some victims can participate in some pre-trial decisions, on the whole, victim participation rights at the pre-trial stage appear highly disjointed in the analysed jurisdictions. No overall vision regarding a structured participation approach can be detected. Notably, and perhaps relatedly, scholarship in the area of victim participation at the pre-trial stage is also very limited. A large number of scholars, especially those with an Anglo-American legal background, seem to contemplate the question of victim participation exclusively through the lens of Victim Impact Statements at the sentencing stage with limited pre-trial focus.

3.2 Rights During Trial and Sentencing in National Criminal Justice Systems

During the trial proper, Chapter 5 found that adversarial criminal justice systems afford victims the fewest avenues for participation. The role of victims in adversarial systems during the actual trial remains dominated by the traditional understanding that victims are witnesses for the prosecution without additional individual rights. Some adversarial jurisdictions, for example the US on the federal level, and some Australian jurisdictions, now allow for legal representation of the victim witness in certain circumstances. The representation, where available, however, is often limited to victim witnesses providing testimony for the state, thus allowing for marginal victim input in key trial decisions and outcomes. It flows logically from this understanding of the victims' role that victims who are not witnesses have no role in adversarial proceedings.

The situation for some victims during the trial stage is different in the analysed European non-adversarial and mixed criminal justice systems (Germany, France, Denmark and Sweden). All of these jurisdictions have in common that victims who aim to claim financial losses stemming from the criminal act during criminal proceedings have the right to participate during the trial in relation to their civil claim. These proceedings are called adhesion procedure or civil party (*partie civile*) proceedings. The origins of adhesion/civil party proceedings vary. In Germany, their introduction seems to be mostly related to restrictions during the Second World War and the possibility to save on procedural costs through combing civil and criminal trials. In France and Sweden, the right appears to have more organically emerged out of the historical separation between civil and criminal proceedings. When participating as civil claimants in criminal trials, victims are generally able to request the introduction of specific evidence at trial or to ask witnesses questions relevant to the outcome of their civil claim. In cases where no financial losses have occurred or where victims wish to pursue their financial losses as tort cases in the civil court system, they are unable to participate in the criminal trial as applicants to the adhesion procedure. In that case, their role is reduced to that of a witness if required during the trial.

Furthermore, in two of the analysed systems, Germany and Sweden, (certain) victims are able to support the prosecution in a role that can be described as a secondary prosecutor. This is referred to as Private Accessory Prosecutor (*Nebenklaeger, PAP*) participation in the German context. The requirements for victims who qualify for this active procedural role vary between Sweden and Germany. In Germany, the role has traditionally been reserved for victims of serious violent and sexual offences as these victims were considered particularly in need of protection in the view of the German Government. More recent law reforms in this area now enable German courts to determine whether a victim of any offence should be able to act as a PAP on a case by case basis. Relevant considerations in this context include whether the court is convinced that victim participation is indispensable to safeguard the victims' interests—especially with a view to the impact the crime has had on the individual victim. The burden of proof to establish that their participation is necessary in the case at hand lies with the individual victim. In Sweden, the decision to support the prosecution seems generally open to all victims without restriction to specific categories of criminal offences. Once victims have declared that they wish to participate in the above-described active role, they, or their legal representative on their behalf, can exercise numerous active procedural rights. For example, they can make requests for certain evidence to be introduced, question witnesses and make a final speech during proceedings. In contrast to the role of the civil party, the victims' involvement in this context in Germany and Sweden explicitly relates to the criminal charges and aims to influence the criminal verdict and not any civil claims the victim may try to pursue. Little information is available on the reasons for the introduction of this active participation right for victims in non-Swedish literature. In Germany, this form of victim participation was introduced in 1986 with the Victim Protection Act (*Opferschutzgesetz*) which amended and extended victims' rights in the German Code of Criminal Procedure. The Act holistically and radically transformed private prosecution as it stood until then in German criminal procedure and introduced a new legal status for certain categories of victims, deemed particularly worthy of protection in the state's view, with related far-reaching procedural rights.

None of the inquisitorial and mixed criminal justice systems analysed in this volume have a separate sentencing phase. Verdict and sentence are handed down after a singular trial process has occurred. As a consequence, in these jurisdictions no specific participatory rights exist for victims during sentencing. All adversarial systems, on the other hand, have a split trial and sentencing phase. While participation possibilities for victims are almost non-existent during the trial phase, these jurisdictions afford victims the opportunity to submit statements during the sentencing phase in which they can explain how the crime has affected them, so-called Victim Impact Statements (VIS) or Victim Personal Statements (VPS). Depending on the jurisdiction, the right can be limited to specific victims, for example, victims of violent offences or available to all victims as well as to the families of deceased victims. The statements only become relevant where the defendant is found guilty and proceedings move to the sentencing stage where no jury is present.

At that stage, the statement is presented to the sentencing judge and, in some jurisdictions, certain victims are granted the opportunity to read out (parts of) their statement in court. The evidential value of these statements and what significance courts are meant to attribute to them remains unclear even some 30 years after their first introduction. None of the inquisitorial and mixed criminal justice systems have afforded victims the right to make a VIS, a statement especially focusing on how the crime has affected them, comparable to that available in adversarial systems. It seems possible that the uptake of VIS schemes in continental European systems has been low due to the belief that victims have already been afforded avenues for participation, for example, in the form of PAP participation or as applicants to the adhesion procedure, making the introduction of the right to submit a VIS superfluous.

In light of the above, some victims in continental European systems have been afforded ample participation rights during the trial phase while others, depending on the jurisdiction, continue to be marginally involved and as witnesses only. In general, victims in adversarial systems very much remain outsiders to the trial and sentencing phase. One of the only active participatory rights they have obtained across the board over the past three decades is the right to make a written submission to the courts of unclear evidential value, which, under certain circumstances, may be read out by them during the sentencing phase.

3.3 Post-trial Rights in National Criminal Justice Systems

Out of all three procedural stages, possibilities for victims to participate across the board seem greatest at the pre-trial and, in some jurisdictions, during the trial phase. Chapter 6 concluded that the least number of participatory rights for victims exist once the trial proper has concluded. The post-trial phase is characterised by few, if any, victim participatory rights in most of the analysed jurisdictions. Furthermore, little scholarship exists analysing the merits of victim participation at this stage. One explanation for this distribution of available rights may be that victims are important actors during the pre-trial and trial stage where their cooperation is needed in reporting crimes and assisting criminal justice authorities with their investigation and prosecution. It may be that victims are afforded some possibilities to participate at the pre-trial stage in the hope that, in exchange, this will lead to their cooperation with criminal justice authorities. In contrast, post trial, the victims' assistance is no longer required as any necessary witness' testimony has already been introduced at trial, and offenders have either been convicted and sentenced or acquitted.

Chapter 6 was concerned with victims' rights to complain against pre-trial and trial decisions directly affecting them, to appeal the verdict or sentence issued against the defendant in the particular case at hand, as well as the possibility for victims to take part in early-release decision making. It concluded that victims in few jurisdictions are able to participate in relation to appeals. In Germany, for example, only victims who participate as PAPs have been afforded a limited right to appeal the verdict, but not the sentence, and only in relation to errors of law or fact relating to those offences which gave rise to their initial participation. This limited form of participation has been justified in Germany with the explanation that an appeal should only be possible where an individual can demonstrate that they have suffered a grievance. It has been argued that victims without special legal status, however, do not experience a grievance, as they are not proper participants in the first place and therefore not aggrieved by the verdict. The situation differs in Sweden, the only other jurisdiction analysed allowing for this kind of active victim participation. There, victims acting in this participatory role are, for example, able to appeal an acquittal which the prosecution is not pursuing to a higher court.

In relation to appeal rights of civil claimants/applicants to the adhesion procedure, the situation differs between jurisdictions. Civil claimants in Germany are unable to appeal verdict or sentence and are referred to the civil courts to pursue their civil claim if they are not satisfied with the decision of the criminal court. While civil claimants in France can appeal court decisions which relate to their civil claim, they generally do not have the right to appeal verdict or sentence as such. In Denmark, civil claimants have the right to appeal specific decisions relating to their civil claim. This, however, does not appear to afford them the right to appeal verdict or sentence.

None of the analysed adversarial systems afford victims the right to appeal either verdict or sentence *per se*. This seems a logical and conceptual extension of the limited role victims have been afforded during the trial stage where they are seen as non-parties and non-participants. Non-participants are not affected by either verdict or sentence and thus do not qualify for receiving any appeal rights.

Complaints against pre-trial and trial decisions affecting victims' rights are possible in some jurisdictions but not in others. For instance, on the federal level in the US, victims have been afforded the right to petition the court of appeals for a writ of mandamus on the basis of an erroneous decision relating to an infringement of their rights in the district courts.

In relation to early-release decisions, all adversarial systems afford (certain) victims the possibility to make a submission in the context of parole/early-release proceedings under certain circumstances. Yet, this does not amount to an enforceable right for victims to make direct submissions in all jurisdictions. Moreover, the content of the submission differs between jurisdictions. In some states, victims are able to comment on whether early release should be granted while in others the submission may only relate to what conditions should be imposed on the parolee. In yet others, the submission seems mainly concerned with what effects the crime had on the victim. Comparable to the problems attributed to victim submissions at the sentencing stage, the evidential value of these statements during early-release proceedings and relatedly how much weight the parole board should attribute to them remains unclear. Furthermore, the right to tender such statements is largely non-enforceable in England and Wales and Australia. In contrast, on the federal level in the US, victims have the enforceable right to be heard during parole proceedings. None of the analysed non-adversarial and mixed jurisdictions (Germany, France, Sweden, Denmark) provide victims with a right to participate in early-release proceedings. While courts in France can elect to hear from the victim prior to making an early-release decision, this remains in the discretion of the court and does not amount to an enforceable victims' right.

4 Possible Reasons for the Fragmentation of Victims' Procedural Rights

The findings in Chapters 4–6 offered a broad picture of available victim participation rights at the pre-trial, trial and post-trial stage in adversarial, inquisitorial and mixed criminal justice systems and exposed existing limitations. The chapters make clear that the way in which victims can participate during proceedings varies greatly. For example, in the German criminal justice system, victims are classed into specific participation or non-participation groups with categorically associated rights. Furthermore, even victims who act as PAPs and therefore have ample participation rights during the main trial are limited in their participation during the pre-trial and post-trial phase. Overall, while it cannot be denied that possibilities for participation do exist to some extent in all of the analysed jurisdictions, the rights remain non-systematic and appear to be introduced without a clear and long-term legislative concept. It seems that victims' rights law reform over the course of the years has amended and introduced new legislation and, at least in some jurisdictions, has created an overall opaque framework in relation to victims' participatory rights during different trial stages. Duenkel (2001, 182) remarks in the German context that '[o]n the whole, the victim's current possibilities of participating are not derived from a uniform concept of joining in the proceedings, rather, they evolved historically from very different roots and political currents'. On this basis, he criticises German victims' rights reform legislation as lacking 'overall vision' while highlighting that this is not an exclusively German phenomenon but is also the case in other European countries (Duenkel 2001, 182).

Based on the analysis in this volume, little suggests that criminal justice is transforming into a truly victim-focussed process model in adversarial, inquisitorial and mixed criminal justice systems. The 'rediscovery' of the victim may have led to an increase in attention to victims and their needs. However, this acknowledgement may have manifested itself more in the area of service and information rights and in obligations requiring respectful treatment rather than in the context of affording victims active participation rights during proceedings.

The lack of a clear vision for victim participation in practice in many jurisdictions is perhaps less surprising when taking into account the changed role of victims throughout the course of history and the potential influence of traditional criminal theories on criminal justice responses to victims of crime. The understanding of criminal law and procedure as a state-based conflict from which the victim, as an individual stakeholder, has been intentionally removed seems to limit participation possibilities for victims *per se*. In addition, in states in which the understanding of criminal justice remains heavily influenced by traditional criminal theories in the form of retributivism or utilitarianism, few philosophical or theoretical underpinnings are available justifying an expansion of the procedural role of victims. It may be due to this traditional understanding of criminal justice that much criticism has been uttered regarding victims' participatory rights in legal-political dialogue and scholarship in Germany and Australia, the two jurisdictions selected for in-depth case study in Chapter 7. The chapter focused on whether the introduction of victims' participatory rights may signify a changed understanding of criminal justice and a reconceptualisation of the existing criminal justice system in Germany and Australia. It identified a lack of consensus towards systematically reintegrating victims into criminal procedure through participation possibilities in either system. Furthermore, it contemplated political opportunism as a reason for introducing and expanding victim participation rights in practice. These findings may be indicative for other Western inquisitorial and adversarial criminal justice systems.

In light of the above, the promise of numerous Western governments to reintegrate victims into criminal procedure is not only lacking an established theoretical and philosophical base and a clear strategy but is also viewed critically by many in society, not the least the legal profession. A consensus on what role victims should play in criminal procedure as well as an established theoretical underpinning for this role is absent. This is the case even in systems in which some victims have broad participation rights during proceedings, such as Germany, ultimately causing a gap between theory and practice. The underlying motives for victims' rights law reforms in this area may be more closely entwined with electoral politics and the wish to show that something is 'being done' for victims than with the desire to holistically transform the criminal justice system and the victims' role within. The promised 'reintegration' of victims into criminal procedure in a holistic fashion has not happened so far and, due to the identified difficulties and limitations, it is unclear whether it can and will happen in the future. Indeed, it may be the case, as some have cautioned, that pursuing victims' rights reforms which are not broadly supported in society will lead to opposition and resistance. This, in turn, may negatively impact the willingness and readiness of advocates to pursue other law reform efforts concerned with less contested victims' rights. Aiming to introduce or expand what some may consider excessive victims' rights, for example, such as those related to extensive participation, may therefore become counterproductive in enhancing the overall position of victims in criminal proceedings in practice.

5 An Enhanced Focus on Protection in the Form Legal Representation for Victims

The expansion of victims' participatory rights may be incompatible with the current understanding of criminal justice in many jurisdictions. Ultimately, this gives rise to the question of whether continuous advocacy in this area will yield the desired results. Accordingly, Chapter 8 contemplated whether, at present, it may be more beneficial to focus on better protecting victim witnesses during proceedings to ensure an enhanced experience in criminal trials. In so doing, the chapter considered legal representation schemes for victims by examining the status quo of such initiatives as well as the legal merits of their introduction in jurisdictions currently lacking such arrangements. The argument was presented that the traditional role of victims as witnesses, a role which exists in all analysed jurisdictions, may be enhanced in practice by allowing victim witnesses to be legally represented during proceedings. In most Western jurisdictions, victims have already been afforded certain rights including information and service rights and rights relating to claiming financial losses. In order to ameliorate the victims' situation, however, these rights must find application in practice. Where victims are not informed about their rights and/or criminal justice authorities fail to comply with them, the situation for victims on the books differs greatly from their situation in practice. A lawyer acting on behalf of a victim witness could contribute to ensuring access to as well as compliance with already existing victims' rights and standards. A likely consequence of having their own legal representation is that victims will be more informed about the different procedural stages and their outcomes but also about their role within the criminal justice system. In addition, specific information and legal advice will be available to victims on how to claim restitution in their specific circumstances. Ensuring that victims receive necessary information enables them to make informed decisions about how they wish to proceed. This may help close potential gaps between victims' rights on the books and in action. Furthermore, the mere fact that victims are entitled to legal representation and, as such, are able to actively seek protection of their rights rather than having to rely on third parties to do so, including prosecutors and the courts, may add up to an improved role in practice. Ultimately, all of these different components inherent in legal representation schemes may contribute to a reduction of secondary victimisation, an aim which is also often cited as one of the reasons for the introduction of more extensive procedural rights for victims. Overall, there is only a limited amount of research available on established legal representation schemes. While the small number of existing studies shows that benefits for victims can be attributed to these schemes, not all operate without difficulties in practice. Yet, none of the identified problems, such as, for example, lack of available funding and lack of adequately skilled lawyers, appear to be of such fundamental nature that they could not be resolved through practical and strategical decision making for the future.

While the focus on protection rather than on more active participation rights may be criticised on the basis that it does not touch on or change the basic position of victims in tradition criminal justice as such, this may also be the advantage of this less intrinsic approach. The introduction or enhancement of legal representation schemes may be less at odds with a traditional understanding of criminal justice while contributing to improving the situation for victim witnesses at different stages of proceedings in practice. Although, this strategy focuses more on aspects relating to service, restitution, compensation and information and less on participatory rights the practical advantages for victims may nevertheless be far-reaching.

6 Concluding Remarks

The perception of victims and their needs have changed significantly since the first half of the twentieth century. Promising to reintegrate victims into criminal justice, a political mantra frequently reiterated by many Western governments, is considered useful in winning elections. Being tough on criminals and good to victims during political campaigns is generally well perceived by the electorate. In political discourse, the term 'victim' has become so influential and powerful that some now call it a magical term.

While much legal-political dialogue appears to focus on the reintegrating of victims into criminal procedure, the procedural situation in practice in the analysed criminal justice systems differs from what one might expect in light of these political promises. It is submitted that crime and criminal justice in many Western jurisdictions continue to be heavily influenced by a traditional understanding. An understanding in which crime is seen as a conflict between the state and the offender from which the victim has been intentionally excluded. Justifications for criminal justice and punishment are based on the interests of the state, the community or the individual offender but not the individual victim. Furthering the victim's procedural role fits squarely into this traditional understanding. Where a philosophical and theoretical base is missing, it flows logically that the procedural role victims currently play at different trial stages is disjointed and without an apparent overall vision in many jurisdictions. While frequent expansions of certain aspects of participatory rights occur in practice in some jurisdictions, these developments are perhaps more related to political opportunism than to an attempt to holistically afford victims a general participation role and change the underlying nature of the criminal trial. In addition, many in society see the expansion of victims' participatory rights critically and what role victims should be afforded in criminal procedure continues to be heavily debated.

Systematic expansion of victims' participatory rights cannot occur in a legal vacuum. Without a changed understanding of crime and justice and a related attitude change towards the victims' role in criminal procedure, it appears likely that victims' procedural rights will continue to be modified in a piecemeal fashion through numerous reform acts in the future leading to an even more disjointed legal landscape. The appropriate procedural role for victims in criminal procedure will likely remain subject to much debate. It is easy to imagine that no homogenous approach to victim participation will emerge between different jurisdictions due to their diverging legal traditions and backgrounds. The current challenge may therefore particularly lie in identifying avenues for enhancing the experience of victims in the justice system without exclusively focusing on the introduction of additional, and arguably highly contested, procedural participatory rights.

Reference

Duenkel, F. (2001). The Victim in Criminal Law—On the Way from Offender-Related to Victim-Related Criminal Justice. In E. A. Fattah, S. Parmentier, & T. Peters (Eds.), *Victim Policies and Criminal Justice on the Road to Restorative Justice: A Collection of Essays in Honour of Tony Peters* (pp. 167–211). Leuven: Leuven University Press.

Index

K. Braun, *Victim Participation Rights*, Palgrave Studies in Victims and Victimology, https://doi.org/10.1007/978-3-030-04546-3

www.ingramcontent.com/pod-product-compliance
Ingram Content Group UK Ltd.
Pitfield, Milton Keynes, MK11 3LW, UK
UKHW020834290926
15470UKWH00004B/1345
* 9 7 8 3 0 3 0 0 4 5 4 5 6 *